THE
REFERENCE
SHELF

DRUGS IN AMERICA

Edited by ROBERT EMMET LONG

THE REFERENCE SHELF

Volume 65, Number 4

THE H. W. WILSON COMPANY

New York   1993

THE REFERENCE SHELF

The books in this series contain reprints of articles, excerpts from books, and addresses on current issues and social trends in the United States and other countries. There are six separately bound numbers in each volume, all of which are generally published in the same calendar year. One number is a collection of recent speeches; each of the others is devoted to a single subject and gives background information and discussion from various points of view, concluding with a comprehensive bibliography that contains books and pamphlets and abstracts of additional articles on the subject. Books in the series may be purchased individually or on subscription.

Library of Congress Cataloging-in-Publication Data

Drugs in America / edited by Robert Emmet Long.
   p.   cm. — (The Reference shelf ; v. 65, no. 4)
   ISBN 0-8242-0843-9
   1. Drug traffic—United States.   2. Narcotics, Control of—United States.   3. Drug abuse—United States—Prevention.   4. Drug legalization—United States.   I. Long, Robert Emmet.   II. Series.
HV5825.D838   1993
363.4'5'0973—dc20
                                                     93-16881
                                                        CIP

Cover: U.S. Marshal guards suspects during a crackhouse raid.
Photo: AP/Wide World Photos

Printed in the United States of America

CONTENTS

5

PREFACE

It is virtually impossible today to be unaware of the prevalence of illicit drugs in American life. Celebrities in sports and entertainment, as well as other public figures, are in the news because of their drug abuse. Radio and television bring daily reports of government seizure of drugs and of gang killings that are drug-related. In 1986 I edited the Reference Shelf volume titled *Drugs and American Society* (Volume 57, Number 6), devoted to the drug epidemic, particularly the emergence of cocaine as the drug of choice in this country. Since then, however, many things have occurred that call for an updated volume on the subject. During the four years of the Bush Administration, the federal government vastly expanded the effort to suppress the flow of drugs into the U.S. The apparent failure of this campaign, despite heroic efforts, raises serious questions about what approach must now be developed to deal with the drug problem.

Section One of this volume is devoted to the government's efforts in the war on drugs. The opening article reports that the U.S. military has been deployed in the Andean countries of Colombia, Bolivia, and Peru to train local enforcement agencies in drug interdiction. The second piece is concerned with the "Andean Initiative" implemented in 1990 to replace the growing of coca leaf with other crops and to intensify the prosecution of drug trafficking. As the article notes, however, the effort has been seriously hampered by interagency rivalries and widespread corruption in the countries involved. Another article proposes that the U.S. government now redirect its resources to curtailing the demand for drugs on the domestic front. Still another piece warns of the threat to American civil liberties posed by the suspension of Bill of Rights guarantees in the crack-down on suspected drug dealers and users. A final article contends that the demand for drugs in the inner cities cannot be reduced until living conditions and employment opportunities of those in the ghettos are addressed.

Section Two focuses upon the Latin American countries that supply cocaine and heroin for U.S. consumption. An opening article deals with the fall of the Medellín cartel in Colombia and its replacement by the Cali organization, an even more formidable antagonist with great skill and resourcefulness in thwarting the efforts of the Drug Enforcement Administration. Another article, also dealing with Colombia, maintains that U.S. economic aid intended to contain the production and distribution of cocaine has been used in many cases to suppress critics of the country's right wing regime. A following article reveals that the war on drugs in Bolivia has foundered; and a piece on Peru discloses that the economic aid the U.S. has provided has been siphoned off in a long, drawn-out war between the government and a leftist guerilla group called the Shining Path. A concluding piece about the trial of Manuel Noriega in Miami points out that after Noriega's removal from power drug trafficking in Panama continues to flourish.

Cocaine and crack are the subject of Section Three, in which the first two articles trace the origins of crack production and distribution in the U.S. Obtained cheaply and ready to smoke, crack has become one of the most widespread drugs in use today; and is controlled by ethnically diverse syndicates, each with its own turf in American cities. Several other articles deal with the effect of crack on the newborn infants of crack-addicted mothers. These "crack kids" are sometimes irreparably damaged, and even those who are not require special health and educational care. What policy ought to be adopted then in respect to "crack mothers"?

Section Four deals with the controversial issue of legalizing drugs. Two of the articles in this section oppose legalization, partly on the presumption that it would vastly increase drug use. Other articles dispute this view, and maintain that the war on drugs cannot be won. Legalization, they claim, would destroy the drug cartels at a stroke and provide hope for improving the lives of the poor and disadvantaged.

The editor is indebted to the authors and publishers who have granted permission to reprint the materials in this compilation. Special thanks are due to Joyce Cook and the Fulton (N.Y.) Public Library staff, and to the staff of Penfield Library, State University of New York at Oswego.

ROBERT EMMET LONG

January 1993

I. THE WAR ON DRUGS

EDITOR'S INTRODUCTION

The first section of this compilation focuses upon the war on drugs, which has been pursued vigorously, but with uneven results, by the Bush Administration. The escalation of the government's response to drugs during the last four years has been aimed primarily at closing off sources of supply from countries in the Andes, which are now the principal growers of coca leaf and distributors of cocaine and heroin into the U.S. This effort has proved an enormous undertaking, since methods of smuggling in drugs are ingenious and take many forms. Despite seizures of drugs in significant amounts, most of the supply has continued to elude the Drug Enforcement Administration (DEA) and other government agencies. Cocaine is still as available in the streets in 1993 as it was before the war on drugs was launched.

In an article in *Newsweek*, Charles Lane discusses the use of the U.S. military in Operation Support Justice in Latin America. American military units have been deployed to train narcofighting agencies in South and Central American countries in their seizure of drugs and destruction of processing plants. As Lane points out, however, conflicts have developed between the military and the DEA, which at times work at cross purposes and, therefore, with reduced effectiveness. This problem has been compounded by corruption in the agencies of the Latin American countries themselves. The next article, by Peter Andreas and several colleagues writing in *Foreign Policy*, paints an even bleaker picture of the war on drugs. While it is true that the $2.2 billion, five-year "Andean Initiative" adopted by the U.S. and the Andean countries in 1990, calls for a significant increase in investment in containing drug trafficking, the record of the DEA thus far offers little basis for optimism. Cocaine production, rather than being reduced, has actually increased, and efforts to introduce a program of crop substitution has proved a failure, because earnings from other crops are modest compared to the large revenues deriving from coca leaf farming. Moreover, some of the money and military supplies provided by the U.S. have been diverted by the Latin American countries to the prosecution of wars against political insurgents, often accompanied by horrifying human rights abuses. Andreas and his colleagues conclude with the observation that no policy of supply reduction by itself can significantly lower the demand for drugs at home. Next, writing in *Fortune*, Louis Kraar proposes that the war on drugs should now concentrate on reducing the demand for drugs at home through preventive education, community involvement, and the rehabilitation of drug users.

Dan Baum, in *The Nation*, explores another aspect of the war on drugs—its flagrant violations of the civil rights of American citizens. Mandatory prison sentences for possession of even the smallest amount of drugs, he argues, are irrational and hysterical. Twice as many people are arrested for possession today as for dealing. The property of individuals is confiscated on the mere suspicion of drug possession, a suspension of civil rights provided in the Bill of Rights. Individuals may also be tried twice for the same offense, in state and then in federal courts. Search warrants on the basis of anonymous tips are permitted, as are the seizure of defense attorneys' legal fees. The entire American judicial process, Baum argues, has been dangerously jeopardized. In the final article in this section, Lewis Lapham in *Harper's* maintains that the war on drugs has been directed against America's underclass. This crusade distracts attention from the need to improve social conditions, housing, and employment opportunities for young black men. The war on drugs, Lapham argues, fails to attack the root causes of drug use among the economically disadvantaged.

THE NEWEST WAR[1]

The American-led battle to oust Saddam Hussein's forces from Kuwait is an increasingly distant memory. U.S. troops may soon be airlifting food to another crumbling former foe, the Sovi-

---

[1]Reprint of an article by Charles Lane, *Newsweek* staffwriter. Reprinted by permission of *Newsweek*, 119: 18–23. Ja 6 '92. Copyright © 1992 by *Newsweek*.

et Union. But the U.S. military is still at war—against the drug lords of Latin America. On the waters of the Caribbean Sea, ships and AWACS planes of the Navy's Atlantic Command search for drug planes and boats, while a military radar aerostat balloon hovers above. In the desert Southwest, Marines and Army Special Forces soldiers burrow into "hide sites," peering at drug smugglers through night-vision goggles. Along the Gulf Coast, Navy SEALs probe ships for cocaine shipments riveted to their hulls. In South America, American trainers mold Latin armies into narco-fighting form.

A two-month *Newsweek* inquiry has documented a Pentagon drug war, parts of it secret, that has quietly escalated to dimensions greater than most Americans yet realize. It involves thousands of U.S. and Latin troops, at a cost of more than a billion dollars per year. Just last month, *Newsweek* has learned, U.S. forces wrapped up a secret operation code-named Operation Support Justice—a U.S.-coordinated cocaine interdiction effort by Latin forces throughout the Andes. While still small by Desert Storm standards, the drug war has nevertheless emerged as the fastest-growing item in an otherwise shrinking post-cold-war Pentagon budget.

With the increased commitment come increased concerns: six recent State Department, Pentagon and congressional reports have documented serious failings in U.S. military or paramilitary drug programs. American efforts, the reports said, are plagued by poor management, policy confusion and faulty intelligence. The drug war may also be doing lasting damage to the unstable politics of America's Latin allies. And where it counts the most— on the streets—the impact, if any, of the military's anti-drug effort is impossible to discern. According to the latest survey by the National Institute on Drug Abuse, the same number of people used cocaine weekly last year as in 1989. The Bush administration wanted to reduce the rate by 50 percent.

Will the military's drug war turn into a quagmire? Ironically, the Pentagon resisted the mission for decades, saying the military should fight threats to national security, and the police should fight crime. But as public concern over drug abuse reached near-panic proportions in the '80s, cries for military intervention intensified. In the last year of Ronald Reagan's presidency, Congress—brushing aside the objections of the then Joint Chiefs Chairman Adm. William Crowe—ordered the Defense Depart-

ment to spend $439 million on the drug war in fiscal 1989.
George Bush was more enthusiastic about a military role. Spending on the drug war has almost tripled since he took office.

No Combat

The Pentagon is now the lead federal agency in aerial and
maritime detection of drug traffickers. Its transportation, com-
munications and intelligence capabilities have been placed at the
disposal of law enforcement. At Southwest border checkpoints
National Guard soldiers armed with brass hammers tap gas tanks
for the resonance of hidden marijuana caches. Abroad, Bush has
launched the Andean Initiative, a five-year plan under which the
United States pushes Latin governments to use their armies—
trained, equipped and sometimes directed by the Pentagon—
against traffickers. For now, the Pentagon will not send troops
into direct combat.

Advocates of a bigger military role argue that the drug cartels
are no match for the Pentagon's technological resources. The use
of those resources against drug smuggling has produced some
results. In the Caribbean, Air Force and Army helicopter pilots
ferrying Drug Enforcement Administration agents and Bahamian police have driven the cartels out of many favorite drop sites
for cocaine in Florida and the Bahamas. On Dec. 2, DEA and U.S.
Customs officials made the second largest cocaine seizure in U.S.
history—12 tons found inside concrete fencing posts at a Miami
warehouse. Pentagon sources say the Atlantic Command provided intelligence and tracking aid for the bust.

Yet building an "electronic screen" around U.S. territory will
be difficult. A network of 18 ground-based radars in South and
Central America and the Caribbean, supposed to be completed in
1992, is a year behind schedule. The Defense Department divided up the drug-detection mission among six military "commands," each responsible for a different geographic area. As a
result, the collection and analysis of intelligence on narco-
traffickers has been "fragmented, duplicative, and not cost-
effective," according to a report by the Pentagon's inspector general.

There is sharp debate within the government about whether
radar raises costs for the traffickers—or for the United States.
Civilian law-enforcement officials regard radar as a redundancy:
it can't see inside a ship or plane; to confirm the presence of

drugs takes an informer or physical evidence. Traffickers evade the Navy's Caribbean radar dragnet by hiding drugs in commercial cargo ships, where they are virtually impossible to detect. "They've got as many sources of getting drugs into the country as there are ways of commerce coming in," says Adm. Leon (Bud) Edney of the Atlantic Command. In September, the General Accounting Office reported that nearly $2 billion worth of Pentagon detection and monitoring over the last two years "have not had a significant impact."

One of the biggest winners from the drug war is the U.S. Southern Command in Panama. SouthCom's traditional mission, countering leftists, has diminished with the cold war. The Andean Initiative gave it a new lease on life. "We're in it for the long haul," says SouthCom commander Gen. George Joulwan, the architect of Operation Support Justice. "And we're serious about this fight."

SouthCom now fields about 500 American soldiers working in counterdrug training and intelligence missions on the ground in Central and South America, according to Pentagon documents obtained by *Newsweek*: some 80 U.S. personnel are stationed in Colombia alone. The military has placed small "Tactical Analysis Teams" in 10 Central and South American countries, working with the DEA and CIA to assemble intelligence dossiers on trafficking organizations. Army Green Berets train Bolivian, Peruvian and Colombian police and military in jungle warfare. Navy SEALs in Ecuador, Colombia and Bolivia have given instruction in riverine operations. Even the Army's supersecret counterterrorist unit, Delta Force, has given the Peruvian Army counterterrorism training, U.S. and Peruvian military sources say. A secret planning document obtained by *Newsweek* revealed that the State Department has a wish list for Honduras as well, including Green Beret training, and the conversion of Honduran units that patrol the Salvadoran border for guerrillas into drug-interdiction teams.

Support Justice is a regional—and ambitious—program: Andean counternarcotics forces conduct simultaneous attacks on traffickers in different countries. In April and May, SouthCom began a massive "intelligence surge" in the Andean countries, involving overflights and the use of U.S. satellites. According to classified Pentagon documents obtained by *Newsweek,* the intelligence was fed to the DEA and Andean security forces, for use in interdiction operations by Bolivian, Peruvian and Colombian air and ground forces, which began in June. SouthCom is finishing its third phase of Support Justice, an attempt to close the cartel's northbound air corridors. Two mobile radars have been slipped into Peru to join a network of radars in Ecuador and Colombia.

SouthCom hasn't yet divulged official results, but a Desert Storm-style "surge" of information may be of limited use to corrupt, ill-equipped Latin militaries. The history of U.S.-sponsored drug raids in South America is replete with impressive-sounding "body count" statistics that crumble upon inspection. In a June Support Justice raid, Bolivian police and DEA agents helicoptered into the town of Santa Ana del Yacuma and seized 15 cocaine labs, 42 aircraft, 9 estates and 110 kilos of cocaine base. Still, none of the biggest traffickers was captured (although they later negotiated a surrender under Bolivia's lenient "repentance law"). The Bolivians complained that the United States had denied them vital intelligence and that DEA agents roughed up a Bolivian Navy officer. U.S. officials counter that the traffickers were tipped off by Bolivian congressmen.

The basic problem for U.S. efforts in Peru, Bolivia and Colombia is that drug consumption is not a serious social problem in those countries, while exports are a source of hundreds of millions of badly needed dollars for hundreds of thousands of people, many of them farmers in remote areas. Fearful that peasant resistance will feed leftist insurgencies—and that U.S. military aid will fatten corrupt, abusive militaries—civilian presidents in all three countries originally balked at U.S. plans to militarize the struggle.

'Hush Money'

Bolivians are baffled at the U.S. insistence on aiding their military, which last made headlines when the "cocaine colonels" took power in a 1980 coup. In October, a Bolivian Air Force plane landed in Paraguay, carrying an unexpected cargo: 16 kilos of cocaine. U.S. officials privately explain that $14 million in aid for the armed forces is "hush money," to silence griping about the police's even bigger counternarcotics budget. Only incidentally do they mention the Army's role in anti-drug work. President Jaime Paz Zamora acceded to the U.S. plan to keep narcotics-related economic-aid packages coming. "Our relations with the U.S. are completely 'narcoticized'," says a senior Bolivian official.

"But it's the only way we can get help in the problems that really concern us."

Meanwhile, U.S. trainers in Bolivia say the drug cartels may be the beneficiaries of their efforts. Of the 900 soldiers now being trained, 85 percent are conscripts, on one-year hitches scheduled to end in a matter of months. Many have relatives working in the drug industry who may well hire the recruits as security guards, paying a premium for U.S. know-how. "With few exceptions, all we're doing is training the bad guys," one adviser says.

The Colombian armed forces receive the biggest share of U.S. counternarcotics aid to that country. At $47.2 million this fiscal year, Colombia is passing El Salvador as the top recipient of U.S. military aid in Latin America. Congress approved the money provided that it be used to fight drug trafficking, not just leftist guerrilla groups. Nevertheless, sources in Bogotá say the U.S. aid has so far been used mostly for counterinsurgency operations— in which hundreds of civilians have also been executed by government forces without trials, human-rights groups say.

Closer Ties

U.S. officials argue that attacking guerrillas is anti-drug work: since "narco-guerrillas" also get rich by protecting traffickers, any attack on the guerrillas is a blow to drug trafficking. Colombia's guerrilla groups do protect airstrips, labs and fields in several trafficking areas, and sometimes even supervise cultivation. A secret Defense Intelligence Agency report claims that the Colombian Revolutionary Armed Forces earned up to $40 million in 1989 on drugs. But Colombian narcos also have close ties to the Army itself; officers sometimes secure landing strips for drug planes, or leak information about coming drug busts.

U.S. policy is also floundering in Peru, where the majority of the world's unrefined cocaine is produced. Narcotics violence is compounded by the war between a terrorist Maoist insurgency, Sendero Luminoso, and a corrupt, brutal military. The multisided fighting is most vicious in the drug-producing upper Huallaga Valley, where guerrillas get drug-protection money to finance their revolution.

As in Colombia, the narco-guerrilla argument was the U.S. rationale for urging the Peruvian Army to join the drug war. The ragged Peruvian armed forces would like U.S. assistance to help fight Sendero, but are less than eager to fight drugs: partly because Army commanders do not believe drugs are as menacing as the insurgency, and partly because so many in the Army are on the take. Traffickers now pay the Army an average of $5,000 per flight to take off from public airstrips in the jungle. DEA agents and Peruvian police have repeatedly been fired on by Army soldiers when they try to raid drug labs.

The debate over aid to the Peruvian Army is academic for now: in September Congress withheld $10 million of $34.9 million in military assistance for the Peruvian Army, citing another chronic problem: human-rights abuses. Pending marked improvements in that record, and clearer answers from the administration about the scope of U.S. involvement in Peru's internal war, Congress does not want to bankroll another Vietnam or El Salvador.

Young Brats

Andean operations are hampered by turf battles between the U.S. military and the DEA. DEA agents openly call American Special Forces troops arrogant young brats with no understanding of intelligence or law enforcement. The military talks grandly of "search and destroy" missions led by 60-man Bolivian Army companies sweeping the jungle. But the DEA opposes letting Bolivian troops wander the jungle without specific intelligence.

The Army sees the DEA as city cops with no real training for jungle operations. Green Berets charge that the DEA raids in Bolivia are too often conducted in daylight and by helicopter, giving the traffickers enough advance warning to flee. As a result, most of the labs the DEA raids "are empty," complains one American officer.

The dispute is about more than just turf: it's a question of basic doctrine. Is the "war on drugs" really a war in anything more than a metaphorical sense? Or is it a matter of police work for which the military is fundamentally ill suited? "The military can kill people better than we can," says a senior DEA official. "But . . . when we go to a jungle lab, we're not there to move onto the target by fire and maneuver to destroy the enemy. We're there to arrest suspects and seize evidence."

The Army categorizes the Andean Drug War as a "low-intensity conflict," a catchall term historically applied to wars against Marxist guerrilla armies. But the drug cartels, unlike guerrillas, are motivated by money, not ideology. They control tens of thousands of well-paid informers, messengers, hit men and corrupt officials in every corner of Latin America and the United States. There isn't enough money in the U.S. Treasury to counter their swag. "One of the principles of low-intensity conflict is that whoever has the will of the people wins the war," says one American military adviser in the Andes. "You know what that means in Bolivia? We've lost the war." So far, in fact, there is no clear-cut definition of "victory" in the drug war. "We've got to be careful here," one Pentagon official confides. "The military is still groping with their final objective." With its prestige on the line, will the military settle for the "support" role Cheney has set for it, or will a logic of escalation take hold? Desert Storm took 40 days, but the drug war "is going to require commitment over a long period of time," says Pentagon drug czar Stephen Duncan. He likens the drug war to the cold war—which took 40 years.

DEAD-END DRUG WARS[2]

The end of the Cold War and the disintegration of the Soviet Union have led to a fundamental reevaluation of U.S. security interests. In Latin America, the perceived security threat of the 1990s is not a revolutionary government or an insurgency with alleged Soviet ties but a substance: illegal drugs.

The spread of crack cocaine and the dramatic escalation of drug-related violence in the 1980s led first Ronald Reagan and then George Bush to "declare war" on drugs. By the end of the decade, more Americans identified drugs as the number-one threat to the country than any other problem. In September 1989, President George Bush devoted his first nationally televised address to the drug problem, outlining a National Drug Control Strategy that called for "an assault on every front." Efforts to curb the cocaine supply at the source of production were stepped up,

[2]Reprint of an article by Peter R. Andreas, research associate at the Institute for Policy Studies; Eva C. Bertram, associate fellow at the Institute for Policy Studies; Morris J. Blackman, associate director of the Institute of International Studies at the University of South Carolina; and Kenneth E. Sharpe, professor of political science at Swarthmore College. Reprinted by permission of *Foreign Policy*, 85: 106–28. Wn '91/92. Copyright © 1992 by *Foreign Policy*.

and the Andean cocaine-producing countries of Bolivia, Colombia, and Peru became a first "front" in the U.S. drug war abroad. Under the $2.2 billion, five-year "Andean Initiative," U.S. aid and advisers have poured into the region. Drug-related military aid jumped from approximately $5 million in 1988 to more than $140 million in 1990.

The Andean region has now replaced Central America as the leading recipient of the U.S. military aid in the hemisphere. The Joint Chiefs of Staff's "Military Net Assessment" presented to Congress in March 1991 highlights the seriousness of the Pentagon's approach to the drug war: "Counternarcotics" leads the list of likely future conflicts.

But the premises and methods guiding the administration's Andean drug control strategy are neither new nor untested and, unfortunately, have a long record of failure. After more than a decade of U.S. efforts to reduce the cocaine supply, more cocaine is produced in more places than ever before. Curiously, the U.S. response to failure has been to escalate rather than reevaluate.

U.S. counternarcotics strategists recognize that the success of the drug war in the Andes depends upon local actors—governments, police, militaries, and peasant producers—possessing the will and the capability to curb production and stop trafficking. Drug-war strategists widely acknowledge that these conditions are currently lacking in the Andean countries. Yet without providing any compelling argument or evidence, they maintain the unquestioned presumption that greater U.S. aid, training, and equipment can create them. The logic of escalation in the drug war is in fact strikingly similar to the arguments advanced when U.S. counterinsurgency strategies, undercut by ineffective and uncommitted governments and security forces, were failing in Vietnam: "We've just begun to fight." "We're turning the corner." Since failure can so easily be used to justify further escalation, how do we know whether we are really turning the corner or simply running around a vicious circle?

The president's National Drug Control Strategy recognizes that America's drug problem has both a demand side and a supply side: Americans are able and eager to buy drugs, and drugs are cheap and readily available. The strategy, however, continues the supply-side approach of decades of past U.S. counternarcotics efforts: About 70 per cent of 1991 federal antidrug dollars target supply reduction, while the remainder is invested in demand-side measures of treatment and prevention. The assumption is that severely restricting supply will lower demand for drugs by making them scarcer and more expensive. Supply-side tactics have included law enforcement programs to disrupt distribution at home and interdiction efforts on U.S. borders. Abroad, the United States has aimed to seize drug shipments by land, sea, and air, to disable trafficking networks, and to destroy the drug supply at its source of production.

"The logic is simple," Bush said in a May 1988 campaign speech, "The cheapest and safest way to eradicate narcotics is to destroy them at their source. . . . We need to wipe out crops wherever they are grown and take out labs wherever they exist." For more than a decade the main foreign targets in the war on drugs have been the Andean cocaine-producing countries.

The U.S. drug war there has been built on the twin components of law enforcement and economic assistance. The enforcement component seeks to cut supply by eradicating coca crops, destroying processing laboratories, blocking the transport of processing chemicals, and interdicting drug shipments. Traffickers are to be arrested and prosecuted, their assets seized, and their networks dismantled.

Past U.S. drug control efforts emphasized aid to Andean civilian law enforcement agencies and judiciaries. Meager results led to a search for ways to increase enforcement capabilities; an early step was to "militarize" the police. Beginning in 1983, the United States helped establish special counternarcotics units in Bolivia and Peru—paramilitary police squads later trained by U.S. Special Forces personnel. When this strategy proved ineffective, U.S. narcotics officials turned to Andean militaries, backed by U.S. equipment and training, to do the job.

Law enforcement has been coupled with economic assistance. A 1990 report by the Office of National Drug Control Policy emphasizes that "economic strategies and resources are required to provide the general conditions for a healthy and viable legal economy throughout the region as well as provide viable alternatives for those currently engaged in illicit drug cultivation."

The track record of American enforcement and economic assistance efforts, however, has been dismal. The United States Drug Enforcement Administration (DEA) estimates that cocaine production in South America skyrocketed from approximately 397 tons in 1988 to 990 tons in 1990. Production is expected to increase by another 10 per cent over 1991. "Coca cultivation is now approaching 200,000 tons of coca leaf a year, enough to satisfy four times the annual estimated U.S. cocaine market," according to a congressional report.

Coca eradication programs have consistently failed even to keep pace with new growth. Interdiction efforts have yielded equally poor results: In Peru and Bolivia, for example, less than 1 per cent of coca paste and base was seized in 1989.

Enforcement efforts in Colombia have shown periodic signs of success, but even these have been short-lived. In the months following the Colombian government's renowned fall 1989 crackdown, cocaine processing and trafficking dropped by more than 70 per cent. Production quickly recovered, however, reaching 80 per cent of the previous level within six months. Even more significant was the State Department Office of the Inspector General's conclusion earlier, in March 1989, that U.S. efforts in the Andes "have had little impact on the availability of illicit narcotics in the United States."

U.S. counternarcotics strategies have not only failed to significantly reduce supply but have been costly to the region and to other American interests there. U.S. aid has allied the United States with corrupt and brutal security forces in the region. Peru has either topped or run second on the United Nations' list of forced "disappearances" for the past five years; its military was condemned by the U.S. State Department's 1990 Country Report for "widespread and egregious human rights violations." Aiding such security forces further strengthens historically antidemocratic institutions against fragile civilian governments and undermines the interests North Americans share with the people of the Andes in promoting democracy.

The Andean Initiative

Despite the record of supply-reduction failures and damaging consequences for democracy and human rights, the Bush administration's response has been escalation, not reconsideration. Interpreting past failure as a consequence of inadequate funding coupled with insufficient local political will and institutional capacity, the administration is implementing a "new and improved" supply-reduction strategy. The president's Andean Initiative provides unprecedented levels of U.S. aid for Bolivia, Colombia, and Peru to escalate enforcement and economic assistance efforts.

The major shift from past antidrug efforts is the dramatic

extension of militarization: The United States has signed separate
military assistance pacts with Bolivia, Colombia, and Peru, assigning a leading role to their respective military forces in the war on
drugs and committing extensive U.S. assistance. The militarization of the drug war also requires a significantly expanded training role for the U.S. Defense Department, and American advisers
have already been sent to the region. In Peru, where the administration has concluded that the Shining Path guerrillas are imped-
ing drug enforcement, the United States will support counterinsurgency.

Once Andean governments implement this militarized enforcement strategy, significant economic assistance will follow.
Projected to comprise about half of the $2.2 billion designated for
this region, most of this aid is targeted at balance-of-payments
support, not alternative development programs. The governments of Bolivia and Peru publicly resisted initial American efforts to draw their militaries into the drug control campaign, yet
their desperate need for economic help has given them little
choice but to sign the antidrug accords.

Will the escalation succeed? Preliminary evidence indicates a
continuation of previous trends: increased success in terms of
crops eradicated, labs destroyed, and traffickers arrested, but little or no impact on overall levels of supply. Official reports of
failure to achieve real supply reductions continue to mount. The
State Department's March 1991 report acknowledged that the
department had underestimated the potential dry leaf coca harvest over the last five years by about one-third. The report projected a large increase in Peru's coca production and noted that
even with increased law enforcement efforts in Bolivia, "trafficking organizations have kept pace by diversifying their marketing
of refined cocaine." Recent successes in curbing the operations of
the Medellín cartel in Colombia, meanwhile, have led only to an
increased market share for the competing Cali cartel. According
to DEA chief Robert Bonner, the Cali cartel boosted its market
share from 30 per cent to 75 per cent in the 10 months after the
government cracked down on Medellín in mid-1989.

Missing: Official Will and Capability

U.S. drug strategists recognize that these trends will not be
reversed unless Andean governments and security forces acquire
the capability and will to fight the U.S. drug war. "Strengthening

political will and institutional capability," notes the 1990 report of the Office of National Drug Control Policy, "is a requisite for all further [counternarcotics] actions" in the Andean region. Andean militaries and police are presently no match for narco-trafficking organizations operating transnationally and backed by private armies, advanced weaponry, and highly sophisticated intelligence systems. Security forces in the region are further hamstrung by operational inefficiency and ineffectiveness.

A November 1989 raid on the Bolivian town of San Ramón, touted by the U.S. embassy as "the largest counternarcotics enforcement operation in recent times," is a case in point. The raid was compromised by a tip-off; the targeted traffickers fled the site hours before the operation. Less than five kilos of cocaine were seized. The 20 Bolivians detained during the raid were released for lack of evidence, and the cost of the operation was more than $100,000.

Countless examples of inefficiency and mismanagement led the DEA in a December 1989 internal review to emphasize the need for "institution-building":

All members of the study team agree that "institution-building," or helping host country law enforcement agencies develop to the point of operational self-sufficiency has been an objective of the United States foreign policy for many years. . . . Despite significant achievements, institution building in the [Andean drug-producing] countries is incomplete. No . . . country is currently able to routinely conduct operations against coca processors without a U.S. presence.

The Bush administration's belief that the United States can manufacture the institutional capability needed for Andean governments to carry out U.S. objectives provides the rationale for the current strategy. But what leverage does the United States have to create such capability? In certain areas, Washington can and may make a difference. It can invest resources in training judiciaries, establishing new courts for drug proceedings, and offering technical assistance for crop substitution. It can improve the efficiency of policy and military enforcement with training, intelligence, and equipment. The size and operational capacity of the counternarcotics units will grow, and improved efficiency should lead to measurable, short-term successes: an increase in the levels of crops eradicated, coca paste seized, labs destroyed, and traffickers arrested.

But such *efficiency* does not automatically translate into institutional *effectiveness* in meeting stated objectives—in this case, cocaine supply reduction. This gap between efficiency and effectiveness is clouded by the very measures of "success" favored by policy advocates. There is a tendency to emphasize the number of crops eradicated and not the amount of new coca planted; the number of labs destroyed and not the number rebuilt or the total processing capacity; the number of seizures and not the totals being shipped; the number of arrests and not the continued effectiveness of the trafficking networks. Washington's measures of efficiency are as misleading in assessing genuine progress in the Andean drug war as "body counts" were in measuring U.S. success in the Vietnam war. With such measures, there is no failure, only milestones that fail to mark progress toward any meaningful goal.

These misleading measures obscure a deeper problem: No degree of technical capability among Andean drug enforcement agencies can achieve the stated objectives of the U.S. Andean strategy without political will—that is, unless government and military officials are committed to making our war their war. And their will to fight the U.S. war seems notably absent. Kirk Kotula, Bolivia program officer for the State Department's Bureau of International Narcotics Matters, noted in a January 1990 memo that the Bolivian government's performance "in almost every area indicates total lack of commitment to the anti-drug war." The DEA has reached similar conclusions about Peru.

The reasons for the lack of Andean commitment to the U.S. drug war are not hard to identify. The Andean economic and political context makes it rational for political leaders, military and law enforcement officials, and countless peasant producers to follow strategies at odds with American counternarcotics objectives. The limits on U.S. ability to create the Andean will to fight America's drug war may be far greater than even the most pragmatic U.S. drug strategies have calculated.

The primary concerns of Peruvian President Alberto Fujimori and Bolivian President Jaime Paz Zamora are to ensure economic and political stability in long-impoverished nations suffering from high unemployment, enormous foreign debts, and falling wages. In the last decade, both Peru and Bolivia have experienced the worst economic crises in their histories. Immediate economic and political interests dictate against a crackdown on coca, both nations' most significant and dependable source of dollars and jobs. The Peruvian coca industry brings in approximately $1 billion annually, or 30 per cent of the total value of legal exports, and employs some 15 per cent of the national work force. The Bolivian situation is starker. Bolivia's $600 million in annual coca revenues is equivalent to the value of all its other exports combined. The coca industry employs 300,000 Bolivians, or 20 per cent of the adult work force.

A swift and effective blow to the coca economy would have a devastating economic and political impact. The livelihoods of hundreds of thousands of citizens would be threatened, triggering massive social unrest. Paz Zamora has compared the effect of eliminating the Bolivian coca industry to that of laying off 50 million Americans by closing down a single industry.

The political impact of fighting the U.S. drug war is further complicated in Peru by the Shining Path insurgency. Peru's coca-rich Upper Huallaga Valley is effectively controlled by the Shining Path; the guerrillas portray themselves as protectors of the peasant growers, often serving as intermediaries on their behalf with the traffickers. Peruvians fear an aggressive narcotics control effort would increase the threat posed by the guerrillas by driving peasants into their ranks. Peruvian politicians, according to a 1989 DEA internal review, have said that

Peru can live with the narcotics problem for the next fifty years, but may not survive the next two years if the economic and insurgent problems are not dealt with now. . . . The will to deal with the drug issues, when faced with problems that threaten the immediate survival of the country, remains the most difficult issue.

The question of political will is more complex but equally at issue in Colombia. The government of President César Gaviria Trujillo draws a clear distinction between narco-terrorism and narco-trafficking. Its priority is not to eliminate drug trafficking per se, but to end the violence associated with the drug trade, which has taken an extraordinarily heavy toll in lives and on internal stability. In the "total war" declared by the Medellín drug cartel in 1989, more than 400 police officers, 100 judges and judicial assistants, and 11 journalists were killed in one year. The government's crackdown on the Medellín group has been formidable, but Colombian officials show little commitment to stopping the drug-trafficking activities of a broad range of other drug networks that, unlike Medellín, have not used paramilitary violence to threaten the government.

The difficulty in creating political will is not lost on U.S. narcotics officials. "Political will, pragmatically speaking, I would define as getting governments to do something they don't want to do," stated State Department narcotics specialist Daniel Chaij in April 1989. He and others, however, proceed as though the right mixture of carrots and sticks can make Andean governments act in accordance with U.S. strategy. They fail to understand the systemic character of the problem: Any U.S. drug strategy designed to significantly reduce the supply of cocaine at its source threatens the immediate economic viability of Andean countries and the political survival of Andean leaders.

Certainly, Andean governments share an interest in receiving U.S. aid and support: Offering millions of dollars in desperately needed aid in return for promises to fight the drug war, not surprisingly, has generated formal commitments and varying levels of cooperation from each of the Andean countries. But the lack of real commitment to U.S. antidrug objectives suggests that only those components of the drug policy that serve existing local interests—such as economic assistance and counterinsurgency support—will be actively pursued.

Andean will to wage the drug war is further undermined by the competing interests of the law enforcement and military institutions charged with carrying out the U.S. counternarcotics strategy. Military and police, for example, frequently refuse to cooperate and even sabotage each other's operations. U.S. field reports document the interagency conflicts as police and military forces vie for resources, prestige, and power in each of the three nations in a pattern not uncommon among Latin security forces.

In some instances, notably in Peru, these interagency conflicts are exacerbated by the contradictory missions of police and military forces. The Peruvian military is absorbed in a campaign against the Shining Path; the responsibilities of the police, meanwhile, include narcotics control missions conducted independently or with DEA assistance. The conflict is played out in the Upper Huallaga Valley. The military's interest is in driving a wedge between the insurgents and the coca-growing peasants whom the guerrillas claim to protect; military forces therefore are reluctant to alienate the growers and have generally permitted them to grow coca unimpeded. The police and the DEA, on the other hand, seek to disrupt both growing and trafficking. Serious conflicts have resulted: U.S. officials acknowledge a pattern of incidents, including armed attacks, in which Peruvian military forces have thwarted DEA operations.

As General Alberto Arciniega Hubi, formerly regional commander in the valley, explained, "There are 150,000 *campesinos cocaleros* [coca-growing peasants] in the zone. Each of them is a potential *subversivo*. Eradicate his field and the next day he'll be one." He further noted that "most of my troops come from this area. In effect, the police were wiping out the livelihood of their families, while I was asking them to fight Shining Path, which was sworn to protect the growers. Shining Path looked like heroes."

Administration attempts to link the antiguerrilla and anti-drug objectives may win military aid from a U.S. Congress alarmed by drugs, but they sidestep the fundamental contradiction between fighting the drug war and fighting the Shining Path. In Peru, the military's primary mission will remain counterinsurgency, although officials will gladly pay lip service to the drug war to gain U.S. aid. Likewise, in Colombia, the clear priority of the military is to battle insurgents, not drugs. In fact, Colombian military officials told U.S. congressional staff members that $38.5 million of the $40.3 million in counternarcotics assistance allocated for 1990 would provide most of the logistical support for a major counterinsurgency operation in an area not known for drug trafficking.

Can a well-crafted U.S. policy solve the problems of institutional rivalry and conflicting missions that undermine the will of the Andean countries to fight the U.S. drug war? There may be some specific actions the United States can take that would have salutary effects on the margins, but the limits of U.S. leverage in the Andean context are obvious. A December 1989 report by DEA agents in Peru is particularly telling:

Without the DEA presence, the Peruvians would not move against the traffickers. If given an airlift capability, the Peruvians would be more likely to move against the insurgents than the traffickers. Without U.S. presence, human rights violations, to include the slaughter of insurgents or traffickers, is likely.

While the United States may succeed in winning apparent compliance with its objectives and tactics, once American agents turn their backs, security forces will revert to their own mission and methods.

Perhaps the most insidious and uncontrollable factor undermining the local commitment to carry out the U.S. counternarcotics strategy is the drug-related corruption that runs through the militaries and law enforcement agencies of all three Andean countries. According to a December 1989 DEA memorandum, "corruption is a major factor within the police, the military and the judiciary" in Peru. The State Department reported in March

1991 that in Bolivia "widespread corruption, compounded by [government] weakness in policy implementation, further combine to hamper [Bolivia's] counter-narcotics effectiveness."

Forms of corruption are wide-ranging. Officials tip off narcotics traffickers before antidrug operations. They re-sell seized coca products for a profit after a raid. They accept payoffs to allow arrested traffickers to escape, or to permit drugs and processing chemicals to be transported through checkpoints. Corruption most commonly involves individuals who accept money simply to look the other way or conveniently disappear during a drug transaction. The motivation is not complicated. In November 1989 congressional testimony, retired Special Forces commander General Robert Kingston described a conversation between a U.S. border patrol agent and a Peruvian official at a checkpoint in Peru:

A colonel from Lima said, I have the opportunity while I'm here to make $70,000 by looking the other way at certain times. You have a family, they are protected in the United States, you have a proper pension plan. My family is not protected and I don't have the proper pension plan and I will never have the opportunity to make $70,000 as long as I live. I am going to make it.

A senior officer in Peru earns about $240 a month. It should therefore be no surprise that officers now bribe their superiors to get assigned to coca-producing zones once avoided at all costs.

Corruption becomes more insidious, however, when elements of an institution are complicit in the traffic itself, and the institution acts as a shield against individual accountability. In Peru, according to U.S. Special Forces commander Colonel Robert Jacobelly, "We know as a fact that the Army gets payments for letting traffickers use airstrips."

Bank records located after the capture and killing of Colombian trafficker José Gonzalo Rodríguez Gacha revealed that he had provided multimillion-dollar payoffs to entire brigades of the Colombian army. In one well-known 1983 case, a Colombian special forces company helped relocate an entire cocaine-processing operation that was threatened by guerrilla attacks. The operation took almost a month and involved nearly 50 army personnel, including six officers; each was paid between $500 and $2,500 by the traffickers. Asked why he did not act to seize the cocaine laboratory, the chief of staff of the Colombian Seventh Brigade responded that "it is not the mission" of the army to fight drugs but rather to battle insurgents.

Corruption reaches its most dangerous form when national leaders use the power of the state to further personal stakes in the drug trade. Although Panama's Manuel Antonio Noriega provides the most notorious example of state-level drug corruption, one of the Andean nations has had its own drug dictator. Andean expert Gustavo Gorriti testified before Congress that the 1980–81 regime of Luis García Meza in Bolivia "was without doubt the most important case in which political power—the control of a country—was used to further, protect, and engage in narcotics trafficking."

Unless the corruption deeply embedded in the government, police, and military can be addressed, many of the very agents on which the United States relies to carry out its strategy will subvert the U.S. drug war in pursuit of personal and institutional interests in the drug trade. The United States has distressingly little leverage in tempering this problem. The United States can and on occasion has secured the removal of individual officials accused of corruption. But such steps are merely temporizing measures perceived by Andean leaders as necessary to secure continued U.S. assistance. They do not address the systemic problem of drug-related corruption: the high profits of the drug trade. Government salaries cannot compete with traffickers' bribes. Moreover, an intensified antinarcotics campaign heightens the risks involved in the drug trade, thereby increasing the need for traffickers to rely on bribes and payoffs. The more aggressive the counternarcotics campaign, the greater the corruption and the higher the institutional stakes in the drug trade—and in subverting the U.S. drug war.

Narcotics officials acknowledge that problems such as corruption pose tremendous obstacles to the success of U.S. policy. As a December 1989 DEA report observes, "The 'moral' factors of corruption and national will are more complex [than the 'physical' factors of training and equipment], requiring progress in tangible and intangible areas beyond the scope of law enforcement." Yet the administration's policy rests on the assumption that focusing on the "physical" aspects will improve the "moral" factors. As the 1990 report of the Office of National Drug Control Policy stated, "increased military and law enforcement capability . . . can strengthen a country's national will to initiate and sustain counternarcotics programs." In fact, the effect can be precisely the opposite: An increased capability can make corruption even more profitable—and institutional will to fight drugs even more elusive.

The Logic of Peasant Production

The success of the U.S. drug strategy is conditioned not only on the will and ability of political elites and institutions, but on the actions of vast segments of the Andean population engaged in the cocaine economy. The United States and the Andean governments must convince hundreds of thousands of people to stop growing, processing, and shipping coca products. The current strategy relies on the same "carrot and stick" approach to peasant production that has underpinned previously unsuccessful U.S. efforts in the region.

The United States seeks to provide peasants with "carrots," through incentives to substitute other crops for coca, despite its profitability. The program of the U.S. Agency for International Development (AID) offers macro-level economic assistance, alternative development and income substitution, narcotics awareness and education, and administration of justice. Funds are used, for example, to identify potential new crops and to provide seeds for distribution. But U.S. officials concede the failure of Andean crop substitution programs: In Peru, for example, $25 million has been invested in the Upper Huallaga Valley over a decade, with no signs of success. Representative Lawrence Smith (D-Florida) stated flatly, "We have put a lot of money into crop substitution and it has gone absolutely nowhere."

The enforcement "stick" seeks to raise the risks and costs of illegal coca growing and processing activities through crop eradication, interdiction of coca products, and destruction of processing labs. Yet these tactics have failed to stem the increase in the overall coca supply. Despite periodic price swings, the profits to be gained from growing, processing, and transporting coca products have remained far higher than alternative economic pursuits.

The U.S. response to this poor record has been, once again, to change the emphasis but escalate the strategy. In recent years U.S. drug strategists have largely abandoned the difficult and time-consuming process of forcible manual eradication of coca crops, for example, in favor of coca seedbed destruction and "voluntary" eradication programs. The United States has set its sights on increased lab destruction rather than targeting primitive processing pits. Rhetorical and financial support for the economic assistance "carrot" is also mounting in Washington. Congressional critics looking for less-dangerous and cheaper alternatives to militarizing the drug war pin their hopes on rural development programs, including crop substitution. Such assistance may be good for the region's people, but as an effective instrument of drug-supply reduction it is doomed.

Consider the market from an Andean peasant's perspective: Coca brings many times the price of competing crops. Easy to harvest and process into paste, coca does not require transport by poor farmers to distant markets: Traffickers fly into remote airstrips regularly and pay peasants up front in dollars. Government intervention in the market to raise the risks of coca growing and enhance the attraction of economic alternatives is unlikely to change this logic; and localized, short-term successes do nothing to affect the rationale of other peasants—in other regions or other countries—who may choose to enter the lucrative market. Consequently, neither the crop-substitution carrot nor the enforcement stick can fundamentally transform the rational interests that poor peasants have in producing the high-profit coca crop.

AID officials acknowledge the impossibility of defying the logic of the market as long as profits remain high. "No single crop can approach the returns from coca production at current prices, and coca growers may suffer short term income losses as they move into legitimate occupations," testified AID official Frederick Schieck in June 1989. Faced with the severe limitations of economic assistance programs, he and others look to enforcement. "Efforts to provide alternative crops and incomes," Schieck emphasized, "cannot succeed unless there is sustained and effective enforcement and interdiction." But enforcement, too, is doomed to fail.

Peasants have developed sophisticated counterstrategies to circumvent drug enforcement efforts. Growers scale down and hide crops or replant in new regions. Processors downsize, camouflage, and relocate labs. The ineffectiveness of enforcement measures is compounded with peasant political responses: Coca growers have resisted eradication efforts not only through strikes and blockades organized by powerful regional coca growers' federations, but at times through armed resistance.

Drug enforcers increasingly find they are squeezing a balloon: "Successful" enforcement in one area causes—and even creates incentives for—production and processing to pop up in another. The drug strategy ultimately exacerbates the very problem it tries to solve as it encourages the spread of coca production, not only within the current producing countries but across borders: DEA agents acknowledge the increasing spread of cocaine processing and trafficking to Brazil, Ecuador, and Venezuela.

The Counterinsurgency Parallel

What debate there is in Washington over drug policy is proceeding in predictable ways. Conservative advocates of the use of force push for greater spending on enforcement and increased militarization. More moderate voices insist that economic development, crop substitution, and technical assistance would be more effective—and less destructive to human life and political democracy. The most serious debates are over the mix and levels of U.S. aid targeted for enforcement versus economic assistance.

But neither of these approaches, nor any mixture of them, can succeed, given that the major actors in the region are not only uncommitted to the U.S. drug war but have both rational and venal interests in thwarting it. Administration officials continue to argue that more arms, more training, and more technical assistance will solve the problem. If challenged, they drag out the false pragmatism of those unable to defend a failed policy through reasoned argument: "We can't know that the policy won't work until we try harder."

But we do not have to wait for more evidence from the Andean drug war front: The current counternarcotics strategy is built on the same flawed premises as U.S. counterinsurgency strategies that have so often foundered on repeated failures to create the needed will and capability among local elites and populations.

Counterinsurgency (CI) and counternarcotics (CN) strategies are distinct. The first aims to defeat a guerrilla movement seeking support among the peasant population; the second aims to arrest and prosecute drug traffickers who offer lucrative markets for the peasants. There are, however, important and troubling parallels between CI's military strategies for defeating guerrillas through search and destroy missions and wars of attrition, and the increasing use of such "low intensity conflict" against drug traffickers. And just as CI strategists seek to woo peasants away from the guerrillas by winning their "hearts and minds" through local development projects, land reform, and technical assistance, so too do CN strategists look to economic reforms and "civic action" programs to lure peasants away from profitable coca production. Not surprisingly, counternarcotics policy planners at the U.S. Southern Command and elsewhere have self-consciously borrowed from counterinsurgency theory and experience.

But what is most important here is the common understanding counterinsurgency strategists share with today's counternarcotics planners: If the strategy is to work, governments must have the ability and will to carry out the military and reform strategies, and peasants must have the will and ability to support the government and reject the insurgents (or traffickers). Efforts to build up local institutions to fight the U.S. drug war parallel the process earlier CI strategists called "nation-building": attempts to create institutions with funds for judicial and electoral reform, economic development, and administrative training. Military institution building meant training in intelligence, operations, and human rights. But as Michael Shafer has demonstrated in his 1988 counterinsurgency study *Deadly Paradigms*, limited success in improving operational efficiency did not translate into effectiveness because the will to carry out the U.S. CI strategy was absent and could not be created. Also, government officials often had other, more important interests that made it rational for them to act contrary to U.S. objectives.

U.S. training, for example, unquestionably created more skillful and efficient government administrators. But corruption was often so systemic that these skills were used to protect "bought" positions and reap personal profit. U.S. efforts to tame rampant corruption have historically failed in Vietnam and elsewhere, as journalist Neil Sheehan pointed out in *A Bright Shining Lie* (1988). U.S. pressure occasionally resulted in the removal of an individual, but "this was a trick. The man would be put in a staff job for a while and then given another province or district. . . . No Saigon official was taken off the wheel of corruption. He revolved on it." Little wonder that the head of DEA activities in Bolivia, Don Ferrarone, pulled a well-marked copy of Sheehan's book from his bookshelf to illustrate to a *New York Times* reporter the problems of corruption his office is now facing.

U.S. counterinsurgency efforts saw perhaps their greatest institution-building successes in the improved operational efficiency of local militaries. Yet it was here, too, that the United

States failed most dramatically in trying to create the commitment to meet U.S. objectives.

As early as the 1950s and the 1960s, U.S. policymakers felt that Third World militaries could help the process of modernization and nation building. U.S. training programs at U.S. staff colleges and later at the School of the Americas in Panama sought to professionalize the militaries and expose them to "democratic" values and attitudes.

But what did Latin American militaries do with their U.S. training? In Bolivia, officers involved in civic action later helped overthrow the civilian government in 1964 and establish an 18-year period of authoritarian rule. In fact, throughout Central and South America, these early U.S. efforts to involve the military in nation building led the military to intervene in politics.

With the increasing militarization of the U.S. counterinsurgency strategy, militaries lost any commitment to winning over the population. Modernizing the Salvadoran security forces, for example, often meant creating a more efficient instrument of repression despite U.S. training in professionalism and human rights. Some of the worst human rights abuses in El Salvador were carried out by members of U.S.-trained units such as the Atlacatl Battalion, whose most notorious crime was the November 1989 murder of six Jesuit priests. In Honduras, it was the soldiers of Battalion 316, trained in Texas as part of a CIA program to "professionalize" the security forces, who formed a major right-wing death squad.

U.S. efforts to curb Latin human rights abuses ran headlong into conflicting military interests. Latin military officers understood that real respect for civilian control would mean submitting themselves to laws that could punish them, politicians who could cut their budgets, and institutional accountability that could end the widespread corruption by which they profited.

Despite the evidence, U.S. strategists nevertheless clung to the idea that proper training could "create in them an awareness of the political process of nation-building" and make them "advocates of democracy and agents for carrying forward the developmental process," according to a key 1962 Kennedy administration policy paper. When this failed, the ultimate myth was that the United States could use the leverage of U.S. aid to force change. As this analysis put it, governments facing expulsion "have no practical alternative to accepting the U.S. recommendations, particularly if specific reforms become prerequisites to the continu-

ance of U.S. aid." But time and again this assessment has proven
wrong. U.S. leverage is limited as long as these militaries know
that defeating the insurgency (and, increasingly, winning the
drug war) is considered a vital national security matter and that
Washington is therefore unlikely to pull the aid plug.

The experience of U.S. counterinsurgency efforts thus provides an instructive critique of current drug war strategy. The
lesson is not the impossibility of defeating insurgents: Insurgents
have been defeated by governments that were able and willing to
make reforms and thus gain the support of the population—and
by governments and militaries with the will and ability to suffi-
ciently brutalize and repress their populations to contain (even if
temporarily) local insurgent movements. The real lesson is that
the local capability and will to conduct an effective strategy cannot be manufactured by the United States where they do not
exist. Indeed, winning the commitment of local governments and
militaries to fight the drug trade by which so many benefit can
only be more difficult than securing the commitment of local
elites to fight insurgents who threaten their existence.

The Politics of Denial

Tragically, the powerful lessons of failures in counterinsurgency strategy and years of unsuccessful counternarcotics
campaigns have yet to penetrate the Washington policy debate.
The Bush administration and Congress remain stubbornly committed to an Andean drug-control strategy that assumes that the
right mixture of carrots and sticks can create the necessary local
will and capability to carry out U.S. policy objectives. Faced with
the evidence of failure—readily available from congressional reports and hearings, DEA and State Department documents,
newspaper accounts, and testimony from U.S. field agents—the
response is a politics of denial. Past failures are either blithely
dismissed or used to justify further escalation. While the mixture
of policy tools may be slightly altered, there has been no fundamental reevaluation of the reasoning behind the supply-
reduction strategy.

To admit the uncomfortable truth that no policy to reduce
supply at the source of production can work without the full
commitment of local actors, and that this commitment cannot be
created by the United States, is to acknowledge that a supply-side
strategy abroad cannot succeed in solving the problems of drug

abuse and violence at home. Few drug officials would risk the budgets of their agencies, let alone their jobs, to argue that what they are doing is destined to fail. Perhaps most important, few politicians would be willing to risk being labeled "soft" on drugs or to surrender the convenience of blaming a foreign enemy.

To overcome this politics of denial and approach a solution to the drug problem, we must begin a real debate: The first step would be to force the Bush administration to confront the fatal flaws in its supply-reduction strategy. The will and ability of Andean governments, militaries, police, and peasants to wage the U.S. drug war do not exist, and years of U.S. attempts have failed to create them. Arms, training, and money may make local security forces more efficient, but the historical record is clear: Efficiency is not the same as effectiveness; better armed and trained security forces are not necessarily less corrupt or more respectful of human rights—or more capable of reducing the drug supply. The administration's "evidence" of success—the number of labs destroyed or tons of cocaine seized—must be exposed as the misleading "body counts" of the drug war.

Policymakers must, finally, confront the analysis of critics such as RAND economist Peter Reuter, who has demonstrated the futility of source-country efforts by showing that there is little relationship between supply reduction in the Andes and demand reduction at home: "Even if source country governments are willing to support them," Reuter testified before Congress in October 1989, "these programs offer little prospect for substantially affecting U.S. cocaine problems." Because the largest portion of the price on the street is added on after the drug enters the United States, Reuter has shown, even an inconceivable 50 per cent reduction in Andean supply would have only a negligible impact on domestic street prices. Even an overwhelmingly successful U.S. Andean strategy would thus contribute little to the ultimate aim of U.S. policy—raising cocaine prices and reducing consumption in North America.

The truth would be a difficult pill for policymakers to swallow: There is no Andean supply-reduction strategy that can significantly lower the demand for drugs at home. The supply-reduction policy defies both the logic of the market and the rational interests of local governments and populations. To continue to frame the central issue as how to reduce the foreign supply at the source is to mistake the means for the end and to

virtually guarantee continued failure. In other words, the drug
problem should be largely in the domain of domestic policy, not
foreign policy.

The required shift in drug policy does not mean abandoning
the Andes. The United States can take immediate actions to end
practices that actually fuel the drug trade: Lax export controls,
for example, make the United States the source of a significant
proportion of the chemicals used for the processing of cocaine
and the majority of the arms used by Andean drug traffickers.

Further, the United States has important interests in the Andes, such as strengthening fragile democracies, encouraging equi-
table growth and development, and discouraging violence and
human rights abuses. If American policymakers were not obsessed with drug-supply reduction, political space would be created for effective policies that genuinely serve U.S. and regional
interests. Andean leaders have requested and deserve assistance
in strengthening judicial and other institutions threatened by the
vast power of the drug cartels—even though such assistance may
not reduce the cocaine supply to the United States. The economic
development assistance needed to provide immediate relief in the
Andes should not be conditioned on acceptance of military assistance or "progress" in the U.S. drug war.

Such foreign policies, however, cannot be allowed to obscure
the focus of U.S. national concern with drug abuse, addiction,
and violence. The central goals of drug policy are to reduce domestic drug consumption and curb drug-related violence. It is
wasteful and inhumane to devote millions of antidrug dollars to
Andean militaries when so many addicts in the United States who
seek help are turned away from treatment centers for lack of
space. U.S. drug policy must finally confront the hard fact that
many drug dealers and users will not "just say no" to drugs unless
they have something better to say "yes" to, such as a decent job, a
decent school, and a chance for a decent life. Aid for the under-
developed territories in American inner cities is desper-
atelyneeded to alleviate the conditions that make drug abuse and
dealing so compelling.

The problems of drug abuse and drug dealing suggest the
need for a domestic policy of treatment, education, and urban
development. Such a policy cannot take shape without much debate and discussion among community leaders, health officials,
and policymakers. And this new dialogue cannot even begin until
the United States abandons its foolish and costly obsession with

solving the nation's drug problem in the distant jungles of South America.

HOW TO WIN THE WAR ON DRUGS[3]

America's so-called war on drugs is looking more and more like the real thing. Troops invade Panama in part to bring Manuel Noriega to justice for his alleged crimes as a drug trafficker. On the Mexican front, U.S. Marines, deployed for the first time in border patrols, engage marijuana smugglers in a firefight. And in mid-February, President Bush flies to Cartagena, Colombia, for an unprecedented antidrug summit aimed at rallying the governments of Colombia, Bolivia, and Peru to escalate their military struggle with the powerful cocaine cartels.

Will all this saber rattling make much of a difference? Don't bet on it. Despite record seizures, the supply of cocaine on America's mean streets—as well as the many not-so-mean ones—has never been more available or less expensive. In a persuasive study conducted for the Defense Department, Peter Reuter of Rand Corp. concludes that even a vastly more stringent interdiction program would at best reduce U.S. cocaine consumption by a mere 5%. Admits Jack Lawn, chief of the federal government's Drug Enforcement Administration (DEA): "Our enforcement efforts will continue to build statistics and fill prisons, but they won't turn around America's love affair with drugs."

Is the answer, then, to raise the white flag and legalize the stuff? Yes, say a small but influential number of professors and politicians, and at least one big-city judge. They argue that legalization would reduce violent crime and divert money from crooks to the government.

But they're probably wrong. The drugs popular today are so cheap to produce—a vial of crack cocaine selling for as little as $3 costs just 35 cents to import and manufacture—that a black market would continue to thrive alongside the legal one. Nor would legalization stop addicts from stealing to support their habits. What it would surely do is swell the use of substances far more

[3]Reprint of an article by Louis Kraar, *Fortune* staffwriter. Reprinted by permission of *Fortune*, 121: 70–71, 74–75, 78–79. Mar 12 '90. Copyright © 1990 by *Fortune*.

dangerous than alcohol. While 10% of drinkers become alcohol abusers, 20% to 30% of cocaine users wind up addicted. Since 1986 at least 100,000 infants have been born to drug abusers. The intensive care they require is costing several billion dollars a year.

Moreover, not all the battles in the drug war have been losing ones. Heroin use, which in the early 1970s threatened to become epidemic, has stabilized at roughly half a million addicts and attracts relatively few new recruits. Casual use of marijuana and cocaine also seems to be declining. The number of Americans who acknowledge using illicit drugs declined 37% between 1985 and 1988, according to household surveys conducted by the government's National Institute on Drug Abuse. The main reason the U.S. is experiencing what federal drug czar William Bennett describes as "the worst epidemic of illegal drug use in its history" is crack, the new plague.

The U.S. *can* gain further ground in the 1990s—but only by waging a more effective fight against illegal drugs at home. That doesn't mean policymakers ought to abandon longstanding efforts to curb the supply from abroad. But it does mean acknowledging that any new fiscal firepower should be targeted at reducing demand in the U.S.

Under President Bush, annual federal spending on the antidrug fight will have climbed 68%, to $10.6 billion, in two years. In a welcome reversal from the Reagan era cutbacks, Bush is increasing spending on prevention and treatment. But he still devotes only 30% of the budget to attacking the demand side of the problem. Instead, Bush is pouring $2.4 billion—a billion dollars more than Reagan—into the effort to interdict drugs before or as they enter the U.S., mainly by relying more on the armed forces.

Fortune would reverse those priorities. We would also invest a few billion dollars more in the struggle than the White House has proposed, though most of that new money will have to come from states and cities on the front line. Treating every one of the country's drug abusers, for instance, would cost $5.6 billion a year— more than half Washington's total spending on the drug war. Happily, much can also be achieved by simply spending and reacting smarter. Here's what we suggest:

Treatment

• **Provide more medical help for addicts.** The toughest challenge is curing the roughly four million Americans who are serious substance abusers. Only about 20% currently get medical help. Many shun it, but most cannot find it. While expensive private treatment centers have plenty of room, public centers—the only ones most addicts can afford—typically have long waiting lists. Says Robert Stutman, a veteran DEA agent in New York: "Imagine if I had cholera and walked into a city hospital and the doctor said, 'Come back in seven months.' It would be a scandal, but that's exactly what happens every day to addicts seeking help."

Though it has increased spending in this area, the Bush Administration is hardly acting like a government faced with an epidemic. Bennett's strategy, shaped more by budgetary constraints than hard evidence, is to focus on the half of the four million addicts whom he deems most capable of being helped. Another million, he argues, can help themselves. The remaining million are "hard-core addicts or career criminals" whom existing methods of treatment can't change much.

Doing better requires new medical techniques as well as more money. Only about half of cocaine addicts stay drug free for up to two years after treatment. Part of the problem is that some 70% of drug users also have an alcohol or mental disorder. Says Dr. Frederick Goodwin, head of the federal government's Alcohol, Drug Abuse, and Mental Health Administration: "We need more effective matching of individuals with particular treatments." A centralized registry of programs and openings in them would be an inexpensive first step.

Drug addiction can be cured, as successful treatment centers such as Phoenix House demonstrate. Says Frank Gough, a former heroin addict and director of an adult treatment center for Daytop Village in New York State: "We return to society productive, responsible people." The big problem is getting those whose judgment has been spiked by drugs to enter and stay in treatment. Most are pushed into it by their family or the threat of imprisonment.

• **Use local laws to allow courts to commit hard-core addicts to treatment.** Few states do this now. But California courts, for instance, can send convicted drug offenders to a special prison that includes a rehabilitation center. This so-called civil commitment program entails frequent drug testing after release and recommitment for those who resume the habit. Says Dr. Mitch Rosenthal of Phoenix House: "If the country wants to get serious, like a good family it has to demand that drug users stay in treatment."

• **Convert surplus military bases to drug treatment sites.** As Nancy Reagan learned in trying to set up a rehabilitation center for adolescent drug abusers in Los Angeles, many communities object to having one in their midst. The Pentagon is supposed to identify surplus facilities but has not acted yet. With a glut of unneeded bases about to hit the market, this is an opportunity not to be missed.

• **Expand research on medical treatments for addiction.** The idea is to treat brain dysfunctions caused by habitual drug use and, by reducing cravings, make patients more receptive to therapy. Medication is already used to treat many of the nation's 500,000 heroin addicts. Democratic Senator Joseph Biden of Delaware proposes spending $1 billion on research over the next ten years, a realistic target. This is a clear-cut case where Washington must take the lead: Pharmaceutical companies are uncertain whether such products would make money and fret they would hurt the companies' image.

Prevention

• **Do more to equip children to resist drugs.** Surprisingly, only about half the nation's public schools provide comprehensive substance-abuse education. Less surprisingly, since the key is building character, it's a struggle to find methods that work. Merely providing information in a classroom does little to curb demand and may even stimulate curiosity to try drugs.

Kansas City has proved that mobilizing parents and the community can make drug education more effective. Starting with sixth- and seventh-graders, schools discourage the use of cigarettes, alcohol, and marijuana, widely considered the path to more dangerous substances. Students get classroom training in skills for resisting drug use, involve parents in discussion sessions, and see their efforts covered in the local media. The result: These youngsters show only half the drug use typical among their age group.

Bringing local police into the classroom helps too. The Drug Abuse Resistance Education program that Los Angeles started in 1983 uses specially trained officers as instructors for fifth- and sixth-graders. By appearing in full uniform, the teachers in blue immediately command attention. They maintain it by dealing with the real world of adolescents, presenting a course that aims at building self-esteem and teaches how to say no without losing friends. The L.A. cops' promising technique has spread to some 2,000 communities in 49 states.

• **Do more to spot drug use early.** Many public schools require a health examination for new students, an ideal checkpoint. The Los Angeles County district attorney's office focuses heavily on truancy, an early sign of drug use, and gets families into fighting it.

• **Shout louder from the most bully pulpit around.** The nonprofit Partnership for a Drug-Free America has created a starkly emotional series of ads now showing on TV all across the U.S. In one, a young woman snorts cocaine in the privacy of her home, while an offstage voice notes that one out of five users gets hooked, then asks, "But that's not your problem. Or is it?" In the last scene, she reappears driving a school bus. Space for this $150-million-a-year campaign is donated by newspapers, magazines, and TV. Surveys suggest that the ads do reduce consumption of marijuana and cocaine, particularly in the markets that run them frequently. By slightly more than doubling the reach of its ads, the Partnership hopes to expose every American to an antidrug message at least once a day.

• **Companies should join the drug war.** Already, federal law requires those in fields such as transportation, nuclear power, and defense to maintain a drug-free workplace. With good reason. In 1987 a Conrail train ran through a restricted switch into the path of a high-speed Amtrak train, killing 16 people and injuring 174. The "probable cause," according to the National Transportation Safety Board's report: The Conrail engineer was suffering from marijuana "impairment."

Now other corporations are getting interested in drug testing as a way to cut health insurance costs and productivity losses. According to a study by the Bureau of Labor Statistics, some 9% of corporate America's employees show up for work with illegal substances in their systems. The cost to the economy: an estimated $60 billion a year.

IBM has a model program that protects both the company and its employees from drug abuse. Since 1984 every job applicant has had to undergo a urine test for illegal drugs. Any employee caught bringing drugs into IBM, including its parking lots, gets fired. Employees who act strangely or perform erratically can be referred to the company's medical department, but are not required to take a drug test unless their job is safety sensitive. Those who admit to having a drug problem, however, get counseling and medical attention. Says Dr. Glenn E. Haughie, the company's director of corporate health and safety: "IBM considers drug use a treatable disease." Among his success stories is a manager who ran up big bills on a company credit card before admitting to a decade-long cocaine habit. After treatment the manager is back at work and drug free.

Enforcement

• **Unclog the criminal justice system.** Crowded courts have taken much of the risk out of the drug business. Arrestees have a 15% chance of going to jail in New York City and face only slightly worse odds in Washington, D.C. Genuine deterrence requires not only more police but also more prosecutors, judges, and jails. The Administration is expanding the federal prisons, which house over 50,000 people, at a cost of $1.5 billion.

But 85% of drug offenders are in state and local prisons. Many are so jammed that courts won't allow them to take in newcomers unless someone already there is released. As a result, drug traffickers convicted in state courts serve only 22 months on average, less time than for robbery or aggravated assault. State and local governments will just have to spend more on jails: $5 billion to $10 billion over the next few years. That's about half the costs of the jails they built in the past decade.

• **Try alternative forms of punishment.** Drug czar Bennett wants swift, sure penalties, but he's willing to see them take forms other than long prison terms. Punishment for recreational drug users, who are more influential than addicts in popularizing drugs, should fit their crime. Says Dr. Herbert Kleber, a Yale psychiatrist who is serving as Bennett's deputy for demand reduction: "The casual user is saying, in effect, that you can enjoy drugs, keep your health and job, have it all."

In Phoenix that kind of attitude can get the casual drug user a heavy fine and a night in jail. In Philadelphia a yuppie shopping at the local cocaine market risks having his BMW auctioned off if he is convicted. Denying teenage offenders a driver's license for a year is another promising deterrent. In Toledo the juvenile court can make parents answer for their children's mistakes by imposing fines or even a few days in jail.

• **Get communities involved in policing troubled neighborhoods.** Operation Clean in Dallas has enabled residents to regain control of areas once overrun by drug dealers. In a six-week operation, the city first pours in cops to put the heat on dealers. It then brings in the full range of services literally to clean up the neighborhood, and finally stations police foot patrols in the community. So far four such cleanups of inner-city areas have reduced violent crimes significantly. Says assistant police chief Sam Gonzales: "We're displacing drug dealers. We can't allow them to take a foothold in part of the city and say, 'It's mine.'"

In Kansas City, the Ad Hoc Group Against Crime runs a hotline that people can use to report suspected drug dealers to police. The organization also provides $1,000 rewards for information leading to convictions. Says Mary Weathers, director of the citizens' group: "The police cannot always get there, so we try to give visible community support." An offshoot of Ad Hoc called Black Men Together, formed to provide virtuous role models for youth, holds frequent antidrug rallies where citizens (backed by police) use bullhorns to shout suspected dealers off the streets.

Seattle is reclaiming drug-infested neighborhoods with bicycle patrols by pairs of officers who befriend local residents and sneak up on drug dealers. Officer Tony Little, who patrols a low-income housing project, says the technique definitely helps cut down drug trafficking. Riding a 21-speed mountain bike "makes you more approachable than if you're driving a patrol car," he argues. Often acting on tips from residents, the bike cops surprise dealers, put them in handcuffs, and radio for a patrol car. The bikes cost around $500 each.

The Drug Enforcement Administration has 2,800 agents, roughly the number of musicians in the U.S. Army. The Federal Bureau of Investigation has assigned 1,100 agents to drug cases. Given those limits, creative efforts by local police are crucial.

• **Seize even more drug profits.** The most vulnerable commodity in the narcotics trade is money. Drug sales in the U.S. generate more than $80 billion in tax-free profits a year. But traffickers must find ways to get their proceeds into bank accounts and legitimate businesses to disguise the source. Tracing and confiscating cash and assets deal drugsters a double blow: Money is much harder for them to replace than drugs, and the government can use it to help pay for the war against them. Says Charles O. Simonsen, chief of the currency investigations branch at U.S. Customs: "We're having a bigger impact taking their money than their drugs. If we can attack the financial infrastructure of a drug organization, we can terminally damage it."

Over the past four years the federal government has seized

more than $1 billion in assets. To do more than skim the surface, states should strengthen asset forfeiture laws for drug proceeds. The Treasury, which acquires an enormous amount of data from banks on cash transactions of $10,000 or more, as well as on "suspicious transactions," often still lacks the paper trail needed for convictions. Requiring more information on international wire transfers of money would help. Under prodding from Senator John Kerry of Massachusetts, the Treasury is also negotiating to get key foreign bank centers to maintain their own paper trails—and make them available to criminal investigations.

International

• **Recognize that the long-term solution is to attack the economic roots of the supply problem.** Sure, there's always room for more military cooperation. But remember that farmers in Peru and Bolivia are hooked on coca as a cash crop, while in Colombia, which processes and exports the stuff, cocaine is one of the main earners of foreign exchange. Rensselaer Lee, a business consultant who has studied the South American cocaine trade, warns, "Trying to eradicate the problem quickly may create worse problems by throwing people out of work and destabilizing governments."

To help those economies go straight, the Bush Administration has promised $2.2 billion in military and economic aid over the next five years. That's not a bad start. But Washington could still show more sensitivity to the legitimate economic needs of drug-supplying countries. Recently the U.S. alienated Colombia by allowing the collapse of an international pact for stabilizing coffee prices. The cost to the Bogotá government: several hundred million dollars a year in legal export earnings.

In the struggle against drugs, what can we expect to achieve by the year 2000? Drug czar Bennett's goal is to reduce drug use in the U.S. by 55% in ten years. Sounds terrific, until you realize that's about what the U.S. has done since 1985. And who feels better off today? Moreover, who knows what cheap, new designer drug could come along to fuel the epidemic? Use of a smokable form of methamphetamine called ice, which gets users high for up to eight hours vs. 20 minutes for crack, could spread rapidly. Says Robert W. Burgreen, police chief in San Diego: "Anyone with a chemistry book and the ability to experiment can make meth."

Still, that's no reason to despair, as some do, that this fight is destined to prove another Vietnam. To the extent that it implies the U.S. can win a reasonably swift and clearcut victory, as it did in World War II, today's drug war rhetoric is misleading. Think instead of another struggle that offered no quick fix but instead required patience, vast resources, bipartisan and international cooperation, but which America saw through successfully—the cold war. Policies based on containment may not stir the blood. Pursued long enough, though, they can ultimately prevail.

THE DRUG WAR ON CIVIL LIBERTIES[4]

Of all the wars the United States has fought since 1945, not one has enjoyed the popularity of the War on Drugs. Americans tell pollsters they're more afraid of drugs than of unemployment or the deficit; drug enforcement, in fact, is one of the few government services for which people say they're willing to pay higher taxes. The consensus crosses racial, gender, class, ideological and geographical lines, so it's sometimes hard to tell the difference between the antidrug rhetoric of, say, Jesse Jackson and George Bush.

Which should come as no surprise. The horrors of drug abuse are so lavishly documented that in a single day it's possible to hear a report on *Good Morning America* about a Coast Guard marijuana seizure off Savannah, Georgia; then read in the morning paper about a drive-by shooting in Los Angeles; glance at a drug-free-workplace poster over the water fountain; listen to a call-in radio confessional about addiction; catch up on Richard Dreyfuss's battle against cocaine while waiting in line at the Safeway; hear from the kids about their D.A.R.E. "drug education" program at school; watch a "kingpin" brought to justice on *Miami Vice*; pop in a video of *New Jack City*; and wind up the day by participating in a crack-house raid on the 10 o'clock news.

This wide and shallow drug education obscures a horror that is harder to dramatize: the gutting of our civil liberties. While the

[4]Reprint of an article by Dan Baum, free-lance writer. Reprinted by permission of *The Nation*, 254: 886–8. Je 29 '92. Copyright © 1992 *The Nation*.

violence and excitement of the War on Drugs hogs the spotlight, the Reagan-Bush-Quayle Administration is backstage building an unprecedented federal apparatus for putting people in prison. More Americans are in federal prison today for drug crimes than were in federal prison for all crimes when Ronald Reagan took office. The United States has a bigger portion of its population behind bars than any other country, including a female prison population that has doubled in six years. And half the Americans in prison today are black, even though only about an eighth of the population is. The United States, in fact, has a rate of black male incarceration five times that of South Africa. More American black men are in prison than are in college. The Justice Department estimates that by 1995 more than two-thirds of all convicts will be inside for drugs. This isn't a war on drugs; it's a jihad against people who use them.

And that includes anybody who has even the most casual contact with drugs. "User accountability" is the buzzword in President Bush's latest National Drug Control Strategy, and people are being arrested for simple possession at twice the rate they were in 1980. Most drug users aren't violent or dysfunctional, the strategy says, but they should be punished anyway because "the casual user imparts the message that you can still do well in school or maintain a career and family." For that, Bush wants casual users imprisoned as criminals, ejected from public housing, deprived of driver's licenses and cut off from both student loans and welfare. Criminalizing victimless drug use uncouples behavior from the societal harm it may cause in much the same way that archaic morality laws against consensual sex did. But a quarter-million Americans aren't in prison for consensual sex; they're in prison for drugs. That single, hopeless fact should at least suggest a serious debate about decriminalization. But instead, the War on Drugs has effectively turned a blue law into the biggest prison-filler in the land and loosed a huge army of federal police to enforce it. Alongside the familiar newspaper stories about innocent victims of drugs, we're beginning to see articles about innocent victims of drug policy, such as landlords whose buildings are confiscated because of tenants who use drugs, or whole families evicted from public housing for the sins of one member.

Meanwhile, the "drug problem" and the violence associated with it show no real sign of diminishing. The drugs are getting more serious, or at least the enforcement is; at the beginning of the 1980s two-thirds of all drug arrests were for pot and the rest were for heroin, cocaine and other drugs. Now that ratio is reversed. What hasn't changed, though, is that although drug "pushers" are supposedly the target of the war, twice as many people are arrested for drug possession as for dealing. Arrest figures and wildly inflated "street values" of seized cocaine have replaced the Vietnam-era body count, and are about as good a measure of who is winning the war. Addiction isn't the government's first concern; treatment and prevention get less than half the funding of enforcement. Instead, the goal is simply to lock people up.

Americans have from the very beginning used drug laws as an excuse to spy on and harass their political or ethnic enemies. The country's first drug ban explicitly targeted the opium of "the heathen Chinee." The first marijuana laws were passed by states fearing an immigration wave of "beet peons" from Mexico. Cocaine was first banned in the South to prevent an uprising of hopped-up "cocainized Negroes."

The War on Drugs has let the government concentrate unprecedented police power inside the Beltway. The total federal drug budget has increased elevenfold since 1980. (The United States spends half again as much on the drug war as it does on the Environmental Protection Agency.) Bush has doubled the corps of federal prosecutors, and while state-level wiretaps decreased during the eighties, federal wiretaps almost quadrupled. Even Chief Justice William Rehnquist—no softy on drugs—took it upon himself in February to chastise the Justice Department for overburdening the federal courts with petty drug cases.

It used to mean something to "make a federal case out of it." Now, though, local police and the idea of "local control" are almost irrelevant; first-offense marijuana possession is on the book as a federal crime, with a mandatory five-year penalty attached. "Every year they find more and more crimes to federalize," says Scott Wallace, legislative director for the National Association of Criminal Defense Lawyers in Washington, D.C. "What's next, a national police in brown shirts?"

Not satisfied merely to take over huge numbers of new drug cases, the Justice Department last year started combing the files of people who have already done prison time in state drug cases; they pin a federal rap on them and send them back to prison for the same crime. Fifty-year-old Donny Clark made a mistake in 1985 and got caught with 900 marijuana plants on his Manatee County, Florida, farm. He served a year in state prison and forgot all about it. But last year, the Feds busted a pot ring in the area and decided Clark had taught the perps their agronomy, and in November, a federal judge sent him to the Federal Correctional Institute at Marianna, Florida, for the rest of his life without hope of parole. "Formally, the charge was conspiracy," Clark's prosecutor, Assistant U.S. Attorney Walter Furr, told me, "but the man was charged based on what was found in the search warrant in 1985." Simply put, Clark has been punished twice for those 900 plants. A Florida judge thought the crime was worth a year; Congress gave him life without parole, even though that mandatory sentence wasn't on the books at the time of his crime. That's not double jeopardy because he was sentenced by "different sovereigns"—the state and federal governments. And his case isn't an anomaly; Justice has a name for the new policy. "We call it Project Trigger-Lock," says Justice spokesman Doug Tillett. "The intent is to get bad guys off the street with apologies to none."

Above all, though, the Reagan and Bush administrations have succeeded in bribing local police to siphon citizens into federal prisons. They did so by slashing general assistance to local police with one hand and offering big drug-enforcement grants with the other. Then in 1986, the Justice Department started offering local police a cut of the cash, houses, cars, airplanes and other assets confiscated in joint operations with federal drug agents— cases that almost always go to federal instead of state court. Junkie-sick for funds, police responded with relish; since Justice started sharing the loot, confiscations have risen seventeenfold, to half a billion dollars a year, of which state and local cops last year got almost half.

In Missoula County, Montana—a place so far removed from the "drug problem" that police say they have never seen crack— two of the sheriff's eleven detectives and one of the county's five prosecutors are paid entirely by federal drug-grant money and assigned full-time to drug cases. Between grants and confiscated assets, the county's chief of detectives told the weekly *Missoula Independent*, drug enforcement is "just about the only type of law enforcement where you get a return on your dollar." Welcome to free-market criminal justice. With police dependent on the drug economy, it's hard to see their incentive for stamping it out.

As drug cases flood the federal courts, the punishments meted out there continue to escalate. Federal judges no longer have much discretion in sentencing; even the most small-potatoes marijuana crime—possession without intent to sell—carries a mandatory minimum. And if prosecutors don't like the sentence, they can appeal, a right that until 1984 was enjoyed exclusively by defendants. There's no federal parole anymore, either, so once you're convicted you're on the federal express; the mandatory machine kicks in and that's the last of you until your sentence is served.

It's gotten to where defense attorneys in federal drug cases can do their clients about as much good as Dr. Kevorkian can do his—quietly shepherd them through to the least painful end. The government gets all the time it wants to prepare its case; a defendant now gets only seventy days. The government can further cripple the defense by confiscating in advance any money the accused would use to pay a lawyer. "It's terrifying," says one Montana defense lawyer. "I've actually thought about resigning from the bar because there is less and less I can do for my clients." Just say nolo contendere.

The Supreme Court, meanwhile, is steadily eroding the protections against police excess promised by the Fourth, Fifth, Sixth, Eighth and Fourteenth Amendments to the Constitution. The Court during the past decade let police obtain search warrants on the strength of anonymous tips (Fourth and Sixth Amendments). It did away with the need for warrants when police want to search luggage, trash cans, car interiors, bus passengers, fenced private property and barns (Fourth). It let prosecutors hold drug offenders without bail (Eighth). It permitted the confiscation of property before a suspect is charged, let alone convicted (Fifth). It let prosecutors imprison people twice—at the state and federal levels—for the same crime (Fifth). It let police fly as low as 400 feet over houses in their search for marijuana plants (Fourth). It allowed the seizure of defense attorneys' legal fees in drug cases (Sixth). It allowed mandatory urine testing for federal employees (Fourth). And in a Michigan case last year, it let stand a sentence of mandatory life without parole for simple drug possession (Eighth).

None of these decisions rated more than a fleeting blip on the political radar. "What we have here is a classic conflict between civil liberties and effective law enforcement," a U.S. Attorney in Montana blithely told me during an interview. "And the will of the people right now, at least as expressed through their elected representatives, is for effective drug enforcement." A Louisiana defense attorney put it another way: "Our rights aren't being taken away," he said, "they're being given away." This for a "war" that, like most others, brings no clear result but violence and misery, even to the people in whose name it is waged.

There hasn't been much criticism of the War on Drugs so far because even as we celebrate the 200th anniversary of the Bill of Rights, any such criticism is essentially forbidden speech. Thomas Kline of Post Falls, Idaho, got a swift lesson in the dangers of speaking out when he wrote a letter to the editor of the *Coeur d'Alene Press* last October advocating the legalization of marijuana. A couple of days later, agents of the Idaho Department of Law Enforcement (IDLE) searched the garbage can behind his house—which is legal without a warrant—and found three grams of pot stems. On the strength of that evidence, they got a warrant, found seventeen joints in Kline's house and busted him. "We'd do the same thing again," said Wayne Longo, the IDLE agent in charge of the investigation, reached by telephone at his desk in Coeur d'Alene. "It's not that often that we see people writing in saying they're using dope." Of course, Kline's letter says nothing about his using marijuana; it's strictly an argument for legalization. Longo, however, wasn't interested in quibbling. "Look," he said. "I've commented on this all I'm going to." And he hung up.

A POLITICAL OPIATE[5]

If President Bush's September [1989] address to the nation on the topic of drugs can be taken as an example of either his honesty or his courage, I see no reason why I can't look forward to hearing him declare a war against cripples, or one-eyed people, or red geraniums. It was a genuinely awful speech, rooted at the beginning in a lie, directed at an imaginary enemy, sustained by false argument, proposing a policy that already had failed, playing to the galleries of prejudice and fear. The first several sentences of the speech established its credentials as a fraud. "Drugs," said Bush, "are sapping our strength as a nation." "The gravest domestic threat facing our nation," said Bush, "is drugs." "Our most serious problem today," said Bush, "is cocaine." None of the statements meets the standards either of minimal analysis

[5]Reprint of an article by Lewis H. Lapham. Reprinted by permission of *Harper's*, 279: 43–48. D '89. Copyright © 1989 by *Harper's*.

or casual observation. The government's own figures show that the addiction to illegal drugs troubles a relatively small number of Americans, and the current generation of American youth is the strongest and healthiest in the nation's history.[1]

In the sixth paragraph of his speech, the President elaborated his fraud by holding up a small plastic bag, as distastefully as if he were holding a urine specimen. "This is crack cocaine," he said, "seized a few days ago by Drug Enforcement Administration agents in a park just across the street from the White House. It could easily have been heroin or PCP." But since nobody, ever, has been known to sell any kind of drug in Lafayette Park, it couldn't possibly have been heroin or PCP. The bag of cocaine wasn't anything other than a stage prop: The DEA was put to considerable trouble and expense to tempt a dealer into the park in order to make the arrest at a time and place convenient to the President's little dramatic effect.

Bush's speechwriters ordered the staging of the "buy" because they wanted to make a rhetorical point about the dark and terrible sea of drugs washing up on the innocent, sun-dappled lawns of the White House. The sale was difficult to arrange because the drug dealer in question had never heard of Lafayette Park, didn't know how to find the place on a map, and couldn't imagine why anybody would want to make such complicated travel arrangements in order to buy rocks of low-grade crack.

Two days later, confronted by the press with the mechanics of his sleight of hand, Bush said, "I don't understand. I mean, has somebody got some advocates here for this drug guy?" The surprised and petulant tone of his question gave away the nature of the political game that he was playing, playing on what he assumed was the home field of the nation's best-loved superstitions. After seven months in office, he had chosen to make his first televised address on a topic that he thought was as safe as mother and the undesecrated flag. He had politely avoided any and all of the "serious problems facing our nation today" (the deficit, say, or the environment, or the question of race) and he had done what he could to animate a noncontroversial platitude with a good visual. He expected people to be supportive and nice.

Apparently it never occurred to him that anybody would complain about his taking a few minor liberties with the facts. Nor did he seem to notice that he had seized upon the human suffering implicit in the drug trade as an occasion for a shabby political trick. He had exploited exactly the same device in his election campaign by transforming the image of Willie Horton, a black convict who committed violent crimes after being released on furlough from a Massachusetts prison, into a metaphor for all the world's wickedness. I can imagine his speechwriters explaining to him that the war on drugs was nothing more than Willie Horton writ large.

The premise of the war is so patently false, and the hope for victory so obviously futile, that I can make sense of it only by asking the rhetorical question *cui bono*? Who stands to gain by virtue of Bush's lovely little war, and what must the rest of us pay as tribute?

The question is a political one. But, then, the war on drugs is a political war, waged not by scientists and doctors but by police officers and politicians. Under more fortunate circumstances, the prevalence of drugs in American society—not only cocaine and heroin and marijuana but also alcohol and tobacco and sleeping pills—would be properly addressed as a public-health question. The American Medical Association classifies drug addiction as a disease, not as a crime or a moral defeat. Nor is addiction contagious, like measles and the flu. Given the folly and expense of the war on drugs (comparable to the folly and expense of the war in Vietnam), I expect that the United States eventually will arrive at some method of decriminalizing the use of all drugs. The arguments in favor of decriminalization seem to me irrefutable, as do the lessons of experience taught by the failed attempt at the prohibition of alcohol.

But for the time being, as long as the question remains primarily political, the war on drugs serves the purposes of the more reactionary interests within our society (i.e., the defenders of the imagined innocence of a nonexistent past) and transfers the costs of the war to precisely those individuals whom the promoters of the war say they wish to protect. I find it difficult to believe that the joke, although bitter, is unintended.

To politicians in search of sound opinions and sustained applause, the war on drugs presents itself as a gift from heaven. Because the human craving for intoxicants cannot be suppressed—not by priests or jailers or acts of Congress—the politicians can bravely confront an allegorical enemy rather than an enemy that takes the corporeal form of the tobacco industry, say, or the Chinese, or the oil and banking lobbies. The war against drugs provides them with something to say that offends nobody, requires them to do nothing difficult, and allows them to postpone, per-

haps indefinitely, the more urgent and specific questions about
the state of the nation's schools, housing, employment opportunities for young black men—i.e., the conditions to which drug
addiction speaks as a tragic symptom, not a cause. They remain
safe in the knowledge that they might as well be denouncing
Satan or the rain, and so they can direct the voices of prerecorded
blame at metaphors and apparitions who, unlike Senator Jesse
Helms and his friends at the North Carolina tobacco auctions, can
be transformed into demonic spirits riding north across the Caribbean on an evil wind. The war on drugs thus becomes the
perfect war for people who would rather not fight a war, a war in
which the politicians who stand so fearlessly on the side of the
good, the true and the beautiful need do nothing else but strike
noble poses as protectors of the people and defenders of the
public trust.

Their cynicism is implicit in the arithmetic. President Bush in
his September speech asked for $7.9 billion to wage his "assault
on every front" of the drug war, but the Pentagon allots $5 billion
a year to the B-2 program—i.e., to a single weapon. Expressed as
a percentage of the federal budget, the new funds assigned to the
war on drugs amount to .065 percent. Nor does the government
offer to do anything boldly military about the legal drugs, princi-
pally alcohol and tobacco, that do far more damage to the society
than all the marijuana and all the cocaine ever smuggled into
Florida or California.

The drug war, like all wars, sells papers, and the media, like
the politicians, ask for nothing better than a safe and profitable
menace. The campaign against drugs involves most of the theatri-
cal devices employed by *Miami Vice*—scenes of crimes in progress
(almost always dressed up, for salacious effect, with the cameo
appearances of one or two prostitutes), melodramatic villains in
the Andes, a vocabulary of high-tech military jargon as reassuring
as the acronyms in a Tom Clancy novel, the specter of a crazed
lumpenproletariat rising in revolt in the nation's cities.

Like camp followers trudging after an army of crusader
knights on its way to Jerusalem, the media have in recent months
displayed all the garish colors of the profession. Everybody who
was anybody set up a booth and offered his or her tears for sale—
not only Geraldo and Maury Povich but also, in much the same
garish language, Dan Rather (on *48 Hours*), Ted Koppel (on *Night-
line*), and Sam Donaldson (on *Prime Time Live*). In the six weeks
between August 1 and September 13, the three television net-

works combined with the *New York Times* and the *Washington Post* to produce 347 reports from the frontiers of the apocalypse—crack in the cities, cocaine in the suburbs, customs agents seizing pickup trucks on the Mexican border, smugglers named Julio arriving every hour on the hour at Key West.

Most of the journalists writing the dispatches, like most of the columnists handing down the judgments of conscience, knew as much about crack or heroin or cocaine as they knew about the molecular structure of the moons of Saturn. Their ignorance didn't prevent them from coming to the rescue of their own, and the President's, big story. On *World News Tonight* a few days after the President delivered his address, Peter Jennings, in a tone of voice that was as certain as it was silly (as well as being characteristic of the rest of the propaganda being broadcast over the other networks), said, "Using it even once can make a person crave cocaine for as long as they [*sic*] live."

So great was the media's excitement, and so determined their efforts to drum up a paying crowd, that hardly anybody bothered to question the premises of the drug war, and several of the more senior members of the troupe took it upon themselves to write diatribes against any dissent from the wisdom in office. A. M. Rosenthal, on the op-ed page of the *New York Times*, denounced even the slightest show of tolerance toward illegal drugs as an act of iniquity deserving comparison to the defense of slavery. William Safire, also writing in the *New York Times*, characterized any argument against the war on drugs as an un-American proof of defeatism. Without notable exception, the chorus of the big media turned its instruments to the high metallic pitch of zero tolerance, scorned any truth that didn't echo their own, and pasted the smears of derision on the foreheads of the few people, among them Milton Friedman and William Buckley, who had the temerity to suggest that perhaps the war on drugs was both stupid and lost.

The story of the drug war plays to the prejudices of an audience only too eager to believe the worst that can be said about people whom they would rather not know. Because most of the killing allied with the drug trade takes place in the inner cities, and because most of the people arrested for selling drugs prove to be either black or Hispanic, it becomes relatively easy for white people living in safe neighborhoods to blur the distinction between crime and race. Few of them have ever seen an addict or witnessed a drug deal, but the newspapers and television networks keep showing them photographs that convey the impression of a class war, and those among them who always worried about driving through Harlem (for fear of being seized by gangs of armed black men) or who always wished that they didn't feel quite so guilty about the socioeconomic distance between East 72nd Street and West 126th Street can comfort themselves, finally, at long last, and with a clear conscience, with the thought that poverty is another word for sin, that their BMW is a proof of their virtue, and that they or, more likely, their mothers were always right to fear the lower classes and the darker races.

As conditions in the slums deteriorate, which they inevitably must because the government subtracts money from the juvenile-justice and housing programs to finance its war on drugs, the slums come to look just the way they are supposed to look in the suburban imagination, confirming the fondest suspicions of the governing and possessing classes, justifying the further uses of force and repression. The people who pay the price for the official portrait turn out to be (wonder of wonders) not the members of the prosperous middle class—not the journalists or the academic theorists, not the politicians and government functionaries living behind hedges in Maryland and Virginia—but (mirabile dictu) the law-abiding residents of the inner cities living in the only neighborhoods that they can afford.

It is in the slums of New York that three people, on average, get killed every day—which, over the course of a year, adds up to a higher casualty rate than pertains in Gaza and the West Bank; it is in the slums that the drug trade recruits children to sell narcotics, which is not the result of indigenous villainy but of the nature of the law; it is in the slums that the drug trade has become the exemplary model of finance capitalism for children aspiring to the success of Donald Trump and Samuel Pierce; and it is in the slums that the police experiment with the practice of apartheid, obliging residents of housing projects to carry identity cards and summarily evicting the residents of apartment houses tainted by the presence of drug dealers.

To the extent that the slums can be seen as the locus of the nation's wickedness (i.e., a desolate mise-en-scène not unlike the Evil Empire that Ronald Reagan found in the Soviet Union), the crimes allied with the drug traffic can be classified as somebody else's moral problem rather than one's own social or political problem. The slums become foreign, alien nations on the other side of the economic and cultural frontiers. The deliberate confusion of geography with metaphysics turns out, again to nobody's surprise, to be wonderfully convenient for the sponsors of the war on drugs. The politicians get their names in the papers, the media have a story to tell, and the rest of us get off the hooks that otherwise might impale us on the questions of conscience or the obligation of higher taxes. In New York last week, I overhead a woman in an expensive restaurant say that she didn't understand why the government didn't arrange to put "arsenic or something" in a seized shipment of cocaine. If the government (or "the CIA or the FBI or whoever does that sort of thing") allowed the poisoned cocaine to find its way back onto the streets, then "pretty soon we'd be rid of the whole damn thing."

If the folly of the war on drugs could be understood merely as a lesson in political cynicism, or simply as an example of the aplomb with which the venal media can play upon the sentiments of a mob, maybe I would rest content with a few last jokes about the foolishness of the age. But the war on drugs also serves the interests of the state, which, under the pretext of rescuing people from incalculable peril, claims for itself enormously enhanced powers of repression and control.

An opinion poll conducted during the week following President Bush's September address showed 62 percent of the respondents "willing to give up some freedoms" in order to hold America harmless against the scourge of drugs. The government stands more than willing to take them at their word. The war on drugs becomes a useful surrogate for the obsolescent Cold War, now fading into the realm of warm and nostalgic memory. Under the familiar rubrics of constant terror and ceaseless threat, the government subtracts as much as possible from the sum of the nation's civil liberties and imposes de facto martial law on a citizenry that it chooses to imagine as a dangerous rabble.

Anybody who doubts this point has only to read the speeches of William Bennett, the commander-in-chief of the Bush administration's war on drugs. Bennett's voice is the voice of an intolerant scold, narrow and shrill and mean-spirited, the voice of a man afraid of liberty and mistrustful of freedom. He believes that it is the government's duty to impose on people a puritanical code of behavior best exemplified by the discipline in place at an unheated boarding school. He never misses the chance to demand more police, more jails, more judges, more arrests, more punishments, more people serving more millennia of "serious time."

Reading Bennett's speeches, I am reminded of the Ayatollah

Khalkhali, appointed by the authorities in Iran to the office of executioner without portfolio. Khalkhali was blessed with the power to order the death of anybody whom he found in the company of drugs, and within a period of seven weeks he killed 176 people. Still he failed to suppress the use of opium, and he said, "If we wanted to kill everybody who had five grams of heroin, we would have to kill 5,000 people." And then, after a wistful pause, he said, "And this would be difficult."

In line with Bennett's zeal for coercion, politicians of both parties demand longer jail sentences and harsher laws as well as the right to invade almost everybody's privacy; to search, without a warrant, almost anybody's automobile or boat; to bend the rules of evidence, hire police spies, and attach, again without a warrant, the wires of electronic surveillance. The more obviously the enforcement of the law fails to accomplish its nominal purpose (i.e., as more drugs become more accessible at cheaper prices), the more reasons the Supreme Court finds to warrant the invasion of privacy. In recent years, the Court has granted police increasingly autocratic powers—permission (without probable cause) to stop, detain, and question travelers passing through the nation's airports in whom the police can see a resemblance to a drug dealer; permission (again without probable cause) to search barns, stop motorists, inspect bank records, and tap phones.

The polls suggest that a majority of the American people accept these measures as right and proper. Of the respondents questioned by an ABC/*Washington Post* poll in September, 55 percent supported mandatory drug testing for all Americans, 82 percent favored enlisting the military in the war on drugs, 52 percent were willing to have their homes searched, and 83 percent favored reporting suspected drug users to the police, even if the suspects happened to be members of their own family. In October, *Newsweek* took note of an inquisition in progress in Clinton, Iowa. The local paper had taken to printing cutout coupons that said, "I've had enough of drugs in my neighborhood! I have reason to believe that (blank) is using/dealing drugs." The paper collected the coupons for the town police, who reported the response as "excellent."

The enforcement of more and stricter laws requires additional tiers of expensive government, and of the $7.9 billion that President Bush allotted to the war on drugs in September, the bulk of the money swells the budgets of the fifty-eight federal agencies and seventy-four congressional committees currently engaged, each with its own agenda and armies to feed, on various fronts of the campaign. Which doesn't mean, of course, that the money will be honestly, or even intelligently, spent. As was demonstrated all too plainly by the Reagan administration (cf. the sums misappropriated from HUD and the Pentagon), the government has a talent for theft and fraud barely distinguishable from the criminal virtuosity of the drug syndicates it wishes to destroy.

Even so, and notwithstanding its habitual incompetence and greed, the government doesn't lightly relinquish the spoils of power seized under the pretexts of apocalypse. What the government grasps, the government seeks to keep and hold. The militarization of the rhetoric supporting the war on drugs rots the public debate with a corrosive silence. The political weather turns gray and pinched. People who become accustomed to the arbitrary intrusions of the police also learn to speak more softly in the presence of political authority, to bow and smile and fill out the printed forms with the cowed obsequiousness of musicians playing waltzes at a Mafia wedding.

And for what? To punish people desperate enough or foolish enough to poison themselves with drugs? To exact vengeance on people afflicted with the sickness of addiction and who, to their grief and shame, can find no other way out of the alleys of their despair?

As a consequence of President Bush's war on drugs, society gains nothing except immediate access to an unlimited fund of resentment and unspecific rage. In return for so poor a victory, and in the interests of the kind of people who would build prisons instead of schools, Bush offers the nation the chance to deny its best principles, to corrupt its magistrates and enrich its most vicious and efficient criminals, to repudiate its civil liberties and repent of the habits of freedom. The deal is as shabby as President Bush's trick with the bag of cocaine. For the sake of a vindictive policeman's dream of a quiet and orderly heaven, the country risks losing its constitutional right to its soul.

II. THE LATIN AMERICAN CONNECTION

EDITOR'S INTRODUCTION

Opium that is grown in Pakistan and the Far East is an important source of the illicit drug supply reaching Europe, but the primary source of cocaine and heroin entering the U.S. comes from South America. The Andean countries of Colombia, Bolivia, and Peru are the center of a vast drug industry that makes up an important part of their economies. Colombia, in particular, plays a key role in the growing, processing, and international distribution of cocaine. Drug cartels in Colombia wield such power that they have openly defied the judicial apparatus of the state. Judges, prosecutors, and public officials at even the highest levels have been assassinated by the notorious Medellín cartel. At present, the ruling cartel in Colombia is the Cali organization, which has proved extraordinarily efficient in circumventing efforts by the Colombian government and the DEA to suppress its activities. The arm of the cartels extends through Central America and countries in the Caribbean in a secret network that ultimately reaches the streets of American cities.

In the opening article of this section, Elaine Shannon, writing in *Time*, discusses the collapse of the Medellín cartel and the rise of the Cali organization in its place. The Cali cartel, a confederacy of crime families, operates like big business, using smooth, calculating, and cerebral methods that are backed up by intimidation and violence. In the second article, reprinted from *The Progressive*, Ruth Conniff charges that American military and economic aid to Colombia intended for the drug war has been used by its right-wing government to suppress those struggling for land reform and social justice. The government's death squads and "cleansing" of people deemed undesirable are, in effect, financed by the U.S. government.

The third piece, by Melvin Burke writing in *Current History*, reviews the recent political history of Bolivia and the present status of its coca production. He points out that coca farming accounts for an estimated 30 to 40 percent of Bolivia's agriculture, and 66 percent of its export earnings. Approximately 1 out of every 5 people in Bolivia are involved in some way with this industry, with coca farmers making a living and cocaine traffickers reaping a vast profit. Much of the country's investment capital comes from drugs. In an article from *The Progressive*, Robin Kirk discusses the situation in Peru, where more than 65 percent of the coca leaf refined into U.S.-bound cocaine is grown. In the Huallaga Valley, the government is engaged in a bloody battle with the Maoist guerilla group called the Shining Path, which has lent its protection to the coca growers. The Peruvian military has acted with extraordinary brutality and been guilty of horrendous human rights violations. Despite years of antidrug efforts, however, the amount of land under coca cultivation has steadily grown. In the final article from *The Nation*, Michael Massing reports on the trial of Manuel Noriega, Panama's former strongman, in Miami. Of his role in channeling drugs into the U.S. there is no doubt, but what strikes Massing as most revealing is that his removal from power has not altered the situation in Panama—or elsewhere in Latin America. Only by redirecting attention to the domestic front, he concludes, is there any hope of containing the drug problem.

NEW KINGS OF COKE[1]

To their admirers, they are Horatio Alger heroes, poor boys who worked their way out of the slums and backwaters of the Cauca Valley. Onetime delinquent José Santacruz Londono studied engineering, went into construction and emerged as Don Chepe, a billionaire whose marble citadel looms high above the sugarcane fields of Cali, the country's third largest city.

Down the road, in the new-rich suburb of Ciudad Jardin, is the modern compound of Gilberto Rodríguez Orejuela. Nicknamed the "Chess Player" because he runs his business—and life—with cold calculation, he parlayed youthful jobs as a drugstore clerk by day and a kidnapper by night into a vast network of enterprises, including a pharmacy chain, office and apartment

[1]Reprint of an article by Elaine Shannon, *Time* staffwriter. Reprinted by permission of *Time*, 137: 28–33. Jl 1 '91. Copyright © 1991 by *Time, Inc.*

buildings, banks, car dealerships, radio stations and Cali's talented América soccer team. His handsome younger brother Miguel is a fixture on the local social scene, and their children, educated in the U.S. or Europe, are often compared to young Rockefellers or Kennedys by Colombians.

Then there are Gilberto's cousin Jaime Raúl Orjuela Caballero and his three brothers, who are prominent impresarios of concerts and sporting events in Cali, travel frequently to New York City and have offices in Los Angeles. Ivan Urdinola Grajales and his younger brother Fabio, cattlemen and landowners from the northern Cauca Valley, are said to be exploring a regional television network. Pacho Herrera, believed to be the son of Benjamin Herrera Zuleta, an Afro-Colombian smuggler known as the "Black Pope," is a wealthy valley rancher with business interests in New York.

They are among the richest families in Colombia, but to the U.S. Drug Enforcement Administration, they are the new kings of cocaine, patriarchs of a criminal consortium more disciplined and protected from prosecution than the Sicilian Mafia and now bigger than the Medellín cartel.

The Cali combine produces 70% of the coke reaching the U.S. today, according to the DEA, and 90% of the drug sold in Europe. The Cali godfathers have a virtual lock on the global wholesale market in the most lucrative commodity ever conceived by organized crime. The cartel is the best and brightest of the modern underworld: professional, intelligent, efficient, imaginative and nearly impenetrable. Says Robert Bonner, administrator of the DEA: "The Cali cartel is the most powerful criminal organization in the world. No drug organization rivals them today or perhaps any time in history."

Most people think the narcotics trade belongs to Medellín. It did in the 1980s, when that city's cartel did more than anyone to put cocaine on the street corners of America. But Medellín's drug power has been shattered by its long and vicious war on the Colombian government. A 22-month counterattack by the authorities has killed drug boss José Gonzalo Rodríguez Gacha, forced the surrender of his fellow cocaine barons, the brothers Jorge, Juan David and Fabio Ochoa, destroyed dozens of labs and airstrips and scattered lesser capos abroad. In the most stunning blow yet to the cartel, Medellín chief Pablo Escobar Gaviria surrendered last week under a plea-bargaining program that promises he will not be extradited to stand trial in the U.S.

After years of murder and mayhem, the government has succeeded in disrupting one center of drug trafficking only to have an even more powerful and insidious gang emerge in Cali. While security forces concentrated on shutting down operations in Medellín, the confederacy of crime families in the Cauca Valley expanded cocaine production and grabbed the lion's share of the market.

Cali has insulated itself from government crackdowns through political influence subtly cultivated over many years. By means of legitimate business ventures, the Cali capos have forged contacts with key people in business, politics, the law and the press. Even police officials speak of *los caballeros* (gentlemen) of Cali in contrast to *los hampones* (hoodlums) of Medellín. "Cali gangs will kill you if they have to," says Robert Bryden, head of the DEA in New York. "But they prefer to use a lawyer."

Drug-enforcement agents believe the architects of Cali's takeover are Santacruz, 47, and Gilberto Rodríguez, 52. Santacruz was the hands-on designer of worldwide trafficking networks; Gilberto Rodríguez handled the finances.

In the mid-1970s, while Medellín's cocaine cowboys were monopolizing drug sales in Miami, Santacruz was sewing up Manhattan. Today the DEA estimates that Santacruz, the Orjuela Caballero brothers and the Pacho Herrera organization import 4 of every 5 grams of cocaine sold on the streets of New York City. From that base, Cali operatives have fanned out across the U.S. and deep into Mexico. The Rodríguez Orejuelas are generally considered partners in Santacruz ventures, but they sometimes appear to operate independently. Their cousins, the Orjuela Caballero brothers, are also major dealers in Los Angeles. DEA agents say the Urdinola brothers work somewhat independently from the rest of the Cali consortium, with their own trafficking and money-laundering organizations across the U.S. They are linked to large lab operations in the northern Cauca Valley and, according to DEA intelligence, are suspected of assassinating a number of Colombians.

The Cali families are now focusing their efforts on cornering the market in Europe and Japan. Last year Dutch officials seized 2,658 kg of coke packed in drums of passion-fruit juice from Cali, the biggest single bust in Europe. Santacruz bank accounts have been found across Western Europe and as far afield as Hungary and Israel. DEA informants report that Cali is looking for sales representatives to man branch offices in Japan, where the going wholesale price for cocaine is as high as $65,000 per kg. "If the Cali cartel makes an alliance with the *yakuza* [Japan's organized-crime network]," warns a Colombian presidential aide, "watch out!"

"El Gordo" (the Fat Man), as Santacruz is known, is a legend in the New York Latin underworld. The word making the rounds is that every so often he materializes in the middle of a drug deal and exchanges a few pleasantries with the customer. Then, as suddenly as he appeared, he is gone again.

These tales filter back to the DEA. Possibly, Don Chepe wants it that way. "He's toying with us," says William Mockler Jr., chief of the New York task force investigating the Cali cartel. He and Kenneth Robinson, a retired New York City policeman who is now a DEA intelligence analyst, have been a step or two behind Santacruz since 1978, when they found out that he was building an air fleet and setting up businesses along the East Coast. Thanks to their efforts, Santacruz was indicted for drug-trafficking conspiracy in 1980, but he fled the country. "He is my Professor Moriarty," Mockler says. "He's the one I'll never get."

Investigators in New York, Los Angeles, Louisiana and Florida have won some battles against the cartel. They have dismantled a succession of distribution rings. Federal narcotics trafficking and conspiracy charges, which form the basis for extradition requests, have been lodged against Cali's reputed financiers Gilberto and Miguel Rodríguez, their four Orjuela Caballero cousins and dozens of other senior figures. U.S. Attorney General Dick Thornburgh has asked the Colombian government to extradite them. Santacruz's half-brother and confidant, Luis Santacruz Echeverri, has been convicted on conspiracy charges in Miami, and his personal financial adviser, Edgar Alberto Garcia Montilla, has been jailed in Luxembourg for money laundering.

Yet these setbacks have not impeded the cartel's steady growth. Cali's leaders have carefully compartmentalized their organization, so that individual losses do not threaten to bring down the whole enterprise. The Cali management style is cerebral, calculating and guileful. In the tradition of the great Mediterranean trading dynasties, the major families have a patriarchal, authoritarian structure that demands absolute discipline and loyalty yet encourages creativity.

The Cali imagination shines when it comes to the art of smuggling. Medellín brazenly shipped cocaine across borders in fast boats or light planes with extra fuel bladders. Caleños prefer the slow but safe merchant marine. The cartel has devised endless ways to hide contraband in commercial cargo and launder it through third countries. U.S. Customs can check perhaps 3% of the 9 million shipping containers that enter U.S. ports annually, making the odds very favorable for Cali.

When U.S. agents do uncover a shipment, the cartel adopts new shippers, different routes and more ingenious deceptions. Federal agents took nine years to crack a Santacruz-designed lumber scheme. In 1979, a Cali operative was arrested with the name of a Baltimore lumberyard in his pocket. There, agents saw piles of mahogany boards sliced end to end, with pockets hollowed out and the tops veneered on. A few more clues popped up over the years, but nothing to pinpoint which planks, among the tons of lumber imported from South America, contained contraband.

Then in April 1988, a load of Brazilian cedar boards arrived in Tarpon Springs, Fla., aboard the freighter *Amazon Sky*. DEA alerted Tampa Customs that an informer had reported drugs were aboard. Inspectors drilled holes in stacks of lumber planks, but found nothing. At the last moment, a Customs man saw a crew member drop a plank and glance about nervously. The inspector drilled into the board and hit white powder. The seizure was a record 3,270 kg of cocaine, but just 700 of the 9,000 planks held any drugs.

Other scams are just as difficult to uncover. In 1988 Customs officers found 2,270 kg of cocaine encased in 1,200 blocks of chocolate shipped from Ecuador. The cocaine bricks had been wrapped in lead to thwart X-rays, but the lead set off metal detectors. The next time, Customs found, the smugglers had switched to heavy plastic wrapping.

The cartel has also buried cocaine in toxic chemicals. In 1989 Customs agents and New York policemen found almost 5,000 kg of the drug inside 252 drums of powdered lye. No sane inspector would poke around in lye, which can inflict severe eye, skin and lung burns. Luckily, someone had tipped off the authorities.

The cocaine bricks unearthed from the lye were marked with a destination code, "Baby I." The same marking had been found on an 18,000-kg seizure near Los Angeles two months earlier. Baby I turned out to be a Santacruz protégé in New York, Luis ("Leto") Delio Lopez, 28. His style, according to DEA agents, embodied the typical Cali cartel executive: businesslike, resourceful, hard-working and discreet.

The Cali families are conservative managers, much like other big corporate heads. In the home office sit the chief executive officer and his senior vice presidents for acquisition, production, transportation, sales, finance and enforcement. The logistics of importing, storing and delivering the product to wholesalers are handled by dozens of overseas branches, or cells, overseen by the home office through daily, often hourly, phone calls.

Each cell is directed by a Caleño like Leto Lopez and staffed by relatives and neighbors whose salaries are banked in Cali. Their accounts are debited when they make mistakes. The code of conduct is strict: nondescript clothing, four-door family cars, no drunkenness, no loud parties. Also no failures, no excuses, no second chances. This unforgiving system produces few defections: the penalty for dissent is death, not only for cell members but also for their kinsmen back home in Colombia.

Leto Lopez looked no different from his Westchester County neighbors: he wore conservative suits, lived in a $775,000 colonial house and drove an Acura Legend. He opened a public fax service to mix his drug messages with thousands of others dispatched by honest customers. He set up an import business and actually imported South American furniture so that the U.S. Customs Service would think he was a legitimate businessman.

After the highly publicized Baby I bust, Leto stayed away from his house and offices, which DEA agents were watching. One day in March 1990, he happened to drive past a DEA team running another surveillance in Queens. As the agents started tailing him, he whipped his Acura into a fast U-turn and melted into the traffic. The next thing the agents knew, Leto was back in Colombia—where his luck ran out. At the request of the U.S. government, police arrested him.

U.S. agents have almost no chance of infiltrating a Cali family. Caleños sell only to people they know, meaning other Colombians. A prospective wholesale buyer must establish his bona fides at an audience with top management in Cali. If he is approved, he is not required to pay cash up front. He will send the cartel payment after he resells the drugs to middlemen. The wholesale buyer must put up collateral, cash or deeds to real property as insurance if he is caught. He must also provide human collateral in the form of his family in Colombia, who will pay with their lives if he ever turns informer.

The system for transferring the drugs is dizzyingly complicated but well-orchestrated. When a load of drugs is shipped to the U.S., the home office faxes to the cell head a list of buyers, the amount of their purchases and their beeper numbers. The cell head signals each customer's beeper to arrange a delivery at a street corner or parking lot. After the customer sells the cocaine down the line, he fixes a second meeting to make payment. The deals take two minutes or less to consummate.

After each meeting, both drivers alert the cell head in code from a mobile phone or beeper. He telephones a desk officer in Cali, then sends confirmation by fax. Detailed ledgers are maintained in both countries. The ledgers have proved the system's main vulnerability, providing a rich lode of data to DEA analysts when seized.

If anyone involved in a deal fails to call in, or catches a whiff of the law, the cell is shut down. Last July, in a raid on a Leto Lopez front business in Queens, agents found a list of Caleños who had rented apartments around Manhattan. By the time agents reached the addresses, everyone was gone, leaving behind cocaine, ledgers, more than $1.5 million in cash, and two steamer trunks full of arms. "Whenever we get close to these people," says U.S. District Attorney Andrew Maloney, "they're on a plane back to Colombia, and we have to start all over again."

The cartel's need for goods, services and go-betweens has spawned a thriving network of cottage industries. Front companies acquire mobile phones by the dozen and "sublet" them to the cells. The traffickers know investigators need four or five days to get a court-ordered wiretap, so they use a phone for two days and discard it. If a mobile phone is eventually traced, the trail stops at the front company.

Document specialists obtain clean driver's licenses and car registrations. In 1989 the FBI and New York City prosecutors cracked a scheme in which employees of the state Department of Motor Vehicles were taking bribes of $100 to write phony registration papers. Hundreds of falsely documented cartel vehicles, fitted with hidden compartments, moved drugs north from Mexico and returned south with cash.

The cartel's second-biggest industry is money laundering. The monthly gross for some New York cells runs from $7 million to $12 million, all in $5, $10 and $20 bills. That translates into 1,000 to 3,000 pounds of bills a month, a logistical nightmare.

In the early years a cell's financier would cart the money to a local bank and wire it to Panama. The cartel had a personal banker there: First Interamericas Bank, owned by Gilberto and Miguel Rodríguez Orejuela. In 1985 the U.S. government forced Manuel Noriega to close Interamericas and required U.S. banks to report all large cash transactions.

Many cells now ship the money in bulk to Cali, where some is invested, some converted into pesos and some wired back to banks in the U.S. or Europe under a relative's name. In January 1989 New York agents seized a Santacruz truck loaded with $19 million as it was departing for Mexico. Last October agents found an additional $14 million inside heavy cable spools on Long Island, along with records showing shipments of $100 million more over the previous nine months.

The immunity the Cali cartel enjoys from prosecution is a matter of intense concern to Bush Administration officials. While Henry Orjuela Caballero is in jail in New York State awaiting trial on federal drug-trafficking conspiracy charges, brother Carlos is out on bail on similar charges filed against him in Los Angeles. Another brother, Jaime, the family boss, is free in Colombia. So are Don Chepe Santacruz, the Rodríguez Orejuela brothers and such rising powers as the Urdinola brothers. "You can't destroy the organization without lopping off its head," says DEA's Bonner. "The tentacles grow back. If the Cali cartel is to be attacked successfully, there must be pressure in Colombia."

President César Gaviria Trujillo's advisers insist the Cali cartel will be given priority now that Escobar is jailed. Bonner argues that the new gangs will prove a more formidable threat to Colombia's security than the Medellín cartel "precisely because they make more discreet use of murder, bribery and intimidation." Says he: "The Cali organizations can be characterized as murderous thugs who are more politically astute in the way they carry out their business."

Colombian national police officials say the Cali capos are not living at home, are not doing business as usual and will be arrested if found. Santacruz has kept out of sight since the government began its antidrug campaign after the assassination of presidential candidate Luis Carlos Galán in August 1989. But others seem to feel safe from prosecution. Gilberto Rodríguez Orejuela is very much at home, defiantly proclaiming his innocence and that of his brother Miguel. Gilberto describes himself as a "captain of industry and banker" and has the portfolio to prove it. He also has reputable friends who are partners, associates or suppliers in his business ventures, which do much to promote development throughout the Cauca valley.

Even when police do close in, the Cali bosses have escaped jail. When Gilberto was arrested in Spain in November 1984, the Colombian government went to great lengths to prevent his extradition to the U.S. According to a Rodríguez friend, Gilberto's son Jaime Fernando appealed to then President Belisario Betancur for help. Betancur declined comment. The elder Rodríguez says, "If Betancur helped in seeing I was extradited to Colombia and not the U.S., he was simply doing his duty as President, supporting an extradition order issued by a Colombian judge." Back in Cali, Rodríguez was tried on charges identical to those filed in the U.S. and was acquitted—along with Santacruz, who was tried in absentia. The acquittal protected both men from further extradition to the U.S. on grounds of double jeopardy.

While the Rodríguez and Santacruz clans seem to enjoy considerable respect in Colombia, they are not universally admired. Some intellectuals protest that if the drug mafia's economic power is accepted, its values will eventually be countenanced as well. Critics are especially wary of the dynastic ambitions of the high-profile Rodríguez family. "They invest in the future," says a Bogotá businessman. "They are thinking of the next generation, and the one after that."

Gilberto's son Jaime Fernando graduated from the University of Grenoble with a degree in international commerce. Two other sons studied at Stanford University and the University of Tulsa, and a fourth son is learning systems engineering. Gilberto boasts that one of his daughters has a master's in business administration and that a second is an engineer. "Most are now working in our businesses," he says.

Critics fear the proud father is grooming his children for political office as well. "Someday their sons will rule part of this country," predicts Luis Gabriel Cano, who has succeeded his assassinated brother, Guillermo, as publisher of Bogotá's crusading newspaper *El Espectador*. Unless the Colombian government can now break the hold of the cartel in Cali, Cano's warning may have come too late.

COLOMBIA'S DIRTY WAR, WASHINGTON'S DIRTY HANDS[2]

In a January 28 opinion piece in *The New York Times*, "Colombian Blood, U.S. Guns," Jorge Gómez Lizarazo wrote that the

[2]Reprint of an article by Ruth Conniff, associate editor of *The Progressive*. Reprinted by permission of *The Progressive*, 56: 20–22, 24, 26–27. My '92. Copyright © 1992 by *The Progressive*.

United States is helping to finance a political war in Colombia and looking the other way while the Colombian military tortures and murders innocent civilians. On January 29, the author's secretary was dead.

At 6:30 P.M., hours after Colombian national radio broadcast Gómez's statements to the *Times*, Blanca Cecilia Valero de Durán stepped out of her office at the Committee on Human Rights in Barrancabermeja, Colombia, where she had worked for the past twelve years. As Valero walked to the curb to hail a taxi, a man who had been waiting outside the building jumped out and shot her in the side of the face.

The woman dropped to the ground, and the gunman approached to finish her off, firing another bullet into her head. Valero did not survive the short trip to the hospital. Witnesses saw the murderer run thirty or forty meters—past the local police station—to a motorcycle, and fumble with the ignition for a few moments before driving away. The police officers who usually patrol the area were nowhere to be found.

Valero was the third member of the human-rights office assassinated in the past year, and one in a long line of casualties of Colombia's "dirty war."

Shortly after Valero's murder, the army commander of Barrancabermeja's Fifth Brigade told reporters that the human-rights office was a front for "subversives" engaged in a "tricky scheme" to discredit the military.

All over Colombia, the army, the police, and paramilitary soldiers trained and supported by the state are killing peasants, union leaders, progressive politicians, and people who speak out about the abuse of human rights. Amnesty International and human rights workers like Gómez and Valero have documented military involvement in thousands of murders.

Meanwhile, the United States Government has increased military funding to Colombia to $282 million over the next four years. In 1990, Colombia surpassed El Salvador as the hemisphere's top recipient of U.S. military aid.

U.S. officials say they must fund the Colombian military in order to fight the "war on drugs." But Colombians are not nearly so interested in narcotics. The Colombian Defense Ministry has made combating "insurgents" its first priority. In 1990, Colombian military officers stated flatly to a Congressional subcommittee that millions of dollars in U.S. "counter-narcotics" aid was, in fact, helping to fight political insurgency.

As a wave of violence engulfs the civilian population of Colombia, some members of Congress are increasingly worried that the U.S. Government shares responsibility for the slaughter.

One week after Valero's death, a small group of U.S. citizens traveled to Colombia on a good-will mission. A lawyer, a minister, an expert in co-ops and credit unions, a university student, and a journalist, we were by no means an official investigative team. What we saw and heard is readily evident to any observer.

On our trip we talked with some of the people who had been directly affected by the violence—former guerrillas, peasants, workers, and local politicians. They told us a story that has very little to do with narcotics or insurgency. Rather, it is the story of an economic war—a war that places the United States squarely in the camp of a profoundly antidemocratic elite, a corrupt military, and, ironically, the drug lords themselves.

On the losing end is the vast majority of Colombians, the poor workers and peasants, who are struggling for basic survival and who have suffered through a terrible repression. They told us their stories in the frank hope that the rest of the world would act to stop the violence.

We got off the plane in Apartadó, dazed for a moment by the Caribbean sun. Miles of green banana plantations surrounded the airport. The mayor of Apartadó walked onto the runway to meet us, applauding, the bright light glinting off his sunglasses. Behind him, a group of men in shirtsleeves followed, carrying machine guns.

Everywhere you look in Colombia there are guns. Soldiers stand by the side of the road, keeping an eye on the homeless squatters camped all over the countryside. Policemen and members of DAS, the Colombian secret service, patrol the streets with heavy combat weapons; armored police vehicles roll through downtown Bogotá. Murder is the leading cause of death here. Counting massacres, homicides, tortures, and forced disappearances, Colombia is the most violent nation on Earth.

One year ago, the former mayor of Apartadó was killed by her own bodyguards. Like the current mayor, she was a member of the Patriotic Union, or UP, a popular third party, whose leaders have been assassinated in localities throughout Colombia. The current mayor has added a few people he knows to the state-supplied protective service that follows him everywhere, to diminish the chances that he will be shot in the back.

Like other areas of Colombia where violence has reached epidemic proportions, the Urabá region around Apartadó contains a

wealth of natural resources alongside extreme poverty and neglect. Urabá is the major banana-producing region of Colombia
(narcotics do not grow in this humid, coastal climate), but it is
nearly impossible to come by a banana in Apartadó. A few
wealthy landlords, most of whom live in Miami, own the vast
plantations. They send their bananas abroad—primarily to the
United States.

We drove down the main street of Apartadó—a dirt road
along a strip of tin-roofed buildings. Most local inhabitants do
without electricity, running water, and other basic resources. In
this atmosphere of deprivation, peasant cooperatives and labor
unions have formed to try to improve the generally miserable
living conditions of the people.

The national government has responded to local protests and
organizing efforts by declaring the region a hotbed of subversion,
and sending in troops. In 1988, military and paramilitary soldiers
massacred twenty-two union leaders on a banana plantation nearby.

We stayed in the guest house of a cardboard-box factory in
Apartadó. Outside, under a roof of palm fronds, the mayor and
other local leaders talked to us about the town, while the omni-
present bodyguards sat inside, watching soccer on TV.

"I came to Apartadó five years ago, a militant member of the
Patriotic Union," said Mayor José Antonio López. "I thought that
in Apartadó there were many things that needed to be done. I
wanted to be mayor. I fought for that. It cost me a lot. For example, the only brother I had was killed during the electoral campaign, without being a militant of any political party. He didn't
even live in this region. He came to visit one day. He got here in
the morning and they killed him that night, while he was sitting in
a tavern, waiting for me."

The mayor's voice broke and tears came into his eyes as he
spoke; he stopped to recover his composure and went on. "But
the moment arrives when you cannot turn back. Although there
are things that try to stop you . . . for instance my family, my
mother, my father, who have reached a certain age, and who don't
have another son. But the moment comes when you are not capable of going backwards, and you continue on."

Today, the violence continues. Peasant co-op leaders told us
about being pulled out of their homes in the early morning by
uniformed men who had disguised themselves by painting their
faces black. Some people were shot. Others disappeared. A few

days before we came, a military plane strafed a rural school building, locals said, killing a three-year-old girl. "What they said in the
papers, and the information that the rest of the country received,
was that they bombed a place where the guerrillas were meeting,"
said a farmer, who witnessed the bombing from a nearby field.
"But it was just us, the peasants. There were no guerrillas. We are
just simple farmers."

Guerrillas have gained a foothold in Urabá, and over the
years, skirmishes between the guerrillas and the military have
claimed hundreds of lives. The people who pay most dearly for
this are civilians, caught in the middle of a war zone.

Apartadó is lucky. Its government has worked out a cease-fire
between the guerrillas in the area and the military. The mayor
and the bishop of Apartadó worked together to achieve this official peace. "We went into the mountains to talk to the guerrillas,
and we offered them jobs on the banana plantations," Bishop
Isaias Duarte explains. "The social injustices that gave rise to the
guerrilla movement have improved. Today there is more social
justice. The difference that this mayor's administration has made
is very positive."

But Apartadó's problems are far from over. More guerrillas
have been assassinated during the cease-fire than died in combat
before the official peace, the mayor says. And the number of
civilians killed outside of battle has always dwarfed the number
killed as a result of outright fighting between the guerrillas and
the military.

"This is a very critical moment," says Harrison Martinez, a
former guerrilla who had his hand blown off by a grenade during
the years of armed conflict. "The peace process must be accepted
as a necessity for the country as a whole, not for us, the guerrillas.
We were part of the violence here. But there are other factors in
the violence that will not be resolved over a table—social factors.
Transforming the struggle is not easy. I believe that the social
problems are worse than ever."

Bouncing over unpaved roads in a jeep, through enormous
potholes and small rivers of mud, past rows of tin and plywood
shacks, we toured the region around Apartadó. Everywhere,
groups of peasants camped on the outskirts of banana plantations, with platoons of machine-gun-toting soldiers watching
nearby. The squatters, with the help of the local government,
hope to negotiate to buy a piece of property from the plantation
owners. If they win, they'll build their shacks and set up a town.

Our jeep stopped on the outskirts of Apartadó, where members of a successful squatters' settlement had built a school. Rows of shacks and a few new cement buildings dotted what was recently a field. Under a large red tent, with the Coca-Cola logo scrawled across it in familiar white letters, schoolchildren in uniforms were standing in line, waiting to greet us. We were late, and they must have been there for more than an hour. They presented us with an elaborate fruit-and-flower arrangement, and then we listened to speeches from members of the community. Two representatives from the Coca-Cola Company spoke last, looking incongruous in their suits and ties against the background of dust and squalor. (They were invited, someone from the town explained later, on account of the tent, which Coke provides free on special occasions.)

"We used to think that the government should take care of our problems," one Coke man said. "We were waiting for someone else to come and give us everything. But now we realize that through privatization and the work of the people of this community, we can provide for ourselves."

Privatization for people in this area meant building their own sewer system. Government-regulated services like electricity, paved roads, and basic sanitation are virtually unheard-of around Apartadó and other areas distant from the capital. So here the people showed us how they had learned to mix cement and cast the cylindrical pipes which lay beside the Coca-Cola tent.

It was a startling illustration of a policy promoted by the Reagan and Bush Administrations all over the developing world. Under President Cesar Gaviria, Colombia is pursuing "economic openness"—encouraging foreign investment and, at the behest of the United States and the World Bank, reducing Government spending on the country's infrastructure. Thus, for the rural poor, the situation promises to get worse.

Despite the dogged optimism of the people, there is little chance that the efforts of the peasant co-ops and community-action groups can make up for a missing infrastructure. Cooperatives are continually running out of capital to complete their projects. The community we visited, for instance, may or may not ever get its sewer pipes into the ground. Much depends on banks, which consider such projects a poor investment risk. Meanwhile, at the new school, 1,000 students have already signed up for spaces at the 100 desks.

The face Colombia presents to the outside world is quite dif-

ferent from the one apparent to natives, and to anyone who takes
the time to travel through the countryside.

"The economic situation is not that desperate here," said one
U.S. official who declined to be named. "The guerrillas' ideology
is more political than economic. They've never been able to
mount an economically based uprising."

But in fact, although the State Department and the World
Bank issue cheerful reports about Colombia's growing economy
and relatively high gross national product, 40 per cent of Colombia's thirty-three million citizens live in "absolute poverty" and 18
per cent in "absolute misery," according to the National Administrative Bureau of Statistics. The top 3 per cent of Colombia's
landed elite own 71.3 per cent of arable land, while 57 per cent of
the poorest farmers subsist on 2.8 per cent, the Washington Office on Latin America reports.

Double-speak about the political and economic situation in
Colombia abounds. "Economic reforms" and the transition to a
"freer" economy mean more abandonment and deprivation for
the poor. By the same token, constitutional reform has accompanied more repression.

As far as the State Department is concerned, Colombia has a
"strong, decades-old democratic system." A new, reform-minded
constitution represents great progress in the protection of human rights, says a State Department report dated March 1992.

Colombians disagree. "In reality, the first three chapters of
our constitution exactly describe human rights, the rights of the
individual, and of the family," says Alfredo Vasquez Carrizosa, a
member of the constituent assembly that drew up the new constitution. "All of this is beautiful—it is a symphony of human rights.
But none of it applies."

A system of military impunity—expanded under the new
constitution to include police officers—protects state security
forces from retribution for human-rights abuses.

"The new constitution has not stopped the official repression,
massacres, and official violence," says the Reverend Javier Giraldo, director of *Justicia y Paz*, a Christian human-rights group.
"Repression has become more clandestine. What is happening
now is that the government simply avoids responsibility."

One way the government avoids responsibility for military
violence, says Father Giraldo, is to blame it on paramilitary
forces—private armies operated by wealthy landowners and drug
lords. But evidence collected by *Justicia y Paz* and other human-

rights groups indicates that the army and the paramilitaries operate together.

"In this way," says Father Giraldo, "a democratic discourse accompanies a bloodbath."

Shortly after Blanca Valero's murder, on February 16, members of the Comando Ariel Otero paramilitary group distributed leaflets to the human-rights office and around town declaring: "We denounce and demand of the office of the attorney general of the nation that it initiate an investigation of the office of human rights and the office of the attorney general in Barrancabermeja, since they are run by members of the [guerrilla group] E.L.N. If this investigation is not undertaken, we will exterminate those guerrillas and we will take justice into our own hands."

Within days, Fifth Brigade Commander Roberto Emilio Cifuentes told the newspaper *Vanguardia Liberal,* "The office of human rights, naively or perhaps some of its members with ill intentions, has been used by the subversives to carry out some of their forms of struggle that are based on slander. I state this because it is all a setup that has no support. Some of those people are heedlessly echoing a tricky scheme in an effort to discredit the [military] institution."

Members of the army brigade do not openly acknowledge any association with the paramilitary. But the two groups have cooperated in several attacks on peasants and oil workers in Barrancabermeja, according to investigations by the human-rights office. These attacks, says Gómez, together with government repression, protect the economic interests of wealthy landowners.

A recent increase in violence in Barrancabermeja coincides with the discovery of a vast new oil field in the area. Alynne Romo, a member of the steering committee of the Colombian Human Rights Network in the United States, believes that the United States, too, has a particular interest in ignoring human-rights abuses and supporting repression in Barrancabermeja: "You don't want the largest oil field in the Western Hemisphere in the hands of leftists," says Romo. "The economic question is the most important thing. It's not that we want to send the military down to Colombia and establish a military hegemony. It's an economic hegemony."

There is ample evidence that U.S. military aid earmarked for the war on drugs is in fact going to support a different sort of war in Colombia.

One particularly embarrassing example of this appears in a

1990 report by the House Government Operations Committee. Colombian Army Chief-of-Staff General Luis Eduardo Roca and Army General José Nelson Mejia, thanking members of Congress for $40.3 million in U.S. anti-narcotics aid, reported that $38.5 million of the aid would be used in "Operation Tri-Color," a program aimed at fighting guerrillas in the northeast part of the country, where narcotics are not grown or processed.

"When asked by the subcommittee staff to explain how a major military operation in an area not known for its narcotics production could advance the anti-narcotics goals of either country, the military representatives stated that *if processing facilities were located* during the operation, they would be destroyed," the report said (emphasis added).

It would not occur to the Colombian military officials that such a transparent alibi might bother subcommittee members. Colombians have never pretended to be serious about the war on drugs. After all, the United States has continued to pour millions into that war despite the fact that, by all available measures, the effort has failed. Narcotics production in South America actually increased by 28 per cent in 1990, after the drug war reached a peak. And U.S. officials have never been sticklers about how anti-narcotics aid is used. In fiscal 1990, the Colombian Air Force received the largest share of U.S. military aid, much of it for eight Cessna A-37B "Dragonfly" airplanes, according to the Washington Office on Latin America. "The A-37B is known in armaments literature as a 'Counter-insurgency (COIN) aircraft,'" WOLA reports. "And one SouthCom official told WOLA that the Dragonfly is 'not a counter-narcotics capable aircraft.'" Colombian human-rights groups report that the Dragonfly has, on several occasions, bombed civilians.

Nor has the United States officially condemned the Colombian military's attacks on civilians. Despite denunciations by such groups as Amnesty International and numerous church and human-rights groups within Colombia, diplomats and embassy officials deny the military has been heavily involved in human-rights abuses.

"The military is not a bad institution," said one U.S. official who declined to be named. "It has a few bad apples, but overall it is a democratic institution."

To justify Washington's support for political violence in Latin America, U.S. officials have developed what is known as the "narco-guerrilla theory." They claim that killing guerrillas is a

necessary part of the "war on drugs" because the guerrillas are in
league with the drug traffickers.

"You've got a full-scale insurgency going on here," said Bob
Danze, press attaché at the U.S. embassy in Bogotá. "And a lot of
these guerrillas are heavily involved in the narcotics trade."

In Colombia, this theory is particularly weak. The drug lords,
who own vast tracts of land in rural Colombia, have long been
affiliated with the political Right. The cartels run paramilitary
death squads, which attack peasants struggling for land reform,
and conduct "social cleansing" campaigns, killing prostitutes, homosexuals, and street children.

After the massacre of twenty-two union leaders in Apartadó,
the attorney general's office discovered that the army major who
commanded the region's military-intelligence squad had hired
the Medellín cartel's paramilitary soldiers to make the hit. The
case was one of the first official investigations to begin to unravel
the complicity between Colombian military, the paramilitary
squads, and the drug lords.

"I can testify to the existence of alliances between members of
the armed forces and industry and narcotics traffickers to con-
struct and finance groups called 'black hand' or 'death squads,'"
ex-intelligence officer Ricardo Gómez Mazuera declared to the
assistant attorney general of Colombia. Officer Gómez reported
that police officers and army personnel made up a group which,
in 1986, carried out a nocturnal massacre of homosexuals in Tu-
luá and threw the bodies in the Cauca River.

To finance the operations of the "black hand," a police major
named Suárez received money from industrialists and drug traffickers in the valley, Gómez said. "One day in June or July of
1987, I myself accompanied him, in a white Toyota, to the company 'Green Taxis' in Bogotá . . . and there he received twenty-five
million from the hands of Mr. Gustavo Gaviria Riveros, a narcotics trafficker in league with Pablo Escobar."

Bodies thrown in the Cauca River, which flows through southwest Colombia, have transformed the waterway into an open
grave, human-rights workers say.

"I don't know how many bodies I saw float down the river
during the [year] I helped retrieve them," a witness told *Justicia y
Paz*. "But I could estimate the number at about seventy."

Fishermen and residents of the Cauca River Valley are afraid
to pull out the corpses that float by, since to do so is to invite
persecution and assassination. So the bodies—usually mutilated

beyond ready recognition—slide downstream, occasionally washing ashore to lie untouched by anyone but the official investigators who may come through every few months.

One of the corpses dragged from the river was the Reverend
Tiberio Fernández Mafla, who disappeared in the region called
Trujillo, in the southwest corner of Colombia, on April 17, 1990.
Photographs taken when the body was found a week later show a
human form missing its head and forearms, lying in the mud at
the feet of an investigator.

Father Fernández had helped organize several cooperatives,
declaring that part of the mission of his parish was to raise the
standard of living of its people. In 1990, he participated in a large
protest march, intended to draw the government's attention to
the extreme neglect of its rural population.

The government responded to the protest in Trujillo by sending in troops. There followed a series of disappearances, murders, and tortures, terrorizing the peasants in the area.

Father Fernández denounced the murders from his pulpit
and called for the return of the disappeared. The local military
commander announced that the priest was a dangerous subversive and a guerrilla sympathizer. Shortly thereafter, Father Fernández disappeared.

On Monday, April 23, 1990, a fisherman dragged the priest's
body out of the Cauca River. A few days later the man who
recovered the body was also assassinated. Headless, sliced open
lengthwise, and castrated, Father Fernández was identified by
members of his family with the aid of x-rays which showed bone
fractures he had suffered in a car accident earlier in his life.

Witnesses who testified before human-rights groups and the
attorney general have no doubt that the military was responsible
for Father Fernández's murder. Daniel Arcila was one such witness. He took part in the tortures and assassinations carried
by military personnel in the area around Trujillo, he said.

Arcila helped round up a group of peasants and brought
them to "La Granja," a farm belonging to a drug trafficker in the
area, he testified. There, Army Major Aliro Antonio Urueña Jaramillo and a paramilitary officer called "el tío" had breakfast together and then tortured the victims:

"The Army major sprayed them in the face with pressurized
water from a hose," Arcila testified. "He pried off their finger-
nails with a pocketknife, he cut off pieces of the bottoms of their
feet with a nail clipper, he poured salt in their cuts, then, with a

gasoline flame-thrower he burned them on different parts of their bodies and their flesh cracked and the skin peeled off, he pointed the flame thrower at the genital area, he cut off their penises and testicles and put them in their mouths, and finally quartered them with a chainsaw.

"I transported the bodies of the people that were tortured and killed. . . . I had to do it because otherwise I was a dead man. . . . They got a truck to take the eleven corpses to the river."

The attorney general opened an investigation of the crimes committed in Trujillo, and brought five suspects before a judge in a court of public order—two paramilitaries, two narcotics traffickers on whose properties the tortures and murders took place, and Major Alirio Antonio Urueña Jaramillo.

The judge threw out Arcila's testimony, on grounds that he was mentally incompetent, over the objections of expert medical testimony called by the attorney general. Then the DAS guards assigned to protect Arcila left him to his own devices. On May 5, 1991, while Arcila was visiting his family in Trujillo, he was captured by local police and disappeared.

Today, no one has been convicted of the crimes in Trujillo. Major Urueña received a promotion to lieutenant colonel. Stories continue to circulate about hideous tortures and murders in Trujillo, and on the Cauca River, bodies continue to drift by.

At 8:30 A.M., on one of our last days in Bogotá, two peasants from the area near Barrancabermeja came to our hotel. We had arranged to meet them through the Foundation for Displaced Persons—a charitable organization that helps some of the thousands of internal refugees who pour into Bogotá each year.

We almost missed the two men sitting quietly, hands folded, on the high-backed chairs in the lobby—an old man with a straw hat, and the younger man beside him. They never approached the desk to say they had arrived. The younger man explained, after lingering awkwardly for a while at the edge of the room, that he was waiting for our assistance, as he wasn't sure how to use the elevator.

Manuel Gallero and his nephew fled Santander one year ago, they told us. The whole family abandoned the small farm on the coast where Gallero had lived for forty years. As a farmer, Gallero had helped form a cooperative association and worked on the municipal council. As a member of the Patriotic Union, he was also elected to the regional council.

"All of this brought me the political persecution which forced me to abandon the region with my family," he said. Gallero's son was killed by assassins in the city of Barrancabermeja, and two of his nephews were murdered.

"I understand that this persecution is in part political and in part because I, as a representative of popular organizations, had a duty to denounce all of the persecution and assassinations of my companions, the other peasants, all of the arbitrary abuses of the same Colombian army," said Gallero. "On various occasions I had to denounce them, in front of the national and regional attorneys general in Barrancabermeja and in Santander, and in Bogotá, before the secretary of human rights for the government."

Gallero told us about numerous abuses by the military, which he had reported to the attorney general and the office of human rights. On January 25, 1989, he said, his own farm was strafed by military helicopters.

They fired from helicopters at the house. That was the twenty-fifth. On the twenty-sixth, they brought not only guns and helicopters, but they began to bomb. And it was on the twenty-eighth that they killed my two nephews, the two brothers of my nephew here." He pointed at the young man sitting next to him. "And they decapitated them. They killed the two, and the witnesses who were there they had at gunpoint on the ground. All of this came out in the denunciation. A car came by, and they made the passengers get out. They made them walk over the two boys. No one said anything if they recognized the boys—because of fear.

"As for the boys, one of them—they cut off his ears, and mutilated him beyond recognition. The other, when they found him, was completely rotten. They had decapitated him, and they found his head a month later. The body they had dressed in a military uniform, so it looked like he was a guerrilla. He was a boy who liked to play ball."

What about the guerrillas, we asked Gallero. Isn't it true that the army is fighting them?

"Yes. We certainly can't deny that there are guerrillas in our country. This is no secret from anyone. But we find that, clearly, the ones who pay the consequences are the civilian people. When a guerrilla comes into your house and asks you for a lemonade or a meal, you must give it to him. And when the army passes through it is the same thing. Whatever armed person comes in and asks for something, you give it to him. The army demands that we tell them where the guerrillas are. If you don't know, they say you are a sympathizer. So that is the pretext for assassinating us. Those of us who are in the middle are the ones who suffer."

Gallero himself was shot and crippled in an assassination attempt not long before he fled to Bogotá. He showed us his useless right arm, massaging it as he spoke.

"In Colombia we must denounce all of the violations and abuses committed by any member of the government, and by any person. Because otherwise these deeds can never be brought to light. But the truth of the matter is, one only denounces these things on pain of death," he said. "We believe—I believe—that it was necessary to do this, to denounce everything—the army, the paramilitary groups. For this reason, I had to give up my land, which I loved, everything we had achieved, all of the work of forty years with my family, and all, all that has happened. And now we find ourselves here. And I am going to say, *a la buena volutad* . . . I believe that we had to do it."

How can you go on speaking out, I asked Gallero at the end of our interview, in the face of such horrible persecution?

"It's very simple," he said. "One way or another, we are going to die. If we speak, they kill us for speaking. If we say nothing, they kill us anyway. But so much the worse if we die without having spoken the truth."

In the last days of our trip, we went to the U.S. Embassy in Bogotá, to find out what officials there had to say about the situation in Colombia. We passed through a series of heavy gates and had to surrender our cameras and tape recorders "for security reasons" before we were allowed to enter.

The U.S. officials we met spoke mostly off the record, as did the people at the State Department back in Washington. Of everyone interviewed for this article, including victims of political persecution, only representatives of the United States Government refused to be identified.

Bob Danze, the press attaché, came out to greet us after we announced ourselves at the embassy. He shook our hands jovially and led us through some serpentine hallways into what looked like a movie theater—all dark except for some dim lighting up on stage—where he sat with his feet dangling over the edge and answered our questions.

"There was a letter in *The New York Times* about two weeks ago, and the author's comment was something to the effect that American bullets are killing Colombians," said Danze. "What I found fascinating—since I am former military, so I happen to be familiar with this—is that they don't use American weapons here at all. They use *balas*, Brazilian weapons, so there is no way American weapons are going to kill Colombians."

Another embassy official, who joined us late, interrupted Danze at this point: "Well, there could be some argument on that point. . . . What's important is that the United States is supplying only *antinarcotics* aid."

Danze then admitted that the U.S. supplies military aid to Colombia, but assured us that it was all going to the war on drugs. Asked about human-rights violations, he summed up the detachment expressed by many of the U.S. officials with whom we spoke:

"I attribute it to the difference between the Northern European and a Latin culture. It comes partly from the Spanish— what you see in the Spanish is a bastardization of Islamic law— not a respect for law, but for who you know. You can see it, for instance, in the driving out in the streets here. People feel they can cut in, and commit all kinds of violations. If you see a red light, that's for the other guy, not for me. I have more important things to do. I guess you can say people are more self-centered."

The first thing U.S. officials say about Colombia is that the situation here is "very complex." So many different factors contribute to the violence—drug lords, paramilitary armies, common criminals, and so on. It is true that violence has permeated Colombian society to a frightening degree. But this does not mask the truth Gallero spoke about. Even to a group of naive North Americans, traveling to Colombia for the first time, the reality beneath the rhetoric about national security and "narco-terrorism" is unbearably clear.

As in other parts of Latin America, the political and economic injustices in Colombia are appalling. The stark contrast between rich and poor—the desperate struggle for economic necessities and social justice by the side that is labeled "subversive" against the rich and powerful—that is the real war. And it is clear which side the United States is on.

Despite this grim picture, our delegation flew home from Colombia with a feeling of hope. We were inspired by the courage of witnesses like Gallero, and by the dedication of the Jesuit priests at Colombia's internationally renowned human-rights research centers—tirelessly cranking out statistics, precisely documenting the name of every person murdered, the date of each disappearance, collecting these details in the faith that this sheer volume of data must eventually overwhelm the wall of impunity and cynical rhetoric that allows the abuse to go on.

And, they told us, there is reason for hope.

"The biggest problem we have in our international work is that the discourse of the government has been convincing to other governments and international groups," said Father Giraldo of *Justicia y Paz*.

International pressure, and particularly letters to Congress in the United States, can make a life-and-death difference for people in Colombia—people like Jorge Gómez, who recently received the Letelier-Moffit Human Rights Award in Washington, D.C. When international eyes are focused on an individual in Colombia, that person tends to live longer. Delegations from such groups as Witness for Peace, which visit people in areas afflicted by violence, also make a difference. Most of all, unabating pressure on the U.S. Government to stop the abuses and to hold the Colombian military and government accountable can make a difference.

Shortly after we returned from Colombia, *The New York Times* reported that the Government had shifted $75 million in antinarcotics aid from the Colombian army to the police. According to the State Department, the *Times* grossly exaggerated the figure. In fact, only a small portion of total military aid—about $20 million—will change its destination. And since all military aid goes into the same pool, to be received by the Ministry of Defense, the shift will be difficult to monitor. But at least the United States was forced to recognize that the Colombian army has not used antinarcotics aid to fight drugs.

Like Colombia, the United States has two faces, explained Cecilia Zarate Laun, a Colombian citizen who lives in the United States and helped arrange our trip. There is the imperialist face that most of Latin America sees. And then there is the democratic face, the face of the people who believe in human rights and who care what happens to the citizens of towns like Apartadó. That is the philosophy behind the sister-city program, the philosophy of people-to-people diplomacy. We all felt grateful to her for saying it. We wanted it to be true.

BOLIVIA: THE POLITICS OF COCAINE[3]

Bolivia's sad and turbulent history continues to repeat itself. The coca boom of today has replaced the tin boom of the last century, which in turn supplanted the exploitation of silver and other precious metals during the colonial period. And as in the past, Bolivia's export-based economy continues to depend on foreigners for everything from bank loans to economic advisers.

It is impossible to understand Bolivia's current economic situation without first understanding the links between Bolivia's prosperity during the 1970's and the inflation, price stabilization and stagnation of the 1980's. The economic prosperity Bolivia enjoyed during General Hugo Banzer Suarez's reign between 1971 and 1978 was financed with petrodollars borrowed from abroad. In less than a decade, public debt increased from $671 million to more than $2.5 billion. Foreign loans were supplemented during these global inflationary years by increased export earnings from tin and crude oil as well as illicit dollars from the booming cocaine trade.

Bolivia's so-called economic miracle, however, was short-lived. It came to an abrupt end in late 1979, when the United States Federal Reserve Board, following a monetarist policy to curb inflation, raised interest rates dramatically, precipitating the worldwide recession of 1980–1982. Prices for oil and tin collapsed, private capital fled Bolivia, short-term foreign debts tripled between 1980 and 1982, and Bolivia fell into a debt crisis and depression from which it has yet to recover. Not even the Bolivian military could contain the social unrest brought on by this economic crash, which manifested itself in political turmoil. The four years from 1978 to 1982 witnessed no less than nine heads of state.

The deteriorating economic situation—combined with pressure from the international community—forced the Bolivian military to return to its barracks in October, 1982. Hernán Siles Zuazo and his Democratic and Popular Unity (UDP) coalition,

[3]Reprint of an article by Melvin Burke, professor of economics, University of Maine. Reprinted by permission of *Current History* magazine, 90: 65–68, 90. F '91. Copyright © 1991 by Current History, Inc.

which had won the 1980 election, then assumed power. President Siles, who had successfully implemented a stabilization program in 1957–1958, was again heir to an inflationary, no-growth economy that was not of his making. As economist Jeffrey Sachs notes:

The Siles government inherited an annual inflation rate of approximately 300 percent (October, 1982, over October, 1981), an inability to borrow on international markets, and an economy declining sharply in real terms (real GNP [gross national product] fell by 6.6 percent in 1982). At the same time, the new government was called upon to satisfy pent-up social and economic demands.

In an attempt to repeat his earlier historic success, Siles implemented six price stabilization plans during his short term of office. They all failed because his government, which included Bolivian Communist party ministers, lacked support from Bolivia's businesspeople and its international creditors. This lack of support led to capital flight, devaluation of the peso and rising prices. In a desperate attempt to stop the vicious spiral of devaluation and inflation, the Siles government fixed prices, wages, interest rates and the official exchange rate. The result was an increase in black market economic transactions, which were not taxed, and a subsequent drop in government revenues. In a futile attempt to finance government deficits, the Central Bank printed more and more money. The outcome of all these measures was the Bolivian hyperinflation of 1984 and 1985.

The New Economic Policy

Hyperinflation forced Siles to call early elections in 1985. In the elections, former General Hugo Banzer Suarez and his Democratic Nationalist Action (ADN) party won a plurality of 29 percent of the vote. Victor Paz Estensorro of the National Revolutionary Movement (MNR), however, became President with only 26 percent of the vote after forming an alliance with the Left Revolutionary Movement (MIR) of Jaime Paz Zamora. Ironically, Paz Estensorro had been Bolivia's President during the previous period of inflation between 1952 and 1956.

President Paz Estensorro took office on August 6, 1985, and proclaimed the so-called New Economic Policy (NEP), which included a devaluation of the peso and a managed floating exchange rate; a cut in government spending and deficits; a freeze on public sector wages; elimination of government subsidies and controls on trade and prices; and privatization of public enterprises. This austere International Monetary Fund (IMF) stabilization program was intended to do more than eliminate inflation.

The policy succeeded in stabilizing prices, but it did so at a high human and social cost. Public sector employment decreased by 10 percent within a year, the peso was devalued by nearly 100 percent and inflation fell to an annual rate of 276 percent in 1986 and 15 percent in 1987. In return for complying with the IMF conditions, Bolivia received increased international financial assistance, including loans of $225 million from the IMF, $257 million from the World Bank and $351 million from the Inter-American Development Bank. The Paris Club of creditor governments also permitted Bolivia to reschedule $2 billion in debt, and it granted Bolivia the unique privilege of repurchasing $450 million of its foreign debt owed to commercial banks at 11 cents on the dollar, with money donated by foreign governments. In short, Paz Estensorro's center-right government was handsomely rewarded for returning Bolivia's economy to an open, laissez-faire and subordinate position in the global capitalist community.

Paz Estensorro's stabilization program also led to the privatization of the national mining company, Corporación Minera de Bolivia (Comibol) and the firing of 23,000 of the company's 30,000 miners. The massive unemployment of miners was only one cost of this stabilization program. Unemployment of workers increased to an estimated 20 percent, real wages decreased, and rural teachers quit their jobs in record numbers. In compensation for their reduced incomes, Bolivian government ministers were secretly paid salaries by the United Nations. If this were not enough, the government imposed a 10 percent value-added tax (VAT) on all economic transactions in mid-1986.

Economist Nicholas Kaldor has observed that orthodox economic policy, like Bolivia's,

is no more than a convenient smokescreen providing an ideological justification for such antisocial measures [as] high interest rates, an overvalued exchange rate, and the consequent diminution in the bargaining strength of labor due to unemployment.

There are indications today that Bolivia's high interest rate of 19 percent discourages real investment and that the "managed" peso is seriously overvalued by approximately 20 percent, thus reducing exports while promoting imports. Moreover, there is substantial evidence that the Bolivian Central Bank is using drug money to stabilize its finances. Short-term (30-day) deposits in dollars and dollar-indexed accounts (no questions asked) increased from less than $28 million in September, 1985, to an estimated $270 million in March, 1987. Since then, dollar deposits in Bolivian banks have increased to about $700 million, and the economy has once again been "dollar stabilized."

This stabilization, however, is not an economic miracle. The return of finance capital (international loans, debt reduction and drug money) to Bolivia after 1985, the freeing of prices and regressive taxes brought price stability to Bolivia. But the program has not brought prosperity or social justice to the country. On the contrary, inequality has increased, and the economy has shrunk. Nowhere is this more evident than on the streets of La Paz, where street vendors and beggars contrast with the fancy boutiques, posh hotels and Mercedes-Benzes. The regressive VAT absorbs nearly 15 percent of the gross domestic product (GDP) and the high-interest dollar deposits discourage productive investment. As a result, "real per capita GDP fell by 5.6 percent in 1986, 0.6 percent in 1987 and 0.1 percent in 1988." From 1986 to 1989, Bolivia's per capita GNP was only 74 percent of the per capita GNP in 1980, and the foreign debt of $3.5 billion absorbs 30 percent of the nation's legal export earnings.

The MNR initially paid for the high cost of its price stabilization, losing heavily in the municipal elections of 1987 after it received only 12 percent of the vote. In the 1989 elections, the MNR emerged victorious, with its new charismatic head, Gonzolo ("Goni") Sanchez de Lozado, winning a plurality of the vote, followed closely by Banzer and the ADN. Paz Zamora of the MIRA, who placed a weak third, however, was declared President when Banzer swung his party's votes to Paz Zamora in a congressional runoff. Unofficially, it has been Banzer who has run the country after he acquired 50 percent (17 portfolios) of the Cabinet in return for his votes. Among the portfolios held by Banzer's ADN are the powerful ministries of finance, defense and foreign affairs.

President Jaime Paz Zamora has vowed publicly to continue the stabilization program and to wage war on coca leaf producers. In return, Bolivia has received increased financial assistance from the United States. In 1989, Bolivia received $100 million in United States aid; $15 million was earmarked for drug interdiction and $40 million was part of a coca substitution program. In 1990, United States aid increased to $230 million; $33.7 million of this will go to the military if it takes part in the drug-eradication program.

War in Bolivia

Bolivia's miners and peasants were the soldiers of the 1952 revolution that brought the MNR to power and resulted in an extensive land redistribution program. However, the MNR government was never comfortable with either the miners or the peasants of the highlands and valleys. In its development programs, the government heavily invested in the lowlands—Santa Cruz, the Chaparé and the Beni—where there were no unionized miners or organized Amayra-Quechua peasants, and no land reform programs.

After 1952, most foreign aid as well as profits from the state-owned Comibol mine went to the lowland regions. Here sugar, cotton and cattle produced on large estates promised to become the new base for economic development in Bolivia. The government's objective was to move highland peasants to the more fertile lowlands, put them to work for agro-industrial entrepreneurs, and make Santa Cruz and the Beni the center poles of development.

Instead of sugar, cotton and cattle, however, the area struck it rich with coca. Today, 80 percent of Bolivia's coca is grown in the Chaparé region, *cambas* (lowlanders) dominate the drug trade, and Santa Cruz is a cocaine boomtown. But the development policy was a dismal failure even before coca arrived. Although the lowland's share of Bolivia's GNP increased between 1965 and 1979, agriculture's share of GNP as a whole decreased, as did traditional peasant agriculture in the highlands. The heavily subsidized sugar crop satisfied domestic consumption but not export needs. Many of the loans for sugarcane, cotton and cattle were unaccounted for and became seed money for the drug-trafficking elites.

The extent to which coca production and trade now dominate the Bolivian economy is astounding. Coca accounts for an estimated 30 to 40 percent of Bolivia's agricultural production, half its GDP and 66 percent of its export earnings. Between 40,000 and 70,000 peasants produce coca, and about 500,000 Bolivians (1 in 5 of the working population) depend on coca for a livelihood either directly or through support industries.

The typical campesino earns between $1,000 and $2,500 per hectare of coca plants, which is about four times the amount he could earn from growing oranges and avocados, the next most profitable alternative crops. He receives $2 for a kilogram of coca leaf, which translates to between $70,000 and $90,000 per kilogram of processed pure cocaine on the streets in the United States. Thus, while the coca farmer makes a living, the cocaine trafficker makes a killing.

The huge profits made from trafficking are used to buy airplanes, weapons, army officers and politicians in Bolivia and abroad. Only one-fifth of the money from the Bolivian drug trade is returned to the country. This leaves about $2.5 billion, which is spent and banked abroad, mainly in the United States.

With so much money to be made in the illicit drug industry, the corruption of Bolivian politics is understandable. It reached its peak on July 17, 1980, when General Luis García Meza came to power in a bloody coup. Garciá Meza's was undoubtedly the most brutal, corrupt, neo-Nazi government in Bolivian history.

During the two years García Meza was in power, the United States stopped all military aid to Bolivia. The populist Siles government that followed was reluctant to accept military aid or to turn the army against the well-organized peasants whom Siles was attempting to woo as supporters. In an attempt to keep the military out of the drug-control business and at the same time convince foreign lenders that Bolivia was willing to cooperate in the war against drugs, Siles created an anti-drug police force, the Mobile Rural Patrol Units (UMOPAR). This force, which was later nicknamed the Leopards, was entirely trained and financed by the United States. But Siles's greatest fears were realized when the Leopards kidnapped him in an abortive coup attempt in July, 1984.

This did not deter Siles's successor, Victor Paz Estensorro, from escalating militarization. In mid-1986, during Paz Estensorro's administration, the Leopards and 160 United States combat troops raided 256 suspected cocaine paste laboratories. They confiscated a mere 22 kilograms of the paste (from which cocaine is refined) and arrested only one narcotrafficker—a peasant worker. The operation, dubbed "Blast Furnace," was a failure in still another aspect. Bolivian society was outraged at the government's unconstitutional use of foreign troops without congressional approval.

Paz Estensorro soon focused his drug-eradication program on two fronts: armed conflict against the peasant coca producers and a program that paid $2,000 for each hectare of coca plants "voluntarily" destroyed. Both programs are financed by the United States government.

The International Response

On February 15, 1990, the Presidents of the United States, Bolivia, Peru and Colombia met in Cartagena, Colombia, to set policy for the drug war. They agreed "to implement or strengthen a comprehensive, intensified anti-narcotics program" to reduce both the supply of and the demand for illegal drugs.

On May 9, 1990, the United States and Bolivia signed an agreement that commits the Bolivian armed forces to fight the drug war. Under this agreement, $33.7 million in United States aid will be distributed in 1990 to eradicate drugs. In 1991 the drug-eradication and coca-substitution aid package is expected to total $95.8 million.

Despite this massive infusion of money and manpower, no one can seriously claim that the war on drugs in Bolivia is being won. Bolivia eradicated between 6,500 and 8,000 hectares of coca leaves in late 1990, although it was scheduled to destroy only 6,000 hectares for the entire year. However, Bolivia produces between 50,000 and 100,000 hectares of coca, which means that at the present rate of destruction, it will take at least 6 to 12 years to eliminate Bolivia's existing coca crop—if no new production is undertaken. And the costs of relocating and compensating coca producers could be as much as $3.5 billion. The Bolivian peasant will most likely continue to produce coca as long as demand in the United States or in other developed countries remains high or until viable alternative cash crops are developed at home.

The battle against cocaine traffickers is making little progress. On December 10, 1989, Colonel Luis Arce Gómez, García Meza's minister of interior, was apprehended and extradited to the United States to face drug charges. He faced similar charges in the Bolivian courts. Erlán Echeverra, Arce Gómez's right-hand man, was recently abducted and extradited to the United States and has reportedly agreed to testify against his former boss. Meco Dominguez, one of Bolivia's top three drug traffickers, was also apprehended.

The arrests of these Bolivian druglords are only the tip of the iceberg. General García Meza still draws his military pension, and his case in the Bolivian Supreme Court drags on. Banzer has been neither arrested nor charged and remains the head of Bolivia's major political party and the recognized power behind President Paz Zamora.

Corruption is most evident in the banking system, where "cocaine stabilization" is the norm. Most Bolivian drug money is laundered in the international banking system, which includes United States and Panamanian banks. The largest private bank in Bolivia, the Santa Cruz Bank, has offices in Panama and Miami.

Drug launderers and their bankers, however, are not targets of the military in its brave new drug war. Drug money is withdrawn from Bolivian banks whenever the government takes action against the druglords or when they do not support or cannot control the government. This capital is repatriated when the druglords feel safe or when they support the government, which has been the case in Bolivia since 1985.

The drug money deposits and repatriation explain why Bolivia's currency and price levels have stabilized since 1985. This policy obviously serves the interests of the new illegitimate bourgeoisie and the "narco-generals" of Bolivia. It also apparently serves the United States national interest, inasmuch as money laundering has not only been tolerated by the United States but has, in fact, been encouraged. The latest program to privatize Bolivia's public enterprises is a case in point.

There is little doubt that much of the investment capital used by Bolivia's new entrepreneurs is drug money. Privatization will further legitimize cocaine profits and make respectable businesspeople of the Bolivian cocaine traffickers. This is not a bad policy in the long run. But drug trafficking is much more profitable than running an airline or a brewery. Bolivia's druglords thus may not abandon their illegitimate drug trade but simply use the privatized companies as new fronts for money laundering.

While the drug traffickers face the prospect of acquiring respectability and legitimacy, the poor peasant coca growers struggle to survive against the combined armed might of the United States and Bolivian militaries. In November, 1990, 1,600 combat regulars of the Bolivian army were ordered to the Chaparé to wage war against the coca growers. Bolivia's peasants will undoubtedly resist this repression as did the Bolivian miners before them.

SOWING VIOLENCE IN PERU[4]

General Jaime Rios likens his job to the one that faced General
Norman Schwarzkopf, commander of the Allied forces in the
Persian Gulf. "The Americans that come here to visit tell me that
after General Schwarzkopf, I have the toughest job in the world,"
Rios says, relaxing in his peaked-roof bungalow in the Huallaga
River Valley of Peru.

Physically, they are nothing alike. Schwarzkopf is a burly
mountain of a man; Rios is lean and lanky, his face toasted by the
intense tropical sun. Instead of desert fatigues, he wears a high-
tech jungle-warfare outfit, comfortable despite the 100-plus degree heat.

But that outfit, like Schwarzkopf's, is made in the United
States. Rios commands the *Frente Huallaga,* or Huallaga Front, the
100-mile-stretch of the Valley where more than 65 per cent of the
coca leaf refined into U.S.-bound cocaine is grown.

America's appetite for cocaine has turned these rolling green
hills, veined with the earth-red rivers that feed the Amazon, into a
modern Wild West where justice is in the hands of those with the
most cash and the greatest firepower. Portly men in embroidered
white shirts and Italian loafers disappear into the bush with brief-
cases. Bodies putrify along the roads, some with placards around
their necks: DEATH TO SNITCHES AND TO ANYONE WHO REMOVES
THIS BODY.

According to reliable studies, up to 220 Cessna flights leave
the Huallaga's innumerable clandestine—and public—air strips
during dry months. Each can carry up to 880 pounds of *pasta
basica,* meaning an annual export of 302 metric tons of pur-
ified cocaine. Air Taxi Iberico in Tarapoto has a motto fit for the
times: DON'T ASK US WHERE WE GO, JUST TELL US WHERE YOU WANT
TO GO.

It is here that the United States thinks it can—and must—win
the "war on drugs." To do so, American officials are forging an
alliance, with the Peruvian military. The drug war has replaced
the Cold War in the plans of the U.S. Southern Command, which

    [4]Reprint of an article by Robin Kirk, associate editor at Pacific News Service.
Reprinted from *The Progressive,* 55: 30–32. Jl '91. Copyright © 1991 by Robin Kirk.

has already sent trainers, weapons, and supplies to Colombia and Bolivia under the International Narcotics Control Act (INCA).

For the past year and more, shadowy characters with experience in Vietnam, Teheran, and El Salvador have circled around the "Super-Base" at Santa Lucia on the banks of the Huallaga, the $3.5 million headquarters of "about twenty" Drug Enforcement Administration agents, heralded as "the new inter-American center for the struggle against drug-trafficking."

Many in Peru and the United States question the wisdom of financing Andean militaries to fight drugs. Although these nations are at least a decade past their military dictatorships, the men in uniform remain powerful. Strengthening them, rather than civil authorities, may tip an already fragile standoff.

Sending weapons to Peru's military means direct U.S. involvement in the dirtiest war in the hemisphere. Shining Path, the Maoist guerrilla movement of Peru, began its war in 1980 and has gained notoriety as the most brutal insurgency in modern Latin American history. Its aim is to establish a totalitarian state modeled on Mao Zedong's revolutionary China.

In the Upper Huallaga Valley, Shining Path has formed an alliance with coca growers, giving protection in exchange for a lucrative cut of the estimated $1 billion made every year off the sale of *pasta basica,* the gray alkaloid cake leeched out of coca leaves for shipment to Colombian refining labs.

The Middle Huallaga Valley is controlled by the smaller, Castro-style Tupac Amaru Revolutionary Movement (MRTA), which also charges area businesses a "war tax." More than 40 per cent of Peru's territory, including the Huallaga Front, is in a state of emergency, meaning that official control has been ceded to the military.

To combat guerrillas, the security forces have unleashed an equally brutal campaign whose daily features are torture, "disappearance," and extrajudicial execution. For four years in a row, the United Nations has put Peru first on the list of countries that "disappear" their citizens. According to the National Coordinating Committee for Human Rights, 246 Peruvians "disappeared" in 1990, putting the ten-year total at more than 3,000.

The U.S. State Department's own 1990 human-rights report singles out Peru's military for their ferocity. Nevertheless, according to U.S. officials, the Peruvian military will provide the "security frame" needed before crop substitution and police antidrug actions can take place.

General Rios says human-rights complaints are a plot funded by drug-traffickers to attack the army. Without help—and soon—he says, coca and insurgency are bound to grow. The Frente Huallaga command base has not yet come under attack, but military and police vehicles are often ambushed by guerrillas.

One of Rios's predecessors was seriously wounded in an MRTA assault last November. Since assuming command in January, Rios himself has been attacked unsuccessfully three times. In May, the MRTA carried out its most ambitious operation, simultaneously attacking five police stations over a twenty-mile area, including the station ten minutes' walk from General Rios's bungalow.

Of the $100 million slated to be sent to Peru, $30 million is for the military. The rest is for "alternative development." But not one dime will be issued until "security" is assured.

The accord has taken more than a year of comic diplomacy to work out. Last year, the U.S. embassy led hundreds of Peruvian and international journalists through a Potemkin Village of cocaine set up at Santa Lucia, to impress on them the idea of "narco-terrorists," meaning just about everyone living within Huey range of the base.

Lifelike huts, each with authentic-looking "narco-terrorists," were stops along a winding trail near the airstrip long enough to land the biggest U.S. Air Force cargo planes. Other props included coca bushes, harvested leaves spread out to dry, and pace pits where the cocaine alkaloid is stamped out in a murky bath of lime and kerosene.

But when newly elected President Alberto Fujimori decided not to sign a military-aid accord, arguing that those "narco-terrorists" were really coca farmers struggling to survive, the "Santa Lucia Drug Experience" was abruptly closed.

Fujimori insisted that guerrillas, not drugs, were Peru's main problem. A political newcomer without an organized party, Fujimori made it his first act upon taking office to ally himself with the military, Peru's most powerful institution. During one week, he received so many honorary medals that the lapel of his pin-striped suit sagged with gilt-encrusted metal.

What he needed was guns—guns and more guns, boots, rockets, rations, uniforms, bullets, better salaries, and helicopter fuel, to revitalize Peru's flagging war against the Shining Path.

"We need the coca-growing farmers' support, to win them back to the system," explains General Alberto Arciniega, a key

Fujimori adviser. "Targeting them would simply push them into the arms of the guerrillas."

Coca farmers insist they have little choice. The village of Cacatachi, for example, used to be the best rice producer in the province. A pleasant clump of blue adobe buildings, Cacatachi is in a fertile valley that empties into the Huallaga. But prices didn't cover costs. To ship rice out on one of the two disastrous roads that link the jungle to the coast is an exercise in futility. The government, which used to buy the rice, still has not paid for last year's harvest.

Not that it matters any more, according to Cacatachi mayor Roaldo Archenti.

"Inflation has made the amount that they owe us into a barbarous joke," says Archenti, a son of Italian immigrants. "There used to be over 15,000 acres planted in rice here. Now, there's not even 2,500. Many farmers have moved down to Tocache to grow coca."

Despite years of antidrug efforts, which included forced eradication and broken promises of development aid, land under coca cultivation has steadily grown. According to Peruvian estimates, there are at least 500,000 acres planted with illegal coca in the Huallaga Valley, which means at least 1,500 metric tons of *pasta basica*.

Most of Peru's coca is now grown "outside" the Upper Huallaga. The village of Huacayacu—I've changed the name of the village and its mayor—is fifty miles by tortuous road from Tarapoto in the Middle Huallaga. Four years ago, farmers opened up new hillside plots for coca. Huacayacu's 3,000 acres produce approximately 200,000 pounds of *pasta basica* per year, sold in an open-air Saturday market for the equivalent of $145 a pound, or $1,300 per villager per year. That is triple what Peru's nurses and teachers make.

"We are in an impossible situation," explains Mayor Severo Constanza. "We're not going to let ourselves die of hunger."

In fact, Peru's economic reforms depend on a cheap and plentiful supply of dollars shipped in bales from the Huallaga—$4 million a day, which the Central Reserve Bank buys. Fujimori's predecessor, populist Alan Garcia, spent the country into bankruptcy, leaving Peru blacklisted with international lenders and with only unsellable gold artifacts, dating from Peru's colonial splendor, in the Central Reserve Bank vaults.

However, economics is Fujimori's weak spot. He needs international credits to keep reforms afloat. The United States has made it clear that negotiations with the International Monetary Fund and other lenders depend on this accord. No drug war—no credits.

For signing the accord, the United States has thrown Fujimori some plums. The United States now admits funding the fight against guerrillas. No longer are coca farmers considered "narco-terrorists," but entrepreneurs in search of a free market.

Three separate "accords," the most important of which covers military aid, will probably be negotiated, signed, and implemented in secrecy. The United States will be the sole arbiter determining how and to what degree Peru complies.

U.S. officials believe the Peruvian military will now "take control" of the Huallaga—the navy of the rivers, the air force of the skies, and the army of the land. Then the Drug Enforcement Administration and police will just say no to coca. Farmers who do not choose other crops will be compelled to pull up their coca; and like a bad dream, the crack nightmare of the American inner city will vanish.

But the Huallaga Valley has a new sense of tension and fear. The drug economy has always shown an ability to adapt to circumstance, popping up in new and more inventive ways. For instance, although the Peruvian air force has forced thirty-two small planes to land in the Huallaga since January, the supply of *pasta basica* has not notably diminished. Drug-running Cessnas, equipped with the latest equipment, simply fly at night, evading the government's outdated Tucanos.

The military and police have never cooperated. In fact, units often face off at gunpoint, in a hail of mutual accusations about corruption. The district attorney's office in Tarapoto rarely receives a drug case. As one official explains, most are quickly "arranged" with police—by payment of a stiff bribe.

However, the office is overwhelmed with human-rights cases. According to Horacio Garcia, the legal adviser for the human-rights office sponsored by the Catholic Church, it receives thirty cases a month, mostly "disappearances." Half "reappear" bearing horrifying tales of torture—shocked with electrical charges, hung with their arms tied behind their backs, pushed out of helicopters, shut in metal containers placed in the jungle sun.

"The general denies that they are detained at the base, but we have hundreds of testimonies," comments Garcia, an elf-like man with a shock of white hair. "The ones who are eventually handed over to the police are often in bad shape. The police commander takes them immediately to the hospital for an evaluation, so that if they die in custody he won't be blamed."

Unlike cases of torture and disappearance, charges that military officers skim off the drug trade—$10,000 per landing, according to rumors—are taken seriously, Rios says. He claims he showed a list of officers tried and convicted of taking bribes to General Maxwell Thurman, head of the U.S. Southern Command, when Thurman visited the Huallaga Front in February.

But unfortunately, like the lists of officers the military claims are tried for human-rights violations, Rios's list is not available to the press. Recently, the U.S. Army made its first "good faith" gift to the general—500 M-16 rifles, now being lugged around Rios's command center by diminutive Peruvian recruits.

"With this weapon, I could pick off that man at the defense perimeter," Rios says, motioning toward a soldier crouched in a weed-choked trench 100 yards distant. He has detailed crews to fix the Outer Highway, ritually washed away every year by intense rains. But he gives this "development" phase six months, and if he gets no results, things will change.

"The next six months would be very different," he comments dryly. "The subversives may take that as a sign that I am weak. But I will show them differently."

<hr>

NORIEGA IN MIAMI[5]

<hr>

It was billed as the drug trial of the century, but two months after it began, *United States of America v. Manuel Antonio Noriega et al.* seems a big dud. Four days a week in the federal courthouse in downtown Miami, government prosecutors interrogate an endless procession of obscure witnesses about inconsequential events that occurred eight or nine years ago. Jurors snooze. Journalists groan. Manuel Noriega, the macho general who gleefully defied two American Presidents, sits at the defense table scribbling notes, a small, inconspicuous presence in the spacious wood-

[5]Reprint of an article by Michael Massing, free-lance writer. Reprinted by permission of *The Nation*, 253: 694–704. D 2 '91. Copyright © 1991 by *The Nation*.

paneled chamber. Initially splashed across the front pages of the
nation's newspapers, the trial now appears inside Section B—
when, that is, it shows up at all. "Manuel Lays an Egg," ran the
headline above a recent story in *The Miami Herald*. "It's 24 hours a
week of legal tedium played to an audience of three men and nine
women who must be trapped between boredom and loss of consciousness," the paper observed.

Yet beneath the surface, the trial is a fascinating affair, its
torpor regularly punctuated by riveting revelations and arresting
asides. In this ornately elegant courtroom, lighted by antique
chandeliers and ringed by the portraits of robed judges, a tense
political drama is being played out. On trial is not only Noriega
but also the American legal system, the invasion of Panama and,
most telling of all, U.S. drug policy as it has evolved over the past
ten years. The Noriega trial, in fact, provides an excellent look at
the ideology of the Bush Administration's war on drugs—and
shows why it is bankrupt.

I

During the week I attended the trial, in October, each day
brought forth some intriguing bit of news. One morning, for
instance, Lorenzo Purcell, a former commander of the Panamanian Air Force (now working at a Fort Lauderdale pizzeria), revealed that the 1984 presidential campaign of Nicolás Ardito
Barletta—a Noriega front man who won through fraud—was
financed in part by money from the Medellín drug cartel. Eduardo Pardo, a former cartel pilot, described how drug lord Pablo
Escobar had a secret compartment installed on his Learjet so that
the plane could transport drug money from southern Florida to
Panama.

Most striking of all was the testimony of Gabriel Taboada,
Colombian car dealer serving a twenty-one-year sentence for cocaine smuggling. Wearing khaki prison garb, the smooth-talking,
tousle-haired Taboada spent a morning describing in great detail
an elaborate scam he had devised for importing luxury cars into
Colombia despite a legal ban on them. Diplomats (who were ex-
empt from the ban) were paid up to $50,000 each to allow the cars
to be brought in under their names and outfitted with diplomatic
plates. In all, said Taboada, he imported forty-seven cars, using
envoys from Spain, Mexico, Honduras, the Soviet Union, Iran
and Iraq.

Among his customers was Fabio Ochoa, a *capo* of the Medellín mafia. After watching an episode of *Magnum P.I.* in which Tom Selleck drove a red Ferrari 308, Ochoa decided he wanted one just like it, Taboada testified. Ferraris were not exactly common cars in Colombia, however, and most ambassadors were reluctant to get involved. Special arrangements had to be made. Summoned to Ochoa's opulent estate outside the city of Medellín in mid-1983, Taboada said, he was led into a meeting attended by a number of top traffickers, including Pablo Escobar and Jorge Ochoa (Fabio's brother), plus a Panamanian dressed in white and introduced as "Manuel"—the defendant. Taboada suggested that the Ferrari be imported through the Panamanian Embassy. Noriega rejected the idea, saying that "would be the same as having a photograph taken of him with his arm around Fabio and having it sent to *The Washington Post* or *The New York Times*."

Shortly thereafter, Taboada continued, a briefcase was brought into the room and presented to Noriega. He opened it, revealing rows of neatly packed 100-dollar bills. "Five hundred," someone said, which Taboada took to mean $500,000. Noriega promised to find a way to bring the car in, and eventually it was imported through the Haitian Embassy in Bogotá.

It was a sensational story, placing Noriega in the traffickers' very lair. "The most damaging testimony against Noriega to date," *The Miami Herald* called it. Such triumphant moments, though, have been rare for the prosecution. From the start, its case has been marred by glaring contradictions, lapses and inconsistencies. Dates do not always jibe, and key details are often missing, raising questions about the government's contention that Noriega turned Panama into a haven for the Medellín cartel.

The government's case focuses on the years from 1982 to 1984. The thirty-page, eleven-count indictment charges Noriega with receiving at least $4 million from the cartel in return for allowing its members to fly cocaine through Panama en route to the United States; to use Panama to obtain chemicals needed in the manufacture of cocaine; to build a cocaine-producing laboratory in Panama; and to launder millions of dollars in Panamanian banks. In addition to Noriega, the indictment names fifteen other Panamanians and Colombians, including Pablo Escobar.

To make its case, the government has called on an unsavory array of bagmen, drug pilots and con artists. Their performances often border on the burlesque. Luis del Cid, a former officer in the Panamanian Defense Forces (P.D.F.) and a self-described "errand boy" for Noriega, claimed to have given him envelopes and suitcases full of cartel money. Questioned by the defense, however, del Cid admitted that he never actually looked inside the packages. How, then, did he know they contained cash? "It couldn't be anything else," he lamely responded.

Equally spotty was the testimony of Floyd Carlton Caceres, once a trusted cartel pilot. After being arrested in 1986, Carlton, a Panamanian, told U.S. drug agents that the Colombians had paid Noriega $600,000 for permission to fly three planeloads of cocaine through Panama. These four flights are at the core of the indictment against Noriega, and Carlton was billed as the government's star witness.

In court, though, his story was full of holes. When he first told Noriega that the cartel had approached him about using Panama as a transit point, Carlton said, the general exploded in anger. Noriega was about to become Commander in Chief of the P.D.F. and did not want to risk tainting his image. Noriega later changed his mind, Carlton said, but during cross-examination he conceded that Noriega had never actually done anything to protect the drug flights; in fact, he had not even known about them in advance. What's more, in December 1983, Noriega ordered a halt to the flights. "Under no circumstances," Carlton said, did he "want to be linked to the people in the Mafia."

The defense—led by Frank Rubino, a raspy-voiced former Secret Service agent—has yet to call any witnesses. In its cross-examinations, though, its main line of defense has become clear: Noriega had no involvement whatsoever with drug trafficking. Rather, Carlton and other unscrupulous associates traded on his name to extract large sums from the cartel. Far from facilitating drug trafficking, the defense maintains, Noriega was a model drug fighter, assisting the Drug Enforcement Administration (D.E.A.) at every turn. When it does get around to calling witnesses, the defense is expected to summon a number of U.S. officials to serve as character witnesses for Noriega.

For years, of course, Noriega was a favorite in Washington. He lunched with William Casey, conferred with Oliver North, met with George Bush. At the Pentagon, Noriega was received as a great potentate, and at Langley as a prized asset. Earlier this year, the C.I.A. and the U.S. Army admitted paying Noriega $320,000 for his services over a thirty-one-year period. (The actual sum may have been much higher.) It was only after Jesse Helms began agitating against Noriega in Congress, and Seymour Hersh ex-

posed him in *The New York Times*, that the White House finally
broke with its man in Panama. When Noriega refused to step
down willingly, President Bush sent the largest posse in history to
get him. Talk about illegal search and seizure!

The government's excesses have multiplied during the trial
itself. Many of its witnesses are convicted felons, to whom the
government has offered reduced sentences and extravagant fees
in return for testimony. Even Carlos Lehder, the murderous,
Hitler-loving drug lord who helped flood Florida with cocaine in
the early 1980s, has been enlisted. In exchange for his help,
Lehder, who was sentenced in 1988 to life imprisonment plus 130
years, has reportedly been moved from a basement cell at the
federal prison in Marion, Illinois, to a third-floor room with a
view and cable TV. Robert Merkel, the former U.S. Attorney who
prosecuted Lehder, told Michael Isikoff of *The Washington Post*, "I
don't think the government should be in the business of dealing
with Carlos Lehder, period. This guy is a liar from beginning to
end."

On a number of other fronts as well, the government's conduct has raised eyebrows. It has frozen Noriega's assets, estimated
at $20 million, making it hard for him to mount a proper defense.
(Eventually, the United States allowed an Austrian bank to release
$1.6 million.) The government has taped Noriega's telephone
calls to his lawyers and obtained a secret list of defense witnesses.
Most curious of all, Noriega's original chief counsel, Raymond
Takiff, surfaced in another case as a government informer. Add
in the lapses of its witnesses, and the prosecution's case would
seem to be in big trouble.

Except for one thing: Noriega is almost certainly guilty. During his time in office, Panama became a cesspool of corruption,
and drugs were no small part of it. Myriad shipments of cocaine
were transported across Panama's borders, and billions of drug
dollars were deposited in its banks. "I believe without a shadow of
a doubt that Noriega is guilty," says Bruce Bagley, a professor at
the University of Miami who is a leading expert on the Colombian
drug trade. "I've heard from any number of sources that he was
covered with cocaine." John Dinges writes in a new edition of his
book *Our Man in Panama* that "after a close examination of the
investigations that led to the indictments against Noriega, I found
no basis to question their general conclusions."

Several reporters covering the trial told me of their deep
skepticism about Gabriel Taboada's testimony. Noriega was too

circumspect, and had too much to lose, to make such a risky trip
to Medellín, they argued. Certainly he would never accept a bribe
in the presence of a complete stranger. Others, though, had little
trouble crediting Taboada's account. Joel Rosenthal, a criminal
lawyer in Miami who travels frequently to Colombia (he once
represented Pablo Escobar), said that such meetings are typical of
the way the cartel does business. "They like to negotiate face to
face," he told me, adding, "I have no question whatsoever that
Noriega was tight with the cartel. They partied together. He gave
them passports, licenses and jeeps. In return, he got pictures of
dead presidents," i.e., dollars.

The really important question raised by the Noriega case is
not so much whether the man dealt in drugs but what effect his
removal has had on America's drug problem. Operation Just
Cause was sold to the American people as a crippling blow in the
campaign against the international narcotics trade. Yet, nearly
two years later, cocaine continues to flow unabated into the
United States. According to a recent report by the General Accounting Office, money laundering has "flourished" since the
invasion and drug trafficking "may have doubled." To understand why this is so—and why the Noriega case is at bottom a
fiasco—it's necessary to examine how the indictment against him
and the cartel came about.

II

Given all the attention the Medellín cartel has received in
recent years, it's hard to recall that, as late as 1984, few Americans
knew of its existence. Even the D.E.A. was largely in the dark.
Pablo Escobar and the Ochoa brothers were on the agency's most-
wanted list, but officials had little notion of how they operated.
Things began to change in March 1984, when Colombian police,
working with the D.E.A., discovered a huge cocaine-producing
facility in the Colombian jungle. At the site they found fourteen
labs, seven airplanes, 11,800 drums of chemicals and 13.8 metric
tons of cocaine—an unimaginable quantity at the time. Called
Tranquilandia by the traffickers, the complex showed that the
Colombian drug trade had achieved extraordinary levels of inte-
gration.

Seven weeks later, Rodrigo Lara Bonilla, Colombia's Justice
Minister and top law-enforcement official, was gunned down in
Bogotá while riding in his official limousine. It was a clear act of

retaliation for the raid on Tranquilandia, and an ominous sign of the traffickers' growing ruthlessness. A uniquely sinister criminal enterprise had taken shape in Medellín, and American drug agents began studying it more intently.

They were assisted in that task by two informants. Barry Seal, a fast-talking, self-assured, 300-pound pilot and Special Forces veteran, had flown numerous smuggling missions on behalf of Escobar and other Medellín-based traffickers. Arrested in southern Florida in 1983, Seal gave the D.E.A. its first real glimpse inside the Medellín connection. (Seal was later gunned down by cartel hit men.) Even more knowledgeable was Max Mermelstein, a Brooklyn-born trafficker who, until his arrest in June 1985, was a member of the cartel's inner circle. "Max's position with the Medellín cartel was akin to Joe Valachi's with the Mafia," Guy Gugliotta and Jeff Leen write in *Kings of Cocaine.* "Like Valachi, whose dramatic testimony before the U.S. Senate in 1963 served as the first public unveiling of the Cosa Nostra, Mermelstein took the feds deeper than ever before into an uncharted area of organized crime." Mermelstein gave the D.E.A. its first truly comprehensive look at what he called the Medellín combine.

He also described the workings of another trafficking group based in the town of Cali. Comparable in size to the Medellín organization, the Cali cartel nonetheless sparked much less interest among federal drug agents. For one thing, the Cali traffickers were far less violent than their Medellín counterparts. Shrewd businessmen who disliked calling attention to themselves, the Caleños eschewed acts such as the Lara Bonilla assassination; as a result, they seemed less threatening.

Furthermore, the Cali group was not very active in southern Florida. New York, Los Angeles and Houston were all Cali markets; Miami was exclusively Medellín turf. And it was Miami—then America's main cocaine gateway—that was getting most of the nation's attention. It was here, for instance, that the White House set up a special task force to combat drug smuggling into the United States. It was here, too, that *Miami Vice*'s Don Johnson and Philip Michael Thomas tooled about in their European-cut suits battling sleazy drug dealers. *The Miami Herald,* which quickly outpaced other newspapers in probing the international drug trade, ran a series of exposés on the Colombian traffickers that focused primarily on Pablo Escobar & Company. Through such hype, the Medellín cartel became synonymous in this country with the Colombian cocaine trade.

It was in this climate that the U.S. Attorney's office in Miami went into action. Until the early 1980s, the office was a prosecutorial backwater, concentrating mostly on street-level dealers. In 1982, however, Stanley Marcus was named the U.S. Attorney for southern Florida. Intent on invigorating the office, he hired a number of top-flight lawyers and urged them to go after top-level traffickers. To head his narcotics section, Marcus named Richard Gregorie, a savvy, ambitious prosecutor with experience in fighting organized crime. Appalled by the drug-related violence engulfing Miami, Gregorie and his assistants decided to target the upper rungs of the Colombian trade. Working from information supplied by Seal and Mermelstein, they fashioned a single giant case from a number of smuggling incidents that occurred between 1978 and 1985. The indictment named Pablo Escobar, Carlos Lehder and the Ochoa brothers—all members of the Medellín cartel. It was handed down on November 18, 1986.

During their investigation, the Miami prosecutors kept coming across references to Manuel Noriega. Throughout the boom years of the early 1980s, the Medellín cartel was constantly seeking new routes through the Caribbean Basin, and Panama—with its strategic location, extensive unregulated banking system and willing government—became a key outlet. It was not until June 1987, however, when Floyd Carlton agreed to cooperate, that the U.S. Attorneys in Miami knew they had a case. "Carlton was critical in linking Noriega to the cartel," recalls Mark Schnapp, a Miami lawyer who worked on the indictment.

All the while, U.S. pressure on Noriega was building. With crack causing havoc in cities across the country, the drug issue quickly soared to the top of the nation's agenda. Eager to display their toughness, politicians found in Noriega an inviting target. In 1987 Senator John Kerry, chairman of the Subcommittee on Terrorism, Narcotics and International Operations, began mounting an investigation into drug trafficking in Panama and other countries in the region. Feeling the competition, the U.S. Attorneys in Miami stepped up the pace of their own probe. Eventually, Gregorie came up with nine witnesses in addition to Carlton (all but three of them convicted felons). By early 1988, the Noriega indictment was nearly complete.

There remained the matter of Washington's approval. Indicting Noriega was, of course, a highly sensitive matter. Never before had a foreign leader been so charged in this country, and moving ahead in this case would have profound repercussions.

But the U.S. Attorneys in Miami were resolute. In 1986 their office had let lapse an investigation into gun-running to the Nicaraguan *contras*. Leon Kellner, Stanley Marcus's successor as U.S. Attorney, was widely accused of caving in to White House pressure; he denied this, but the criticism made him doubly determined to see the case through. In late January 1988, he and Gregorie traveled to Washington to brief Justice Department officials on the case. They encountered little resistance. And so, on February 5, 1988, Manuel Noriega was indicted on drug trafficking and racketeering charges.

At the time, of course, it seemed highly unlikely that the case would ever go to court. The State Department was pressing Noriega to step down, and the indictment seemed little more than a bargaining chip. But then came the U.S. invasion and Noriega's capture, and suddenly the U.S. government faced the prospect of actually trying the man. The Miami prosecutors hoped that the search of Noriega's quarters in Panama would turn up evidence of his involvement in drug trafficking. Days after the invasion, in fact, Army investigators announced they had found a fifty-pound stash of cocaine in one of Noriega's offices. On closer examination, though, it turned out to be a flourlike substance used in cooking. What's more, the many thousands of documents seized in Panama contained no smoking gun. Gradually, it became clear that the government would have to rely on oral testimony. Squads of F.B.I. agents fanned out through Florida's prisons, looking for inmates with dirt on Noriega. By the end of the summer of 1991, the government had lined up more than sixty witnesses.

Finally, on September 16, in a courtroom packed with reporters, lawyers, government agents and spectators, Assistant U.S. Attorney Michael Sullivan delivered the prosecution's opening statement. Manuel Noriega, he declared, "is the last military strongman from Panama. He looks small here in this cavernous courtroom, but he was a giant in Panama."

III

Oddly, during the trial Noriega has often seemed absent. On most days his name comes up only two or three times, usually in some offstage role. Overall, the trial has left the clear impression that Noriega's part in the drug trade, though real, was quite modest. The events described in the indictment all took place before the summer of 1984, with the exception of a single drugs-for-

arms deal said to have occurred in March 1986. According to
Sullivan, Carlos Lehder will testify that Noriega was "just another
crooked cop"—one of hundreds paid off by the cartel. In *Our
Man in Panama*, Dinges estimates that Noriega earned at most $10
million to $15 million from drugs—"substantial sums, but leaving
him a mid-level player in the billion-dollar league of the Latin
American drug entrepreneurs." According to Dinges, once Noriega's primary drug involvement ended, in the early 1980s, he
"became a trusted and overtly zealous DEA collaborator." That
such a committed enforcer is no longer in power may help to
explain why drug smuggling in Panama has boomed since the
invasion.

Meanwhile, Pablo Escobar—the other top figure named in
the indictment—sits in a prison outside Medellín. He turned himself in this past summer after a determined two-year offensive by
the Colombian government. The organization he once controlled
is itself reeling—its airplanes seized, its labs destroyed, its transportation links severed. The D.E.A., having sought the Medellín
cartel's defeat for so long, has finally gotten its wish. None of this,
though, has had much effect on the amount of cocaine entering
the United States. A kilogram of the drug costs about the same in
Miami and Los Angeles as it did in 1989, before the campaign
against the cartel got under way.

One reason, of course, is the Cali cartel. With the Medellín
cartel routed, the Cali combine has absorbed much of its market.
At long last, the D.E.A seems to have discovered the Cali cartel. In
July, *Time* featured a cover story on the cartel that described it in
the same lurid terms once reserved for the Medellín cartel. "They
are among the richest families in Colombia," *Time* reported, "but,
to the U.S. Drug Enforcement Administration, they are the new
kings of cocaine, patriarchs of a criminal consortium more disciplined and protected from prosecution than the Sicilian Mafia
and now bigger than the Medellín cartel." Relying heavily on
D.E.A sources, the article quoted its head, Robert Bonner, as
saying that "the Cali cartel is the most powerful criminal organization in the world. No drug organization rivals them today or
perhaps any time in history." Clearly, the agency is planning to
open a new front in the Latin American drug war.

It's likely to prove no more successful than the earlier campaigns, for the Colombian cocaine trade is far more amorphous
and decentralized than the feds seem to believe. Major syndicates

operate not only in Cali but also in Bogotá and Pereira (located about 125 miles west of the capital); in addition, Colombia is home to myriad small entrepreneurs working independently of the giant combines. The Medellín cartel itself, though down, is far from out. Many observers expect that the jailed Escobar, freed from his preoccupation with eluding the authorities and enjoying a free rein in his custom-built prison, will prove an even more effective mover of cocaine than when he was on the loose.

Then, too, Colombia is hardly the only country involved in trafficking these days. With the heat coming down there, the drug lords have been moving their operations into Brazil, Ecuador, Venezuela, Bolivia and Peru. Clearly, the Bush Administration's drug-busting strategy in Latin America has been exactly that—a bust.

The Democrats, meanwhile, have offered few alternatives. Although outspokenly critical of Republican policy, they share many of its assumptions. Consider, for example, Senator Kerry's narcotics subcommittee. As a vehicle for exposing U.S. complicity with thugs like Noriega, the subcommittee's hearings in 1988 had a salutary effect. As a forum for analyzing the international drug problem, they were a muddle, full of lofty war-on-drugs grandstanding. Here is a sample passage from Kerry's opening remarks:

> We hope to show the imminent danger posed by continued inattention to the international narcotics relationship. We will hear testimony about the destabilization of whole countries, regions, the support for terrorism, and the subversion of our own laws and institutions. I believe . . . that not only do we face a national security threat ourselves . . . but that other countries are threatened to such a degree that the stability of the Western Hemisphere, certainly the southern Western Hemisphere, is at issue.

Criticizing the Administration for its ineffectiveness, Kerry called for more, not less, U.S. intervention in Panama and other trafficking nations. Not surprisingly, his position was heartily endorsed by such fire-breathers as Jesse Helms and Alfonse D'Amato.

Kerry's hawkish stance is hardly exceptional. This past September, for instance, during a hearing in the House of Representatives, Stephen Solarz urged Administration officials to use herbicides on Peru's coca fields—a potentially disastrous strategy that could drive coca-growing peasants into the arms of the Shining Path guerrillas. Charles Rangel, who has commendably called for more spending on drug treatment and prevention, has also campaigned tirelessly—and thoughtlessly—for an expansion in the D.E.A.'s activities abroad.

Scholarly examinations of the global drug trade tend to be no less simplistic. Over the years a peculiar species of drug-war literature has emerged. Representative of the genre is *The Politics of Heroin: CIA Complicity in the Global Drug Trade*, by Alfred McCoy, a professor of history at the University of Wisconsin. The book was first published in 1972. McCoy, then a young graduate student, spent eighteen months in Southeast Asia's Golden Triangle investigating links between the C.I.A. and the opium trade. After McCoy testified in Congress about his findings, the C.I.A. demanded to see the manuscript he was working on. McCoy's publisher, Harper & Row, complied, but when the agency insisted on numerous changes McCoy stood firm, and the book was published without revision. Earlier this year, an expanded edition was released to take advantage of renewed public interest in the subject.

At 634 pages, *The Politics of Heroin* is a weighty tome, but its theme can be easily summarized. "Over the past forty years," McCoy writes, "American and allied intelligence agencies have played a significant role in protecting and expanding the global drug traffic." Both in the late 1940s, when it connived with the Corsican and Sicilian mafias in Europe, and in the early 1980s, when it joined with the Afghan rebels, the C.I.A. provided a political and legal shield to groups trafficking in heroin. The pattern was repeated in Central America in the 1980s, when the Nicaraguan *contras*—protected by the C.I.A.—smuggled cocaine into the United States.

"The CIA's Contra support operation," McCoy writes, "coincided with a major expansion in the Caribbean cocaine trade. . . . By using Contra support aircraft to carry their cocaine, the Medellín cartel's smugglers reduced the risk of seizure." McCoy concludes: "Simply by launching a major covert operation in a strategic drug zone, the CIA contributed, albeit indirectly, to a major expansion of America's cocaine supply."

This is absurd. However much the *contras* may have been involved in drug trafficking—and the record remains sketchy—their contribution to the overall hemispheric trade was altogether insignificant. Every year, the Colombian traffickers send hundreds, if not thousands, of loads northward, by plane, boat and truck. The vast majority of these shipments have nothing what-

soever to do with the C.I.A. Similarly, the Afghan rebels no doubt
plied opium, but to conclude that the agency actively protected
their trade requires an ideologically inspired leap of faith. The
heroin industry, like that for cocaine, is a multibillion-dollar enterprise with an insatiable base of consumers around the world.
Certainly it doesn't need the C.I.A. to open markets for it.

In the end, the problem is not the C.I.A. Nor is it the size of
the D.E.A. or the restraints imposed on its activities abroad. The
problem is that the international drug trade is virtually immune
to attack. Heavily armed and fantastically wealthy, the drug lords
generally operate in remote fastnesses well beyond the reach of
the law. Based in impoverished societies with high rates of unemployment, they can draw on a bottomless pool of recruits; no
matter how many workers are killed or arrested, others are always
willing to take their place. After ten years of waging war on the
narcos, it's time to recognize that such a strategy cannot work. It's
time, in fact, to recognize that *nothing* we do outside our borders
can significantly diminish the amount of drugs entering the country. Only by redirecting our attention from Latin America to the
domestic front can we hope to alleviate the crushing problem of
drug abuse in America.

Our needs at home are immense. They begin with treatment.
Despite greatly increased federal spending in this area, clinics
remain grossly underfunded, and waiting periods of weeks are
common in cities throughout the country. In the nation's
prisons—virtual colonies of drug addicts—treatment remains
largely unavailable. Even those who do successfully complete re-
covery programs often relapse because of the lack of support
services. Without more spending on vocational training, continuing education and medical care, the drug problem will continue
to fester, especially in our inner cities.

One way or another, it's time to be done with all the foreign
sideshows, from the C.I.A to the Cali cartel, the *contras*, the Afghan rebels, the secret armies, the hidden conspiracies—and
Manuel Antonio Noriega.

The Noriega trial is expected to drag on through the fall. Its
outcome seems foreordained. Drug trials in this country have
extremely high conviction rates, and this one will probably be no
exception. If convicted on all counts, Noriega could receive up to
140 years in prison. A draconian sentence, it might seem—unless
one puts it in the broader context of Panamanian politics. One of
the great ironies of the Noriega trial is that it ignores the man's

really serious crimes—his intimidation of opponents, his stealing of elections, his crackdown on the press, his plundering of Panama's wealth. As a drug trafficker, Noriega was a modest player. As a tyrant, he was indeed a giant in Panama. Should he spend the rest of his days in prison, justice will, in a sense, have been served.

It should, however, have been left up to the Panamanians to make that decision.

III. COCAINE AND CRACK

EDITOR'S INTRODUCTION

The prevalence of heroin was a major concern in the 1970s, but was replaced by the use of cocaine. Most recently, cocaine in the form of crack has been the focus of particular attention, since it can be obtained cheaply and thus reaches a large population of users. In the opening article in this section, Gordon Witkin in *U.S. News & World Report* discusses the emergence of the crack phenomenon. While cocaine powder required an investment of at least $75 a gram, crack—obtained from cocaine by an uncomplicated technique and ready to use when smoked—costs as little as $5 a "hit." As Witkin notes, its introduction was effected by a number of different ethnic groups. By 1986, crack selling became big business. Los Angeles and New York street gangs sold the drug on the West and East coasts, and then fanned out across the country until today half a million Americans are estimated to be using the product.

In a related article in *New York* magazine, Michael Stone notes that from 80 to 90 percent of the cocaine brought into New York City is handled by Colombia's Cali cartel. Crack dealing has a strongly ethnic aspect. Chinese gangs are in control in Chinatown, Dominicans in Washington Heights, blacks in Harlem, and Jamaicans in Brownsville and Bedford-Stuyvesant. They operate separately but all use a hierarchical system of upper and middle-level managers, with street-level managers, each supervising teams of dealers. In a following article, David Whitman in *U.S. News & World Report* points out that although cocaine consumption has declined in middle and working-class households in recent years, crack use has exploded among inner city criminals. The full scale of its use, according to a recent study, appears to have been greatly underestimated, since U.S. surveys have not counted in most criminals. Were they to do so, estimates of crack use might well have to be doubled.

In an article in *Time,* Anastasias Toufexis explores another aspect of the crack epidemic, that of babies born to crack-using mothers. Toufexis observes that 1 out of every 10 newborns in the

U.S.—375,000 a year—is exposed in the womb to one or more illicit drugs. In the case of "crack kids," damage can be quite serious. Some have physical deformities, while others reveal behavioral aberrations that require special schooling. Hospital care for crack babies, many of whom are born prematurely, is 13 times more expensive than for normal infants. With the right treatment and special education, many lead normal lives, but their disability involves a high cost to society. On the same subject, James Willwerth, also writing in *Time*, examines the issue of whether crack babies should be taken away from their addicted mothers and put into foster care. In 19 states laws allow child-abuse charges to be pressed against any woman who gives birth to a child with illegal drugs in its bloodstream. But Willwerth notes that taking children from their mothers would probably involve their being boarded in hospitals and nursing homes, a practice that would not only overwhelm the health care system but also the children. Preferred alternatives are putting the child with a grandmother and requiring the mother either to give up her child or enter a treatment program.

THE MEN WHO CREATED CRACK[1]

The most amazing thing about crack cocaine is that it did not begin rotting America's urban landscape sooner. It has been recognized as a scourge in cities—and none too few suburban and rural areas—for only five years. But the supercharged cocaine, sometimes called "rock," wasn't really new. References to the recipe that used heat and baking soda to turn cocaine hydrochloride, or powder, into the smokable form of freebase called crack appear throughout the 1970s in underground literature, media interviews and congressional testimony. It did not catch on back then, researchers believe, because it was not as pure as other, more processed forms of freebase. Freebasers, who fancied themselves connoisseurs in those bygone days, called it "garbage rock."

What turned crack into a craze was mass marketing that

[1]Reprint of an article by Gordon Witkin, *U.S. News & World Report* staffwriter. Reprinted by permission of *U.S. News & World Report*, 111: 44–53. Ag 19 '91. Copyright © 1991 by *U.S. News & World Report*.

would have made McDonald's proud. Crack was not invented; it was created by a sharp crowd of sinister geniuses who took a simple production technique to make a packaged, ready-to-consume form of the product with a low unit price to entice massive numbers of consumers. Cocaine powder required an investment of at least $75 for a gram, but a hit of crack cost as little as $5. Equally alluring was crack's incredible "high"—an instantaneous euphoria because it was smoked—that could create addicts in weeks.

There were three classes of criminals who created the crack epidemic. The first was composed of anonymous kitchen chemists and drug traffickers in the Caribbean and later in the United States, who used rudimentary science and marketing savvy to help hundreds of small-time criminals set up crack operations. The second was made up of indigenous crime organizations, common in most medium and large American cities, which began to seize local markets from the smaller operators. The third consisted of gangs from both coasts that franchised crack operations into every corner of the country.

The story of how crack infiltrated America is one of daring and enterprise. It also raises distressing questions about the capacity of police agencies to detect and combat massive criminal infiltration into the nation's neighborhoods. It contains lessons for Americans confronting an impending flood of heroin and Europeans tackling a cresting tsunami of cocaine. And it is a cautionary tale about what happens when hopelessness grips whole communities—how it lays them open to the allure of easy money and unspeakable violence.

CHAPTER 1
Early Days: Smoking Coca Paste

Two products, coca paste and cocaine freebase made with ether, came before crack—and led indirectly to its debut. Coca paste is an inexpensive, first-stage creation in cocaine processing that sells for as little as $1 a gram. First reports of its use came from Peru in 1971. By 1974, Lima faced a paste-smoking epidemic; by 1980, the practice had spread to Colombia, Bolivia, Ecuador and Venezuela.

Soon after, Colombia initiated a temporarily successful effort to cut off importation of ether, the primary solvent used to process coca paste into cocaine hydrochloride powder. At the same time, intensified law enforcement efforts began to seal off the Colombia-Florida cocaine pipeline. The result was the widespread transshipment of unrefined coca paste to various Caribbean islands, and then South Florida, for refinement into powder, according to Miami researcher James Hall and University of Delaware criminologist James Inciardi.

Colombian traffickers promoted the idea of cocaine smoking through this new distribution network, hoping to expand sales. Dominican dealers in New York have told sociologist Terry Williams that Colombian wholesalers would include paste in kilo-size shipments of cocaine powder and tell them to give it away free to see how the customers liked it. Paste never did take hold in America, in part because of its harshness. Its future in the Caribbean, though, was bright.

CHAPTER 2
Getting Closer: The Freebase Era

In the early 1970s, American consumers who had seen coca-paste smoking in Latin America apparently came upon the recipe for cocaine freebase through trial and error. Recreational smoking of this type first appeared in 1974 in California. Freebase is created through a chemical process that "frees" base cocaine from the cocaine hydrochloride powder. Crack is a form of freebase, but back in those early days, most freebase was made not from the easy baking-soda recipe but from a more volatile chemical process involving ether and elaborate paraphernalia, such as acetylene or butane torches. This process created freebase purer than crack, and cocaine aficionados mistakenly believed that the purity made it healthier. It was a big hit in Hollywood in the mid-to-late-1970s, helped along by a burgeoning industry that sold pipes, chemicals and extraction kits. By 1980, experts believed between 10 and 20 percent of all cocaine users were doing freebase exclusively, though others resisted it as too complicated and dangerous.

Their fears were confirmed on the night of June 9, 1980, when comedian Richard Pryor set himself on fire while freebasing at his San Fernando Valley home. Pryor suffered third-degree burns over his entire upper torso and parts of his face. It appears likely that the Pryor incident sent many drug users searching for a safer way to freebase, and thus led to wider dissemination of the simpler and safer, though less pure, baking-soda method for making freebase—the recipe that came to be used for crack.

The final and most important force behind the push for crack was the growing street demand for a simple form of smokable cocaine. By 1982, in New York City selling or "copping" zones, as many as 80 percent of the customers wanted "base," according to sociologist Williams, whose book "The Cocaine Kids" provides a riveting window into Gotham's crack culture. That meant the dealers had to cook it up batch by batch for the customers, while they cooled their heels in the dealers' apartments—a level of sustained exposure to outsiders that dealers loathed. One example was Tony, a 29-year-old dealer observed by New York anthropologist Ansley Hamid of the John Jay College of Criminal Justice. "The change in consuming preference placed a fresh burden upon Tony," Hamid wrote in the Spring 1990 issue of *Contemporary Drug Problems*. "Now he was obliged to suffer even larger throngs of customers to remain in his apartment while he, like a crazed apothecary, cooked up their purchases of powder into freebase."

The result of this pressure to handle customers quickly prompted dealers to search for a new product. "They tried to figure out an efficient way to create large batches of cocaine freebase and then package it in such a way that it could be sold at retail in a market they didn't necessarily interact with directly," according to researcher Bruce Johnson of New York-based Narcotic and Drug Research Inc. Crack was the answer.

CHAPTER 3
The Caribbean Test Market

Offshore, there were other forces driving the development of crack. Researchers believe that residents of the Netherlands Antilles, after experimenting with coca paste, came up with a crack prototype around 1980—a conversion of paste using baking soda, water and rum that came to be known there as "roxanne," "base-rock" or "baking-soda base." In the early 1980s, reports of "rock" began to surface regularly in the southern Caribbean. Dr. Charles Wetli, deputy medical examiner for Dade County, Fla., remembers hearing about it during a trip to the Turks and Caicos Islands as part of a teaching team sponsored by the Drug Enforcement Administration: "A local cop asked about a drug that looked like a pebble, and people would smoke it and go crazy. None of us had ever heard of it."

Meanwhile, rumblings of a similar nature were shaking the

Bahamas. By the early 1980s, the vast share of cocaine destined for the United States was being transshipped through the Bahamas' 700 islands and 2,000 cays, with a hefty chunk of it being diverted and consumed by the local population. In 1979, the freebasing of cocaine rock made its debut, and the practice slowly gathered momentum over the next three years.

In the fall of 1983, Bahamian rock abuse surged, especially in the poorer neighborhoods of New Providence and Grand Bahama islands. At Princess Margaret Hospital's community psychiatry department, 35 patients were treated for cocaine addiction in all of 1983; in the first six months of 1984, the total was more than 200. Stumbling addicts, rail thin and malnourished, congregated to smoke rock in tattered abandoned buildings on Grand Bahama, Andros and New Providence islands—in places that came to be known as "base houses," the forerunner of crack houses on the mainland.

Public-health officials groping for answers turned to a burly Bahamian named Chris Finlayson. Dr. David Allen, the islands' leading drug-abuse expert, had met Finlayson when he came in for treatment after claiming his clothes spoke to him during an acute freebase psychosis. Allen helped the personable and fast-talking Finlayson beat his rock problem temporarily, and then followed as his former patient led him deep into the Bahamas' base house culture.

Finlayson convinced Allen and Dr. James Jekel, a Yale Medical School epidemiologist, that the rock epidemic had been caused by a fundamental switch in marketing strategy by local drug pushers. The doctors already knew that in early 1983, the glut of cocaine powder in the Bahamas had dropped the street price per gram to only one fifth of its previous level. Finlayson told them that at that same time, "the pusher man switched to pushing only rock," relates Dr. Jekel. "You couldn't get powder on the street." Other addicts confirmed Finlayson's story. "The pushers knew that crack addicts keep coming back for more and more, so figured, 'Let's create a demand by getting people to go to crack,'" says Jekel. "How do you get them to go to crack? They figured, 'Let's just sell that and nothing else.' It was a marketing decision."

For Finlayson, that was lethal. He succumbed to drugs on a boat trip and died in 1986. His dying words to Allen in Princess Margaret Hospital were: "When the world tastes this, you're going to have a lot of trouble." Allen and Jekel tried to sound the alarm to a wider audience in the United States, but no one seemed particularly alarmed.

CHAPTER 4
Rock Arrives in Los Angeles

While the Caribbean story was unfolding, crack was beginning to show up in California. Addicts reported in Los Angeles that as early as 1978, a process called "smearing" or "pasting" was catching on. It used the baking-soda formula. "Instead of letting it form a rock, you would pour it out on a mirror and take a finger and smear it," recalls one former addict. Then, the dried mound of the drug was smoked. Some contend that this was the transitional product between freebase and crack.

Rock made its L.A. debut around 1980, mostly because it was a faster, easier way for addicts to get their kicks. By 1982, Los Angeles hospital emergency rooms reported the nation's greatest increase in cocaine overdoses, a 90 percent rise over the previous year, according to the National Institute on Drug Abuse, due to "more and more users shifting from snorting to injecting or freebasing." By early 1983, the *Los Angeles Sentinel,* the south central neighborhood's community paper, was reporting a problem with "rock houses"—residences used for dealing crack.

But no one was really prepared for what happened in 1984, when sales of $25 rocks swept south central Los Angeles. Dozens of rock houses "went up overnight," says former LAPD Capt. Noel Cunningham, many of them so fortified that the police for a while used a 14-foot steel battering ram attached to an armored personnel carrier to break in. Teenagers, many of them gang members working for older, tougher former members, openly dealt rock at dozens of hot spots like 98th Street between Avalon Boulevard and Main Street, making thousands of dollars in the process.

Authorities now believe several below-the-surface developments helped crack's rapid ascent. The big Colombian smugglers were responding to increasing heat in Florida by bringing more and more cocaine over the Mexican border into Los Angeles. They found it convenient to tap into the existing gang structure because gang-ridden areas already had heavy concentrations of drug users and because the gangs had experience manufacturing and selling other drugs like PCP. Finally, the market had been thrown wide open by the December 1983 arrest of Thomas (Tootie) Reese, south central's pre-eminent drug kingpin for the previous two decades.

While all these sands were shifting, law enforcement had something else on its mind: planning for the 1984 Summer Olympics. "There was an awful lot of organizational focus on just keeping the city safe from terrorists," says the DEA's William Coonce, "I think the normal law enforcement took a second seat." Ex-LAPD official Cunningham agrees.

CHAPTER 5
Storming the Miami Coast

In the late 1970s and early 1980s, South Florida was already reeling under a deluge of cocaine powder. "Cocaine cowboys" were shooting it out for control of the trade. Hidden behind the mayhem was the conversion of some of the street-level cocaine business from powder to base. The steady flow of Caribbean peoples to Miami, heightened by the early-1980s flood of fleeing Haitians, brought with it the burgeoning knowledge of how to convert paste into "baking-soda base." Crack wasn't far behind.

One early inkling came in November 1982, as researcher Inciardi interviewed a prostitute on a bench near the Miami Marina. "She started talking about something called 'garbage freebase,'" he relates. "Suddenly it clicked. That was an old San Francisco term from the '70s for a rock variety of freebase."

The biggest clue that crack had arrived came around 1982, when a Miami Police Department street narcotics unit busted five drug houses and apartments in the city's Little River and Liberty City neighborhoods, all of them run by a Caribbean-island immigrant who called himself Elijah. He bragged to police that he'd invented rocks, and though the claim is impossible to confirm, former Sgt. Mike Ahearn, who ran the unit, says those were the first rocks he saw. Ahearn recalls the first bust of one of those houses: "I couldn't believe it, there were 30 people in this house, and they didn't look like junkies. These were people with jobs—white, black, upper class, lower class, young girls. I remember thinking, 'What the hell have we got here?' They said they were doing rocks. They called it a 'rock house.'" By 1984, crack had spread more widely to poor neighborhoods like Overtown and Liberty City, selling for as little as $10, sometimes under brand names like "Rambo" or "Miami Vice." Most of the crack retailers were American blacks, small-scale dealers who bought cocaine

powder and picked up the crack recipe from Caribbean wholesalers whom they had first met in the marijuana business. Many
Caribbean people were attracted to the illicit economy of the
crack trade because their illegal-immigrant status cut them off
from legitimate jobs.

CHAPTER 6
The New York Flood

Authorities think there was probably a race between Califor-
nians and Caribbeans to see who got to introduce crack to the
New York market the fastest. The first official to spot its arrival
was Bill Hopkins, a former Bronx narcotics cop who headed a
state "street research unit" set up to monitor drug trends. As he
drove up Arthur Avenue in the Tremont section of the Bronx in
December 1983, Hopkins recognized some of the drug abusers in
Crotona Park and stopped to hear the men talking about two
other abusers who had "freaked out." "You know what that was,
don't ya?" asked one man.

"Yeah, that was that crack," said the other.

"My ears perked up, because this was something new, and
that's rare," recalls Hopkins. "They said it was 'rock cocaine.'" It
was almost another year before Hopkins got a firsthand look at a
man who was smoking it. "I learned for the first time it was done
with baking soda, not ether," says Hopkins. "And I examined
what he had, and it was in vials. I knew we had something new on
the market." Within a year, crack had saturated the city.

Nowhere did crack grab hold as tightly as it did in the northern Manhattan area called Washington Heights, a teeming neighborhood with a distinctly Caribbean flavor. When night fell,
"copping" zones like West 168th Street or 174th Street and Amsterdam Avenue became choked with traffic. Some 70 to 80 percent of the consumers powering the market were white professionals or middle-class youngsters from Long Island, suburban
New Jersey or New York's affluent Westchester County—all of
whom could easily drive into the community. The neighborhood
was diverse enough ethnically, says Hopkins, that "a white guy
could come into that neighborhood without standing out like a
sore thumb."

Though several groups lived in the Heights, it was Dominicans who came to dominate the crack trade. The drug-dealing
Dominicans, like their many legitimate shopkeeping counter-

parts, proved to be ambitious and well organized. They delivered consistently high-quality crack, and they proved adept at moving easily in both black and white worlds. Most important, perhaps, the cocaine wholesalers—Colombians from Jackson Heights, Queens—preferred doing business with them rather than with American blacks. They had already established links with the Dominicans through earlier marijuana trafficking, and they shared a common language.

The market in 1985 and early 1986 was still in its formative stages, however—marked not by massive organizations but by hundreds of cash-hungry young entrepreneurs. They worked out of apartments, using kitchen utensils. "Anyone could buy the cocaine and make crack," says the city's special narcotics prosecutor, Sterling Johnson. "Back then, there was no General Motors of crack, just a lot of mom and pop operations."

CHAPTER 7
The Feds Finally Catch On

In October 1985, when Robert Stutman took over as the special agent in charge of the federal Drug Enforcement Administration's New York office, one of the first things he heard about was crack. After reading a host of intelligence reports and getting a four-hour briefing from a DEA chemist, he decided to start rattling some cages at headquarters. But Stutman's reputation stood in the way of his cause. DEA Administrator Jack Lawn liked his New York man, but others at headquarters were jealous and suspicious of Stutman's yen for publicity—a trait that earned him nicknames like "Stuntman." As a result, much of what he said about crack in those early days was viewed skeptically in Washington.

Federal officials also had a hard time figuring out how widespread the crack problem had become because they couldn't decode street lingo. Was crack the same as the "rock" the DEA was hearing about in California? Were cocaine rocks the same as "rock cocaine"? The confusion "probably slowed down the law enforcement response," says William Alden, DEA's chief of congressional and public affairs. "It's difficult to establish a strategy when you can't define the target correctly."

Disagreement also raged over whether crack deserved to be treated as something new and different—or simply as a subset of the war on cocaine. "The thing that weighed most heavily against a massive response was the argument that to solve crack, you had to first solve the overall cocaine problem because crack was just a marketing technique," recalls David Westrate, then DEA's assistant administrator for operations. "If this was a completely new drug, we might have had a different response." Others felt crack was an issue better addressed by state and local law enforcement, while the DEA followed its mandate to focus on large traffickers.

Still, Stutman finally prevailed. On June 19, 1986, Lawn and a handful of headquarters brass flew an agency plane to New York for an all-day briefing by DEA agents and chemists, New York police and private treatment providers. As the meeting broke up, news arrived of the sudden death of University of Maryland basketball star Len Bias. Those at the meeting immediately suspected cocaine. "When Jack [Lawn] left," recalls Stutman, "he said, 'You've convinced me we've got to do more.'"

For the next few months, however, the federal effort remained confused. As late as July 15, 1986, Westrate was testifying to Congress that "at this time there is no comprehensive analysis of the crack problem, either from a health or enforcement viewpoint." A DEA intelligence review two months later, while acknowledging crack's availability in 12 cities, nonetheless called it "a secondary rather than primary problem in most areas." Just days later, though, the National Drug Enforcement Policy Board, a multiagency group then directing federal strategy, said the "present crack situation, in short, is bleak."

Lawn himself did follow through. Early that fall, he made an emergency request for $44 million to fund 200 agents who would organize a host of state and local crack task forces nationwide. However, the Justice Department's budget monitors, acting on behalf of Ronald Reagan's budget office, denied the request. "[The budget officials] didn't treat it like a major issue," says Lawn, especially under the tight antideficit strictures of the Gramm-Rudman-Hollings law. Stephen Trott, who chaired the Justice Department's budget board, declined comment.

The DEA's next move was to jury-rig a few special crack programs using its existing budget and some new funds from the Anti-Drug Abuse Act of 1986. In 15 cities across the United States, the agency created two-person crack teams to assist local police. Some feel the effort was inadequate. "Then, as now, there is not the same type of commitment to crack as one would see with cocaine generally," says Democratic Rep. Charles Rangel of New York, chairman of the House Select Committee on Narcotics. "In

my opinion, that's because it's in the poorer, minority communities."

CHAPTER 8
Bigger Organizations Muscle In

By the fall of 1986, the National Cocaine Hotline estimated
that 1 million Americans had tried crack, in large part because the
drug's marketing structure was changing and distribution was
expanding. The outlandish profits and inevitable elbowing over
turf led to the creation of larger crack organizations that began to
overshadow the small-time operators. Some grew by simply dominating a territory and gradually forcing out competitors, through
intimidation if necessary. Others were born of mergers. Either
way, organization brought structure—CEOs, lieutenants, distributors, lab operators, runners, enforcers and street dealers. The
business even went high tech as telephone beepers became tools
of the trade. Finding the workers for these groups wasn't difficult. Many inner-city teens felt shut off from legitimate economic
opportunity and came to see drug dealing as the only path to
prosperity.

Once crack selling became big business, it created operations
that finally were sophisticated enough to merit extensive attention from federal law enforcement authorities. Many of these
home-grown organizations came to be dominated by charismatic
supercriminals who ruled with an iron hand. One city that saw the
rise of a highly structured organization was Houston, where prosecutors say Johnny Binder and Martha Marie Preston became the
"king" and "queen" of the city's crack business. In Detroit, brothers Billy Joe and Larry Chambers emerged from humble back-
grounds to craft a disciplined empire that grew to dominate Mo-
town's lucrative crack trade. And in New York, the pre-eminent
early figure was a canny street tough named Santiago Luis
Polanco-Rodríguez, an immigrant from the Dominican Republic
who used marketing savvy to rule Washington Heights.

CHAPTER 9
Gangs Up: Crips and Bloods

As bad as the indigenous organizations were, the spread of
gangs was truly disastrous. America was caught in a pincer movement; Los Angeles street gangs moved east and Jamaican posses

moved west from the East Coast, and between them, by the end of the decade, they had introduced much of the rest of the country to crack.

The chief Los Angeles gangs were the Crips (approximately 30,000 strong now) and the Bloods (about 9,000). Their expansion took off in 1986. Earlier this year, the Justice Department said that investigative reports had placed Crips and Bloods in 32 states and 113 cities. Their reach extended to places as small as Hobbs, N.M., and Ashton, Idaho. Some experts think the L.A.-based gangs now control up to 30 percent of the crack trade.

While the movement conjures up images of a master plan, authorities say it was really more a matter of happenstance. Neither gang is rigidly hierarchical. Both are broken up into loosely affiliated neighborhood groups called "sets," each with 30 to 100 members. Many gang members initially left Southern California to evade police. Others simply expanded the reach of crack by setting up branch operations in places where they visited friends or family members and discovered that the market was ripe—and the prices they could charge were higher than those in locations where the market was saturated. When authorities unraveled an L.A. ring that introduced crack to York, Pa., they discovered not a grand plan but a love-struck Crip named Benjamin West, who had followed his L.A.-based girlfriend to York, where she was visiting her mother on a summer vacation. Since crack hadn't yet come to York, authorities say, West stayed to set up his own operation.

Compared with Los Angeles, other cities were easy pickings, especially for "rollers" or "OGs"—older gang members in their 20s—with a thirst for more-serious cash and existing connections to Colombian suppliers. "Gang members candidly concede that they choose their new homes because of market conditions and perceived weakness in the community's ability to deal with them," says a government sentencing memo in one Seattle gang case. "The word that a particular community is an easy mark spreads by word of mouth." Some Los Angeles gang members also struck out for new territory because they had hit the glass ceiling back home. "If you're a third stringer in L.A., you may figure you'll never reach the heights there, but somewhere else you can be the biggest and baddest," says the DEA's James Forget.

Portland and Seattle proved to be two of the most inviting targets. The march from L.A. to Seattle began in early 1987, masterminded by Derrick "Vamp" Hargress, an older member of a Crips set known as the Nine-Deuce Hoovers. They brought an unprecedented level of violence and a strong criminal infrastructure to Seattle's drug trade, authorities there say. In Portland, police weren't sure what it meant when a Northside apartment raid in December 1987 turned up a man who said he was a Blood from Los Angeles. But they found out soon enough. By mid-1988, some 100 L.A. gang members were in Portland dealing crack, and they attracted at least 230 Portland youths to the gang lifestyle, turning north and northeast Portland into veritable free-fire zones.

CHAPTER 10
Jamaican Posses

From the other coast, the great crack sales-branching scheme was put together by transplanted Jamaicans in the mid-1980s. The discovery of it came in one of those classic investigations that begin with a small piece of evidence and grow like kudzu. In the spring of 1984, Agent J. J. Watterson of the Bureau of Alcohol, Tobacco and Firearms was asked to investigate the origins of a dozen smuggled guns found in shipping containers at the port of Kingston, Jamaica. When he began checking gun store records in Dade and Broward counties in Florida, Watterson found the guns were part of a larger purchase; 50 to 75 weapons had been bought by Jamaicans. The few purchasers who could be tracked—many had given false addresses—seemed to live in virtual fortresses, and it wasn't unusual for a Mercedes or BMW to be parked outside. Pretty soon, the guns began turning up in drug and murder cases in Washington, D.C., New York, Detroit, Miami, Chicago and Los Angeles. "It was an amazing scenario," says Watterson. "We had murders everywhere."

What Watterson had discovered were Jamaican "posses": a network of mobile Jamaican gangs that came to dominate gun trafficking and crack dealing over wide swaths of the United States, leaving a trail of blood-spattered bodies wherever they turned up. The posses take their name from American Westerns. Today, approximately 40 of the posses, with an estimated membership of 22,000, operate in the United States. ATF officials think they control a third of America's crack trade. The posses are believed to be partly rooted in Jamaican marijuana trafficking groups and were nurtured in the grinding poverty in Kingston and the violence-soaked politics of the island in the period around 1980.

Seeing crack's profit potential, Jamaican traffickers moved quickly. They focused first on the large Caribbean populations in Miami and New York. By mid-1987, at least five groups were operating in South Florida, led by the notorious Shower posse, so named for firefights that showered an area with bullets. The posse was run by a couple of smart but cutthroat gangsters named Vivian Blake and Lester Coke. It began by smuggling marijuana but turned to cocaine in 1985, and, according to authorities, grew to 5,400 members nationwide. In New York, the Jamaican traffickers came to be particularly dominant in Brooklyn. One of the biggest and toughest groups there was the Renkers posse, run by an especially ruthless character named Delroy Edwards, better known as "Uzi" for his taste in weapons.

Nearly all the posses displayed an extraordinary penchant for violence. On August 4, 1985, a feud between two posses resulted in a frenzied shootout at an Oakland, N.J., picnic attended by some 5,000 Jamaicans. Shower posse members fired well over 700 rounds; three people were killed and 13 wounded. In New York, a man who tried to steal $20 worth of crack from two members of the Spangler posse was kicked unconscious, placed in a bathtub, decapitated and dismembered. The following morning, a street person found the victim's head in the garbage and began kicking it down the street. Since 1985, the ATF has documented more than 3,000 posse-related homicides nationwide. Gun running, meanwhile, has become a lucrative sideline.

Often, the posses were able to establish new beachheads because it took local authorities some time to figure out what was happening. It hardly seemed unusual when Dallas detective P. E. Jones was rousted from a deep sleep at 2:30 a.m. on July 20, 1985, to investigate a murder at the Kool Vibes Club on Second Avenue; it was Saturday night, after all, in a tough neighborhood. But the victim, Howard Gordon, 28, was Jamaican, and the ensuing investigation turned up scores of out-of-town Jamaican drug connections. The homicide probe led to much more. By the time investigators were finished, they had uncovered 500 to 700 Jamaicans—many of them teenagers called "street worms"—involved in 27 Jamaican drug rings that operated 75 crack houses turning $400,000 in profits a day.

Kansas City was much the same story. In that heartland city, the Jamaicans, with their dreadlocks and accents, stuck out plainly. They were being arrested on drug charges in significant numbers as early as 1983, all of them with phony IDs and passports. But no one knew quite what it meant. By 1986, investigations of a string of 15 murders involving Jamaicans showed police that the posses had brought 450 members into town and were operating at least 50 crack houses. The brains behind the Kansas City invasion were members of the Waterhouse posse (who came from the Waterhouse region of Kingston), which was led by a creative yet vicious thug named Errol "Dogbite" Wilson.

Other cities showed similar patterns. Prodded by Watterson and his Florida cohorts, ATF launched a national investigation of the posses in January 1987. Since then, the effort has resulted in the prosecution of approximately 1,200 Jamaican defendants. "We made some significant cases, but the fight isn't over," says ATF's Chuck Sarabyn.

By late 1987, two other groups had also gotten involved in interstate trafficking. Dominicans, from their base in New York, moved into New England, dominating the crack trade in places like Providence, R.I., and Stamford, Conn. And migrant farm workers—many of them Haitian—took the crack recipe from Florida into Georgia, North Carolina, southern Delaware, western Michigan and the Dayton, Ohio, area.

Today, though the worst may be over, crack still holds at least half a million people in its grasp. The despair pervading America's inner cities, made worse by the blight caused by crack, continues to provide fertile soil for something similar to grow in its place. Anthropologist Philippe Bourgois, who has been studying East Harlem crack dealers for six years, argues that it is unrealistic to expect a youngster growing up in an environment of evil to develop a healthy concept of equal opportunity and personal responsibility. "The 'common sense' emerging among this newest generation is that 'The System' hates them," writes Bourgois in a recent issue of *The American Enterprise*. That is the reason, he says, that so many inner-city blacks believe there is a secret white conspiracy to destroy them and crack is part of it.

But crack's hold on inner-city kids is logic, not conspiratorial hocus-pocus. High-wage, low-skill manufacturing jobs have disappeared from inner cities. Crack selling became rationalized as the only ticket to prosperity. Those who have studied crack operations uniformly say these kids weren't lazy and drifting; many worked back-breaking hours in the drug trade and yearned to make something of themselves. Given half a chance at productive futures, they just might go for it. If not, some other illicit activity will come along—heroin, ice, gun running, something—and this pathological crime cycle will get another jolt.

COKE INC.:
INSIDE THE BIG BUSINESS OF DRUGS[2]

Acting on a tip from the Brooklyn district attorney, federal Customs agents raided a warehouse on 44th Drive in Long Island City early last November. They were looking for cocaine, and they found it—400 pounds stuffed in cardboard boxes lying in plain view. But that was only the start. Against a wall, the agents found hundreds of twenty-gallon cans filled with bricks of cocaine packed in lye so corrosive it had begun to eat through the metal containers. It took a police unit seven days to move out the drugs. By then, the agents had uncovered nearly 5,000 bricks: 4,840 kilograms—5.3 tons—of cocaine.

Richard Mercier, the agent in charge of the operation, says that in 1973, he put a dealer away for 34 years for possession of three ounces of cocaine. In those days, the seizure of a kilogram of drugs—2.2 pounds—was a major bust. After the Long Island City raid, Mercier recalls, he surveyed a 24-foot truck piled four feet high with cocaine. "How much more is out there?" he wondered.

Three months after that bust, in the early-morning hours of February 3, a police anti-crime unit rounded the corner at Lenox Avenue and 128th Street in Harlem and saw a young man we'll call Willie waving a .357 Magnum at a group of youths across the street. Someone yelled, "Yo, burgundy!"—the code name for the officers' red Chevy—and Willie darted into a nearby tenement. The cops cornered him in a second-floor apartment, and Willie dropped a brown bag containing almost 300 vials of crack. On a bench next to him, police found a plastic bag containing 2,900 more vials of crack. In a wastebasket they discovered more than $12,000 in small bills. It was Willie's second arrest. He was fifteen.

These events evoke the images New Yorkers most commonly associate with the city's drug trade: mountains of white powder smuggled by a faceless international cartel, and the dead-end kid hawking crack in the ghetto. But the smuggler and the street

[2]Reprint of an article by Michael Stone, freelance writer. Reprinted by permission of *New York* magazine, 23: 20–29. Jl 16 '90. Copyright © 1990 K-III Magazine Corporation.

dealer are only the most obvious players in the city's bustling drug business. Between them, an army of unseen workers—middlemen, money counters, couriers, chemists, money launderers, labelers, and arm-breakers—tend the vast machinery of New York's dope trade. Seven days a week, 24 hours a day, they process, package, and distribute the hundreds of kilos of heroin and cocaine required to feed the city's habit.

A legion of entrepreneurs also supply New Yorkers with tons of marijuana, as well as a dazzling assortment of pharmaceuticals: barbiturates, amphetamines, LSD, ecstasy. You can still buy PCP on West 127th Street, and officials have run across "ice," a potent new methamphetamine derivative, in East New York. But today, the huge heroin and cocaine/crack markets are the focus of law-enforcement efforts, for these are the drugs that are corroding city life.

During the past decade, New York's drug business has undergone a revolution. Ten years ago, cocaine was still exotic, a drug popular with celebrities and people trying to be hip. Crack wasn't even an idea. Though heroin was plentiful, users tended to be older and more discreet about their habits. A *Times* survey in December 1981 asked New Yorkers to rate the most important problems facing the city, and drugs didn't make the top ten. The appetite for drugs that's since sprung up has developed together with a business that aggressively marketed its products and worked feverishly to keep pace with the demand it was creating. At times, dealer and user seemed locked in a fatal embrace, each egging the other on to new and dangerous highs.

The breakneck expansion in sales and revenues destabilized New York's entrenched distribution networks, ushered in an era of intense competition, and sparked episodes of unprecedented violence. Thousands of organizations—from mom-and-pop candy-store operations to vast criminal conspiracies—sprouted to meet the demand. The drug trade also became an equal-opportunity employer: As the Mafia pulled back from—or was muscled out of—the business, blacks and other minority-group members who'd previously been relegated to the lower levels of distribution were drafted into key roles. And with cocaine and heroin selling at several times the price of gold, street-smart young men suddenly found themselves awash in cash.

At the same time, these dealers influenced the type, price, availability, and quality of drugs in the city. Crack was an immediate success here, though in Boston and Chicago the drug is relatively rare. The taboo on selling dangerous drugs to minors, observed a generation ago, was breached, and now teenagers and even younger children play important roles in the trade.

Despite the efforts of the authorities and the opposition of community groups, the city's drug lords—many of them uneducated and seemingly unemployable—have developed and managed remarkably efficient markets. Gone are the periodic shortages that hit the city when organized crime ran the drug supply. The new traffickers not only increased profits but lowered prices and raised product quality. One wonders what might have been accomplished if all that energy, innovation, and daring had been harnessed to a worthy enterprise.

Everyone agrees that the drug business is big business, but there's wide disagreement over its exact size. The most quoted estimate—which comes from the House Narcotics Committee—is that retail drug sales nationally for 1987 amounted to $150 billion, a figure that one committee aide claims has grown substantially since then. There are no official figures for New York, but Sterling Johnson Jr., the city's special narcotics prosecutor, thinks the city's share may be as much as $80 billion.

Other experts argue that these numbers are grossly inflated. "If New Yorkers were spending $80 billion a year on drugs," says Peter Reuter, a researcher at the Rand Corporation, "then every man, woman, and child in the city would have a habit." Reuter calls the government's estimates "mythical numbers," created by agencies whose budgets and influence grow with the perceived size of the problem.

In fact, there simply isn't enough information to get an accurate reading of the size of the drug trade, although there are ways to make rough guesses. The most common method estimates the amount of drugs smuggled into the area and then multiplies that figure by the street value of the drugs to get a total price. For example, on the basis of figures from several law-enforcement agencies, it's estimated that officials intercepted around 14,000 kilograms of cocaine in the metropolitan area in the past twelve months, an amount experts assume to be around 10 percent of all the cocaine shipped here. Since the street value of a kilogram of cocaine runs from $80,000 to $190,000, cocaine sales in the city, according to the formula, ranged between $11.2 billion and $26.6 billion.

There are several problems with this method, however. For one thing, different government agencies often take credit for the same bust, thus inflating the overall figure for the amount seized. What's more, recent studies indicate that a substantial portion—perhaps 40 percent—of the cocaine and heroin brought into the country never reaches the street. Instead, it's consumed by dealers and their cronies or used as payments for services like prostitution. Finally, there's no good reason to believe that there's a fixed ratio between seizures and imports.

A second method for computing the size of the drug business focuses on heroin and is based on the number of users and the average cost of their daily habit. The state Division of Substance Abuse Services estimates that there are 200,000 heroin addicts (as opposed to recreational users) living in the city. If they spend an average of $50 a day to satisfy their habits, then addicts alone account for $3.6 billion in heroin sales each year.

Once again, however, the experts disagree on the data. Working from studies of the criminal activities of narcotics addicts, Reuter calculates that the common estimate of the number of heroin addicts and the cost of their addiction is far too high. "If there were 200,000 addicts in New York, each spending $50 a day, the city would have ceased to exist," he says. "The junkies would have stolen it long ago."

The average cost of a heroin habit is anybody's guess. "It might be $150 to $200 per day," says Paul Dinella, a former addict who until recently worked for the Division of Substance Abuse. "All I know is that a junkie will spend whatever he can get." Dinella also points out that most addicts vary their drug use over time. Some "dry out" periodically; around 40,000 heroin users entered treatment facilities around the state last year. Thousands more were jailed. When surveyed, though, addicts tend to exaggerate their habits, citing what they spend when they're binging. One study found that a group of addicts overstated the amount they spent on drugs by a factor of four.

A third approach attempts to place drug sales within the context of the economy as a whole. New York's gross economic product is about $180 billion. Given Sterling Johnson's drug-trade figure—$80 billion—that would mean that New Yorkers spend nearly half of what they produce on drugs. Many experts think that's impossible. Rather, they estimate that the city's underground economy is around $18 billion and that drug revenues are some fraction of that.

The wild card here is out-of-town sales. New York is a shipping point for many drugs, one of three or four main distribution centers in the United States. Revenues from these wholesale deals add billions to the total drug trade here and go some ways toward reconciling the difference between estimates based on interception and consumption.

Inevitably, the experts view the size of the drug problem through their personal lenses. The cop and the prosecutor see the crack crews on every corner and think the world has gone crazy. The economists and academicians look for the paper trail that tens of billions of dollars should leave and can't find it. Still, even moderate estimates place drug sales in New York at around $12 billion; by contrast, restaurant and bar revenues in the metropolitan area total around $7 billion.

In any case, the business has grown explosively in the past decade. Even heroin use is on the rise after declining for years. There are a few small positive signs: a recent reduction in casual cocaine use among high-school seniors, a decline in cocaine-related emergency-room visits after a dramatic rise, and a flattening out of the growth rate of crack consumption. But these developments may simply show that the market is saturated. "So we've stabilized crack use at record levels of consumption," says a House Narcotics Committee aide. "Is that something to be proud of?"

Almost every cocaine deal that takes place in New York begins in Colombia. Although the coca plant grows mainly in Peru and Bolivia, Colombians process about 80 percent of the region's crop and export it around the world. Of the estimated 450 tons of cocaine produced last year, as much as 75 tons may have passed through New York, says Arthur Stiffel, top Customs agent at Kennedy airport.

The Colombians smuggle cocaine in ways limited only by the imagination. Government agents have found the drug concealed in the cages of poisonous snakes and in blocks of chocolate. Every year, they intercept hundreds of human "mules" who swallow cocaine-filled condoms to sneak the stuff past Customs. Typically, Colombia's cartels smuggle boat- or planeloads of cocaine into a southern border state, then truck the drug up to New York. Recently, according to Stiffel, the smugglers have also been flying shipments directly into local airports. In June 1988, a Customs unit in Miami seized 1,200 kilos of cocaine that were en route to Suffolk County Airport in Westhampton, the first installment of a 15-ton load targeted for Long Island's East End summer population. The huge cargo ships that visit New York–area ports are another favorite vehicle for traffickers. "Not even counting what's hidden in the merchandise, a one-inch dropped ceiling in a standard container could hold thousands of pounds of cocaine," says Customs agent Richard Mercier. "But we only have the resources to inspect 3 percent of the containers that come in."

Mercier's arithmetic explains the government's dilemma. Because the markup on cocaine is so high—a kilo that costs $4,000 to produce in Colombia sells in New York at wholesale for $14,000 to $23,000 and recently even as high as $35,000—the cartels would make a hefty profit even if Mercier's colleagues beat the odds and intercepted half the illegal drugs entering the city. The Colombians, of course, aren't indifferent to government seizures, but it costs them more to lose customers and sales to competitors than to lose an occasional shipment.

Some officials attribute a recent rise in the wholesale price of cocaine to the effectiveness of the war on drugs here and in Latin America. Others say it's too soon to tell if the war is helping, and in any case, drug prices vary widely depending on the location of the deal and the status of the buyer.

Most of the cocaine brought into New York—80 to 90 percent, says the DEA—is imported by the Cali cartel, an association of traffickers from Colombia's third-largest city. Headed by the two Rodriguez-Orjuela brothers and José Santa Cruz-Londoño, the group was formed in the early eighties to set drug policy and coordinate smuggling.

Before the cartel took over, most traffickers shipped their drugs to Miami, then sold them to middlemen with connections around the country. This arrangement worked fine as long as the market remained small and import prices stayed high. But as more and more traffickers got into the act and production levels jumped, import prices in Miami plummeted. As a result, the demand for cocaine rocketed, and local distributors racked up huge profits.

Today, the DEA maintains that the Cali cartel controls the first line of distribution in New York. Operating through teams, or "cells," of salaried employees, the cartel sells to the legions of mid-level dealers who ultimately supply the city's street dealers and retail organizations. Kenneth Robinson, one of the DEA's Cali experts, says that each cell typically includes a supervisor, or underboss, six to eight managers, and assorted workers. The supervisor takes possession of the drug shipments and stores them in safe houses—generally, private homes or warehouses. The managers place their orders through coded phone calls directly to the cartel in Colombia, which relays them to the supervisor. The supervisor then contacts the managers and arranges delivery at a safe house or at some public place, such as a mall, where the proliferation of shopping bags can help hide the transfer of drugs and money.

The cartel managers are the bureaucrats of the drug business. Contrary to the popular image of cocaine cowboys with flashy lifestyles and flamboyant personalities, typical managers live modestly, blending into the suburbs where they often live. Overall, the cartel's operations are disciplined and difficult to trace. Money and drugs are kept separately, beepers are leased from legitimate businesses, written records are limited, and workers are trained in countersurveillance. When FBI undercover agents posing as money launderers recently met with cartel members, the Colombians brought along their lawyers.

But beneath the corporate veneer, the Colombians operate according to a code of violence and intimidation. Stiffel speculates that many of the cartel leaders came of age during Colombia's civil wars, when killing was a way of life. "They're not like the Mafia," says Robinson. "The Mafia isn't going to touch your family. But the Colombians will kill you, your wife, your children, and your dog. They're not going to leave anyone to take revenge later on."

Their methods are effective. Robinson points out that of the 400 or so cartel members arrested in the United States, only a handful have cooperated with the police. And in a business often disrupted by ripoffs and blunders, the Colombian operation seems to run smoothly. "I've busted dozens of Colombians over the years—peasants guarding rooms with tens, twenties, fifties piled floor to ceiling," Stiffel says. "But I've never yet found one of them with more than a few dollars in his pocket."

Government officials don't know how much money the cartel actually makes from its New York operations. DEA agents busted a Cali money-laundering outfit in Great Neck and found records that indicated revenues of $44 million in less than two months. The 5.3-ton load in Long Island City—also identified as part of a Cali operation, though no one has been arrested in connection with the raid—would have brought around $200-million at wholesale prices. Robinson thinks that the Cali cartel has three or four cells operating independently of one another in the New York area and that, on average, it takes two or three months to distribute a major delivery.

New York's huge market has attracted other importers as well. In fact, Stiffel disputes the view that the Cali cartel controls New York's cocaine hierarchy. Rather, he argues that New York's traffickers are caught up in a kind of feeding frenzy, with all of Colombia's major cartels, as well as other groups and individual importers, competing for coca dollars. Two years ago, an apparent turf dispute between Cali and the Medellín cartel, the world's largest cocaine producer, sparked a rash of murders in Queens.

Last May, FBI agents busted a Medellín-operated ring based in Manorville, Long Island, that supplied cocaine to Jackson Heights, Flushing, and Jamaica, Queens. Agents say the group handled 6,400 kilos of cocaine during one five-month period in 1988. Jules Bonavolonta, the agent in charge of the investigation, estimates conservatively that the ring was generating revenues of $200 million to $250 million a year.

The Mafia has also continued to bring cocaine into the city. Law-enforcement officials speculate that at the time former Bonanno-family soldier Costabile "Gus" Farace murdered DEA undercover agent Everett Hatcher in February 1989 ("Death of a Hood," *New York,* January 29, 1990), he was building a cocaine-distribution ring in South Brooklyn and Staten Island. Farace was allegedly supplied from Miami by Gerard Chilli, his former prison mate and a reputed capo in the Bonanno family. Farace was gunned down last November because his actions had brought too much heat on the mob, investigators say.

After cocaine leaves the cartel's cell, it generally passes through a series of middlemen before reaching the street. Along the way, a dealer—who generally works on consignment—has three ways to make money. He can broker his supply intact and tack on a commission. He can divide it into smaller units and mark up the price. Or he can "cut" (dilute) the cocaine with harmless adulterants like milk sugar—in effect, increasing the amount of cocaine he has to sell.

In one typical sequence, using low-end prices, a high-level broker buys 100 kilos of pure cocaine at $17,000 per kilo and sells them in ten-kilo lots at an average price of $19,000 per kilo, earning $200,000. The second dealer sells the ten kilos for $23,000 a kilo, earning $40,000. His customers cut the cocaine by a third, producing, in all, 133 kilos, which they break into around 4,700 one-ounce units and sell to dealers for $800 each, for a total profit of about $1,460,000. Finally, these dealers add another one-half cut, creating in all 200 kilos, or about 7,050 ounces, of adulterated cocaine. That cocaine is converted into crack at a rate of about 350 vials per ounce of cocaine. The crack vials are sold on the street for, say, $5 each, earning the dealers $8,577,500, of which around 20 percent goes to the street sellers.

This pyramid form of distribution has two main virtues: It maximizes the dealer's access to his market while minimizing his involvement in potentially dangerous transactions. No one at an intermediate level deals with more than a handful of contacts. Yet, after just five transfers, the system has supplied hundreds of street sellers who are reaching tens of thousands of customers. And the original 100 kilos of cocaine valued at $1.7-million have produced more than $12 million in revenues—a markup of around 700 percent.

Sharing in these profits are literally thousands of new, ethnically diverse mid-level dealers. Until the cartels arrived, cocaine distribution had been a closed shop, largely controlled by Cubans. But when the Colombians opened up the market in the early eighties, they created what one dealer at the time called the "ethnicization" of cocaine. Saddled with an oversupply of drugs, the cartels fronted "trusted friends" and associates, who sold to anyone—Latinos, blacks, Italians, even cops—who could deliver the cash. "Our undercover guys were always being told by dealers, 'I think you're "the man," '" says Joseph Lisi, a New York police captain. "They'd say, 'Right, I'm the man. But I've got $80,000 in this briefcase, and if you don't want to deal with me, I'm out of here right now.' They'd never make it to the door."

Meanwhile, as prices began to fall, demand surged, and small-time street sellers suddenly found business soaring. If the Colombians were looking for dealers who could move "weight"—large quantities—those dealers were looking for high-level suppliers who could help them expand. All over the city, small cocaine retail outfits began cropping up—Dominicans in Washington Heights, blacks in Harlem and South Jamaica, Jamaicans in Brownsville, Bedford-Stuyvesant, and East New York.

The appearance of crack in late 1984 accelerated the process. No one group could control its spread. An ounce of cocaine that could be bought on the street for $1,000 yielded 320 to 360 vials of crack—more if cut—that sold for $10 each in hot locations. (The price is lower in poor neighborhoods that don't get suburban traffic.) Anyone with a few hundred dollars and a hot plate could go into business and triple his money overnight. Thousands of people did, and the old order—already shaken—crumbled completely. Crack turned the lower level of the cocaine trade into a freewheeling, decentralized business, with new outfits springing up and established groups growing into multi-million-dollar, city-wide organizations.

DEA agents discovered just how sophisticated some of these groups had become when they started investigating the Basedballs organization in 1985. The brainchild of Santiago Polanco, now 29, Basedballs started out in 1982 as an outfit selling grams and half-grams of cocaine along Audubon Avenue, east of the George Washington Bridge—a prime drug location because of its suburban traffic from New Jersey. The operation was small, but profitable enough to enable Polanco to walk into an Englewood Cliffs car dealership in 1984 and plunk down $43,000 in cash for a Mercedes-Benz.

When crack appeared on the scene, Polanco was one of the first dealers to recognize its potential and aggressively market the drug. He packaged his product in red-topped vials, calling the stuff Basedballs—a play on the term "free-basing"—and took pains to ensure brand quality. He hired "cooks" to process the cocaine, and when one dealer was caught tampering with the product, Polanco had him beaten with a baseball bat. Among the customers driving over from New Jersey, Basedballs quickly became one of the most sought-after brands.

Basedballs employees were the only dealers on Audubon Avenue around 173rd, 174th, and 175th Streets. Organization members later told DEA agents that they had bought the territory from its former owners, but, just in case, Polanco imported a team of hit men from his family's village in the Dominican Republic to protect Basedballs's turf and ease its expansion. By 1986, the organization had wrested control of the intersection of Edgecombe Avenue and 145th Street—a prime spot, easily accessible to the Bronx across the 145th Street Bridge—from a group of black dealers and opened a string of new spots in Harlem and the South Bronx.

As Basedballs's business expanded, so did its organization. Polanco secured a major supplier, a Dominican who dealt directly with the cartels in Colombia. Polanco also centralized Basedballs's operations in a headquarters at 2400 Webb Avenue in the Bronx. There, his workers cooked, packaged, and stockpiled crack in separate apartments. And he arranged with one of the dozens of money-changing companies along upper Broadway to launder Basedballs's revenues through an investment company he set up in the Dominican Republic.

Meanwhile, Polanco began distancing himself from Based-balls's day-to-day operations, adding layers of bureaucracy and spending more and more time in the Dominican Republic. By the summer of 1986, Basedballs employed as many as nine mid-level managers to deal with street-level managers at a score of locations around the city. Each location manager, in turn, supervised teams of dealers, none of whom were supposed to know the people more than one level above them.

It took law-enforcement agents and their informants nearly two years to penetrate the highest levels of Basedballs's organization. They can only guess how much money the operation made, but by one estimate, Polanco may have been clearing $20-million a year. One DEA agent saw the fruits of Polanco's activities in the Dominican Republic: two nightclubs, a jeans company, a 30-unit condominium complex, an office building, a palatial home, and a gold-plated gull-wing Mercedes. Today, Polanco is believed to be serving a 30-year sentence in a Dominican prison for homicide, and U.S. law-enforcement officials have dismantled his organization and locked up more than 30 of his associates. But agents estimate that there may be dozens of organizations as large as, or larger than, Basedballs operating in New York.

At the bottom of the distribution pyramid stands the street seller, subject to arrest, to ripoffs, to calculated violence by competitors. This is especially true for crack dealers. Over the past five years, law enforcement has focused on the cocaine trade, with street dealers the most visible target. They are also the first to get shot when a fight breaks out over turf, which is far more common in the cocaine trade than in the older, more established heroin business. Even the crack dealer's clients present special risks. "I wouldn't deal that crack s---," says Reuben, a former heroin dealer in the South Bronx. "Once a [heroin addict] gets his fix, he's cool. But when those crackheads start bugging out, you don't know what they're going to do."

In contrast to the myth, most street dealers make only modest profits. The stories about their vast incomes probably arise in part because they generally don't point out the distinction between the large sums of cash they handle and the relatively small commissions they earn. "After factoring in the long hours, they may come out a couple of dollars an hour ahead of the minimum wage," says Philippe Bourgois, an anthropologist studying East Harlem's drug culture.

Willie, the fifteen-year-old caught on gun- and drug-possession charges in Harlem last February, was probably earning about

$300 to $350 per week, according to his arresting officer Terry McGhee. "We see these kids out there in the cold, not moving from one spot, selling for ten hours at a stretch with nothing but a space heater. Maybe at the end of the night, they'll get paid $50," McGhee says. "I'll tell you one thing: You couldn't get a cop to do that."

But to compare dealing to a mainstream job may miss the point. Many youngsters drift in and out of the drug trade as a way of making pocket money or supporting their own drug habits. Part-time work is hard to find in the slum neighborhoods where most dealers live, and a full-time job often means a long commute and menial work. What's more, though a dealer's hours are long, they are often spent with friends on the streets. Willie, for example, belonged to a group called Boogie-Down Productions—the BDP—a gang of up to twenty teenagers that still pushes drugs on 128th Street and Lenox Avenue. "A lot of these young kids who become dealers are joining a crew," says McGhee. "It gives them access to power. Access to guns. It means no one can push them around anymore."

Crews like these are not simple throwbacks to the gangs of the fifties. They're richer and far better armed, and they're manipulated by adult criminals for profit. But their gang structure ensures discipline and loyalty. The graffiti on the walls of an abandoned BDP hangout—THIS BLOCK BELONGS TO THE BDP— indicated that Willie and his pals were protecting their turf, not just a business enterprise.

In even the poorest markets, however, some dealers make out well. "Everyone who goes into the crack business perceives that he's going to get rich," Bourgois says. "And some of them will. Kids who are responsible or street-smart or especially tough can still get promoted very quickly to manager and get a cut of the profits." Also, street dealing is the entry point into the trade, a way to make contacts or amass enough capital to go into business for oneself. Some street dealers get regular salaries or per diems, but many work on commission—usually between 10 and 20 percent. One of Basedballs's dealers boasted to DEA agents that he cleared $1,400 in commissions during one eight-hour shift on Audubon Avenue.

Before crack, heroin was the drug of choice in the slums, and its popularity is said to be rebounding. According to Division of Substance Abuse data, roughly one in every sixteen working-age men in New York is a heroin addict. The ratio has remained

constant over the past five years, but the high mortality rate associated with heroin—especially since the outbreak of AIDS among
IV-drug users—may conceal an increase in new addicts. Meanwhile, heroin use among twenty-year-olds—a better indicator of
trends in demand—has been rising.

Some experts think the change comes as a reaction to crack, as
former crack users switch to a relatively milder drug. Others attribute the comeback to an improvement in the quality of heroin.
Greater purity not only gives users a better high but enables them
to snort the drug instead of shooting it. At least two factors account for heroin's better quality. For one, Southeast Asia—noted
for its pure heroin—now supplies about 70 percent of the New
York market. For another, the recent decentralization of heroin
distribution in the city has increased the supply and fostered
competition among dealers.

Throughout the sixties and seventies, the Mafia dominated
the heroin market as the major importer and distributor. In the
early eighties, however, the so-called Pizza Connection prosecu-
tions weakened the mob's hold and cut the flow of heroin from
Sicily into the United States. Law-enforcement officials say that
the ethnic Chinese took over as the industry's new leaders.

In fact, New York's Chinese have been smuggling heroin into
the city for years, but until recently, they distrusted the distributors—most of them black—who supplied the street networks; as
a result, Chinese smugglers delegated a few of their elders to
broker the drug through the Mafia. But around the time that
the Mafia began pulling out of the trade, Chinatown began to
change.

"Thirty to 40 years ago, Chinatown was very provincial," says
Michael Shum, an agent in the DEA's New York Southeast Asian
Heroin Task Force. "People from different regions spoke different dialects. In my grandmother's day, if you were Fukienese and
you went into a store owned by Toy Shanese, they wouldn't sell
you groceries. Forget about drugs—if you didn't speak their language, you couldn't buy a tomato."

Today, Shum says, the old rivalries have broken down and
cash has become a universal language. In one recent case, DEA
agents turned up a connection between Puerto Rican heroin
dealers and members of a Chinese youth gang; the young men
had met in school and later "married up" in jail.

The big Chinese move into heroin has had two profound
effects on the market. By stepping up their smuggling activities,

the Chinese have flooded the city with Southeast Asian heroin. And by dealing directly with minority distributors, they have bypassed the Mafia middlemen who were notorious for heavily cutting their product. As a result, the average drug sold on the street has gone from being as low as 2 percent pure heroin in the early eighties to around 40 percent today.

Still, the heroin trade remains highly profitable. A kilo of pure heroin that costs around $11,000 in Bangkok can be sold for between $85,000 and $125,000 to an Asian broker in the United States or for $150,000 to $240,000 to a mid-level dealer acting as an intermediary between the importer and the street. Markups like these have attracted a grab bag of international trafficking organizations in addition to the Chinese, and even diplomats and businessmen have joined the trade. "We map out ten to twenty major trafficking routes and find out there are ten to twenty more," says DEA agent Dwight Rabb. "We're being inundated with dope."

Government agents have seized heroin hidden in imported cars, wheelbarrow tires, and the caskets of servicemen killed overseas. The "condom eaters" have also been busy. "Last year, we arrested 123 Nigerians alone at JFK, most of them carrying internally," says Arthur Stiffel, whose Customs agents use X-ray machines to search suspects. "This year, they're running at double the rate."

Though the Chinese dominate the heroin trade in the city, no single group controls the supply. Various foreign nationals—including Nigerians, Ghanaians, Pakistanis, Indians, Thais, and Vietnamese—and assorted American organized-crime groups all smuggle heroin independently of one another. What's more, the Chinese in the trade often operate separately. Unlike the Mafia, Chinatown's criminal organizations—descended from Hong Kong's ruthless triads—do not require their members to pay tribute or even, in many cases, to get permission to deal. Indeed, the new generation of Chinese traffickers may have broken into the violent American market at the expense of their ties to traditional criminal hierarchies. "When the young American Chinese go to Hong Kong now, the guys over there don't want to have anything to do with them," says Dwight Rabb. "The Hong Kong Chinese call them 'bananas'—yellow on the outside, white on the inside."

From the mid-level to the street, heroin distribution has mainly been controlled by black organizations. However, law-enforcement officials report that lately Chinese gangs have been selling in northern Queens and that Hispanic groups—often backed by cocaine money—have broken into the business. But the big heroin markets are found in the predominantly black slums, and dealers from outside are unwelcome.

Older and more established than their crack counterparts, these networks give the heroin business a stability unique in the drug trade. Many of them were Mafia franchises and developed along the same organizational lines as the mob. Until their recent bust, a handful of powerful dealers in southeastern Queens divided the lucrative market there into territories. In Harlem, where several groups often run outlets on the same street or even in the same building, agreements over turf are strictly regulated.

What's more, heroin's high price and narrow distribution make the business easier to control than the crack trade. For one thing, there's simply less heroin around. For another, top distributors are especially guarded about the people with whom they deal. Even if an enterprising young street dealer could find a connection, a kilo of heroin might cost him $200,000 or more wholesale—about six times as much as a similar amount of cocaine.

Heroin's high prices are reflected in the dealer's huge profit margins. While cocaine is rarely cut more than once, heroin can be "stepped on" two or three times. Mid-level transactions are based entirely on relationships; a trusted broker need never touch the product and only rarely the cash. From 1985 until recently, Lorenzo "Fat Cat" Nichols, the legendary Queens drug trafficker, ran a multi-million-dollar operation from prison. In 1988, according to the FBI, he was moving an average of 25 kilos of cocaine and 3 kilos of heroin a month. He bought the heroin from Chinese broker "John" Man Sing Eng—whom he'd met in prison—and, using two lieutenants as go-betweens, sold them to more than a dozen customers.

The big heroin money, however, is made by the dealers who process the drug and market it through networks of street sellers. Take the case of Earl Gibson, a veteran black dealer whose operation included a heroin mill in Queens and selling locations in Brooklyn, in the Bronx, and on the Lower East Side. Before his conviction on drug charges two years ago, Gibson cut, packaged, and sold about a kilo of heroin every four days, earning $150,000 to $200,000 a week. Gibson's occasional partner, Raymond Sanchez "Shorty" Rivera, a Puerto Rican dealer based on the Lower East Side, generated that kind of revenue every day. Based on the testimony of workers for Rivera—who has also been convicted—

the FBI estimates that he was grossing more than $60 million a year.

With money like that to be made, the drug business is a powerful lure. In 1987, when he was seventeen, a young Dominican we'll call Pedro had already tried several times to get into the drug business, passing his requests through an acquaintance who worked as a courier for one of the leading distributors in the Bushwick–East New York section of Brooklyn. The distributor, a fellow Dominican in his mid-twenties who knew Pedro and his family, eventually agreed to front him a small supply of heroin.

Pedro took in a partner who knew a location for selling—a spot on his East New York block that had opened up when the previous dealer was nabbed by police. Since neither youth had any extensive experience, they hired a seller recently out of jail. In those days, two distributors in the area were selling different brands, one called Goodyear and the other Airborne; Pedro handled Airborne.

The distributor supplied Pedro with heroin already cut and packaged in units called packs, each of which contained 100 $10 bags. Pedro took the packs on consignment and eventually returned 80 percent of the proceeds to the wholesaler. He paid a further 10 percent to his seller and split the remaining 10 percent with his partner—leaving him just $50 profit per pack sold.

Nevertheless, business was solid—on a good day, he could sell fifteen packs. Most clients were local addicts who could afford only a bag or two at a time, but, Pedro recalls, some were middle-class men in business suits. Others were out-of-town dealers who bought in bulk and who got discounts from Pedro.

Over the next two years, Pedro was able to open five locations, including spots on Knickerbocker Avenue and in Bushwick Park— prime areas that are restricted to well-connected dealers. At the height of his operation, he was personally clearing $600 a day.

Over time, though, competition picked up and cut into Pedro's revenues. By the time he got out last year, he was making $200 a day; now, he says, most dealers are just trying to survive.

"They're making $1,000 a week, if they're lucky," he says. "That may seem like a lot, but to a dealer, that's nothing." In Pedro's world, a successful dealer must project a certain image: He's got to be tough and free-spending. Fancy cars, gold jewelry, and designer warm-up gear are only the most obvious marks of his position. He's also got to pay for trips to Florida (stressed-out street dealers like to relax at theme parks) and pick up the tab at restaurants and clubs.

Beyond all that, a high-flying life-style can be especially expensive in the slums. Pedro's Cutlass Supreme was stolen right after he'd sunk $3,000 into customizing the tires and sound system. At a party, his $1,500 gold chain and medallion were lifted at gunpoint. And several times, he says, he was ripped off for the drugs he was carrying.

Meanwhile, Pedro's risks were high. Once, early on, some competing dealers tried to move in on one of his locations. Under the terms of their agreement, Pedro's wholesaler was supposed to provide him with protection. Instead, he supplied him with guns—expecting Pedro and his cronies to take care of themselves.

"Like most young guys from the neighborhood, carrying a gun made me feel power," he recalls. "At the time, I only thought about shooting other people. I never thought about getting shot myself."

Over time, twelve of the young men he worked with were arrested and jailed. He says that since their release, two have been killed trying to re-enter the drug trade and another was killed because he owed money to Pedro's former supplier. In fact, the police have determined that more than quarter of New York City's record 1,905 homicides last year were drug related.

The demise of his associates and the decline of his business finally led Pedro to give up dealing. But he still recalls the many times he rebuffed his mother's tearful pleas to stop. "That really made me sad, to see my mother cry," he says. "But not my mother or any job was ever going to give me the money that drugs was bringing to me."

THE STREETS ARE FILLED WITH COKE[3]

Trick question time for taxpayers seeking to judge the progress of the war on drugs:

According to national surveys conducted for the federal gov-

[3]Reprint of an article by David Whitman, *U.S. News & World Report* staffwriter. Reprinted by permission of *U.S. News & World Report*, 108: 24–26. Mar 5 '90. Copyright © 1990 by *U.S. News & World Report*.

ernment, which of the following is true about cocaine and crack use in the U.S.?

    a. *The number of current cocaine users (those who used cocaine within the last month) fell by 50 percent from 1985 to 1988*

    b. *The annual use of crack among high-school seniors fell sharply in the nation's 12 largest cities from 1986 to 1989*

    c. *Cocaine use among blacks dropped from 1985 to 1988. In fact, only 2 percent of all blacks are current users of cocaine*

    d. *All of the above are true*

    e. *All of the above are true—and also misleading.*

As the correct answer (e) illustrates, the tale of cocaine use in America is a little like the fable of the six blind men and the elephant. The first blind man falls against the elephant's sturdy side and concludes the elephant is nothing but a wall; the second feels the animal's tusk and concludes the elephant is like a spear, and so on for the rest of the blind men. In much the same fashion, policymakers have sometimes misconstrued the full picture of cocaine abuse in the U.S. by relying on one-dimensional data from government-sponsored surveys of drug use in American households and among high-school seniors. Drug czar William Bennett, as well as those in Congress, now routinely uses the survey results to gauge progress in the drug war. Just this month, Bennett claimed the national data showed cocaine use was "down in urban America, black America . . . and poor America."

The problem with such contentions, however, is that the numbers that Bennett and others cite invariably reflect an undercount of the very populations most likely to regularly use cocaine—the homeless, heroin addicts, school dropouts and prisoners. Those omissions, it now appears, are not minor. In fact, a forthcoming study obtained by *U.S. News* suggests that gaps in the government's surveys may have led to a massive undercount of cocaine abusers in America. The study, by Eric Wish, a visiting fellow at the National Institute of Justice, could well prompt federal and local officials to re-examine where they will concentrate their antidrug efforts, who will be tested and what kind of drug treatment will evolve for criminal addicts.

According to Wish's analysis, which is scheduled to appear in *The International Journal of the Addictions* this summer, there may be nearly twice as many frequent cocaine users in the U.S. as show up in national surveys. He projects from urinalysis test results of arrestees that as many as 1.3 million Americans arrested in 1988 in the nation's 61 largest cities used crack or cocaine on a weekly basis—well above the official 862,000 weekly user figure projected by the National Institute on Drug Abuse (NIDA) for all U.S. households. Wish's estimates, however rough at this point, show a vast number, perhaps the majority of regular crack and cocaine users in the U.S., may not be counted in the government's regular drug surveys. The consequence, he says, is that federal and local officials must now begin to "concentrate far more attention on testing and treating the criminal cocaine user."

In part, the discrepancy between Wish's numbers and those in household surveys conducted for NIDA reflects the inevitable limitations of polls on drug use. Senator Joseph Biden (D-Del.), chairman of the Senate Judiciary Committee, asserts that "the NIDA surveys present the most optimistic picture you can find out there—and I think they especially grossly underestimate the number of hard-core cocaine users." The agency's household survey, for instance, purportedly covers 98 percent of the U.S. population, but its limited sample size sometimes requires officials to make heroic extrapolations from tiny subsamples. In the 1988 household survey, only 65 of the 8,814 individuals randomly polled acknowledged using cocaine or crack weekly, yet NIDA projected from that small group that roughly 862,000 Americans were weekly cocaine users. Moreover, as cocaine and crack have lost the luster of a glamour drug, some criminologists now contend that users are less and less willing to acknowledge cocaine use. "A lot of people," says Prof. Mark Kleiman of Harvard's Kennedy School of Government, "just won't tell the nice man from the government that they smoked crack recently."

In contrast to the NIDA polling approach, Wish's numbers are drawn from a 21-city Justice Department pilot program (known as the Drug Use Forecasting System or "DUF") that tracks actual cocaine use through urinalysis tests. DUF tests of more than 10,000 male arrestees show that, while cocaine consumption may have plummeted in recent years in middle and working-class households, crack use has exploded among the inner-city criminal class. On average, almost 50 percent of male arrestees in DUF cities have cocaine-positive urinalyses (which can detect cocaine and crack use within the previous two to three days). In the 21 DUF cities alone, Wish projects that law-enforcement officials arrested some 800,000 frequent cocaine users in 1988, roughly the same number that NIDA officials say existed in the entire U.S. household population that year. And unlike the national survey data, urinalysis tests have not shown a significant downward trend for cocaine use during the last year in DUF cities (with the exception of Washington, D.C., where demand for crack may have reached a saturation point). Perhaps the best that can be said about cocaine and crack use among the inner-city "underclass" is that it is not growing in major urban areas as rapidly as in the past.

A Two-Front War

In a fashion, Wish's numbers underscore the notion that the nation, as Bennett put it several months ago, is "now fighting two [drug] wars, not just one." The first battle—against casual drug use among middle and working-class Americans, black and white—has generally gone well. But the second, far more intractable struggle against inner-city crack addiction is foundering. Get-tough measures aimed at casual users, such as fining those caught with small amounts of drugs or revoking the student loans and driver licenses of drug offenders, have so far had little impact in the ghetto. As Yale Medical School Prof. David Musto puts it: "Cocaine and crack users in the inner city aren't the folks who will pay attention to an ad campaign. Now you're confronting the users who are least likely to be affected by educational initiatives and changing attitudes."

Nowhere, Wish suggests, is the disparity between the two fronts of the drug war broader than in the area of drug testing. In some cities today, a policeman or fireman is more likely to be tested for drug use than a criminal. Unlike offender-testing programs, urinalyses of private and public-sector employees have typically registered very low rates of cocaine use. When the Department of Transportation recently randomly tested some 22,000 employees over a two-year period, fewer than 50 employees, or 0.3 percent of those tested, were cocaine-positive, a rate roughly 150 times below that of DUF arrestees.

Yet while millions of employees and job applicants now face drug tests in the workplace, only a small proportion of arrestees, prisoners, parolees, or those out on bail are required to submit to urinalyses or prove they are drug-free as a condition of their release. Currently, just five metropolitan areas (Washington, Tucson, Phoenix, Milwaukee and Portland, Oreg.) and one county (Prince George's County, Md.) routinely test substantial numbers of adult arrestees. And only two cities, Washington and Phoenix, randomly test juvenile arrestees, who might be easier to reach with drug treatment. Last year, President Bush proposed legislation that would have required states to adopt offender drug-testing programs as a condition of receiving federal criminal-justice funds. His bill, though, died in Congress following complaints it was costly and cumbersome to administer.

Treatment Backlog

Of course, in the bifurcated drug war of the 1990s, an insensate crackdown on inner-city cocaine users could be as ineffective as the current policy—a kind of benign neglect of drug abusers following their arrest. Requiring parolees and those on bail to be drug-free is eminently sensible, yet it is also unworkable. Inevitably, offender testing is expensive and creates added burdens for law-enforcement officials. Urinalysis tracking involves repeated follow-up tests, and identifying a cocaine abuser is of limited value if there are no treatment slots available. In 1989, the District of Columbia alone spent nearly a million dollars on lab services and personnel costs for some 50,000 clients, including costs for monitoring arrestees, referring them for treatment and supervising those out on bail. Most cities, however, are unprepared to make a similar investment, and urban areas around the country report they already have thousands of cocaine addicts awaiting treatment.

To his credit, drug czar Bennett helped boost federal funding for treatment last year by 51 percent (although he has not increased treatment moneys nearly as much as some critics would like). He also has stressed the need to get more-accurate numbers on cocaine and crack use among high-risk populations in the inner city. His current drug-control plan calls for doubling the sample size of the household poll, conducting extensive surveys of drug use in urban areas, and targeting spot surveys on groups like the homeless. But the results of the new studies will generally not be available until next year. Until that time, the best litmus test for judging the extent of America's cocaine and crack problem may be Bennett's own response to a recent query about the world supply of cocaine. "Nobody," he replied, "gains anything from underestimating the size of the problem."

INNOCENT VICTIMS[4]

At a hospital in Boston lies a baby girl who was born before her time—three months early, weighing less than 3 lbs. Her tiny body is entangled in a maze of wires and tubes that monitor her vital signs and bring her food and medicine. Every so often she shakes uncontrollably for a few moments—a legacy of the nerve-system damage that occurred when she suffered a shortfall of blood and oxygen just before birth. Between these seizures, she is unusually quiet and lethargic, lying on her side with one arm draped across her chest and the other bent to touch her face, sleeping day and night in the comfort of her cushioned warming table. At best, it will be three or four months before she is well enough to leave the hospital, and even then she may continue to shake from time to time.

At a therapy center in New York City, the saddest child brought in one morning is three-year-old Felicia, a small bundle of bones in a pink dress, whose plastic hearing aids keep falling off, tangling with her gold earrings. She is deaf, and doctors are not sure how much she can see. She functions at the capacity of a four-month-old. Like a rag doll, she can neither sit nor stand by herself: her trunk is too weak and her legs are too stiff. A therapist massages and bends the little girl's legs, trying to make her relax. Next year her foster mother will put Felicia in a special school full time in hopes that the child can at least learn how to feed herself.

At a special kindergarten class in the Los Angeles area, a five-year-old named Billie seems the picture of perfect health and disposition. As a tape recorder plays soothing music in the background, he and the teacher read alphabet cards. Suddenly Billie's face clouds over. For no apparent reason, he throws the cards down on the floor and shuts off the tape recorder. He sits in the chair, stony faced. "Was the music going too fast?" the teacher asks. Billie starts to say something, but then looks away, frowning. The teacher tries to get the lesson back on track, but Billie is quickly distracted by another child's antics. Within seconds, he is off his chair and running around.

[4]Reprint of an article by Anastasias Toufexis, *Time* staffwriter. Reprint by permission of *Time*, 137: 56–60. May 13 '91. Copyright © 1991 by Time Inc.

These children have very different problems and prospects, but they all have one thing in common: their mothers repeatedly took crack cocaine, often in combination with other drugs, during pregnancy. That makes them part of a tragic generation of American youngsters—a generation unfairly branded by some as "children of the damned" or a "biologic underclass." More often, they are simply called crack kids. A few have severe physical deformities from which they will never recover. In others the damage can be more subtle, showing up as behavioral aberrations that may sabotage their schooling and social development. Many of these children look and act like other kids, but their early exposure to cocaine makes them less able to overcome negative influences like a disruptive family life.

The first large group of these children was born in the mid-1980s, when hundreds of thousands of women began to get hooked on the cheap, smokable form of cocaine known as crack. The youngsters have run up huge bills for medical treatment and other care. Now the oldest are reaching school age, and they are sure to put enormous strain on an educational system that is already overburdened and underachieving.

Their plight inspires both pity and fear. Pity that they are the innocent victims of society's ills. Pity that the odds will be stacked against them at home, on the playground and in school. Fear that they will grow into an unmanageable multitude of disturbed and disruptive youth. Fear that they will be a lost generation.

The dimensions of the tragedy are staggering. According to the National Association for Perinatal Addiction Research and Education (NAPARE), about 1 out of every 10 newborns in the U.S.—375,000 a year—is exposed in the womb to one or more illicit drugs. The most frequent ingredient in the mix is cocaine. In major cities such as New York, Los Angeles, Detroit and Washington many hospitals report that the percentage of newborns showing the effects of drugs is 20% or even higher.

The cost of dealing with these children is rapidly escalating. In California drug-exposed babies, many of whom are born prematurely, stay in the hospital almost five times as long as normal newborns (nine days, vs. two days) and their care is 13 times as expensive ($6,900, vs. $522). And that is only the beginning, since many of the crack kids are placed in foster care. In New York City annual placements of drug-affected babies run to 3,500, compared with 750 before the spread of crack. That brings the city's foster-care tab to about $795 million (up from $320 million in

1985). The New York State comptroller's office expects that New York City will spend $765 million over the next 10 years on special education for crack kids.

Among the most visible victims are black and other minority children born into crack-plagued ghettos. It is bad enough that the drug assaults children in the womb, but the injury is too often compounded after birth by an environment of neglect, poverty and violence. "I sometimes believe that babies are better protected before they are born than they are after," says Dr. Barry Zuckerman, head of the division of developmental and behavioral pediatrics at Boston City Hospital.

Even after they give birth to drug-impaired children, many mothers go right on smoking crack. Melinda East, a former crack addict now in treatment in Long Beach, Calif., supported her habit as an often barefoot street prostitute. Her first baby was born with "the shakes," she says, but that did not turn her away from crack. She remembers selling milk and Pampers back to the grocery store for drug money.

Local governments often take crack kids away from still addicted mothers, but that does not guarantee stability for troubled children. Charlie, a five-year-old Los Angeles–area boy with severe behavioral problems, went through three foster homes before an elderly couple became his guardians. He seems to be making progress, but his prospects appear limited. He sometimes erupts into frenzied episodes of thrashing about, pulling his hair, biting and banging his head against a wall.

While poor, black ghetto children have attracted the most attention, they are far from being the only members of the crack generation. Cocaine abuse is common among members of the white upper and middle classes, but it is hidden better. Their babies are usually born at private hospitals that rarely ask mothers about drug use or screen them and their children for illegal chemicals. A 1989 Florida study found similar rates of drug use among pregnant white and black women of equal socioeconomic status, but only 1% of white abusers were reported to authorities, compared with nearly 11% of blacks.

Billie, the kindergartner, is a white child whose mother was addicted to crack, among other drugs. Soon after birth, Billie was whisked away from her and given to wealthy adoptive parents. Growing up in a stable environment, however, has not prevented him from being kicked out of four preschools for disorganized, rowdy behavior. Only when he started at this new school, where his teachers are trained to handle drug-exposed children, did he begin to calm down.

The crack kids are not the first children to be devastated by drugs while their mothers were pregnant. For many years, the unborn have been exposed to opiates, barbiturates, inhaled cocaine and a panoply of other drugs. And fetal alcohol syndrome, brought on by drinking during pregnancy, is believed to be a leading cause of mental retardation in the young.

But the coming of crack made a bad situation worse. This readily available, easily ingested chemical has lured far more women into addiction than any other hard drug has. By the latest estimates, more than 1 million U.S. women use cocaine. Moreover, crack has spurred the use of other drugs. Women who take cocaine are likely to use heroin to prolong a high, then tranquilizers and alcohol to come down. They may indulge in marijuana, PCP and amphetamines. As a result, many crack babies steep in a stew of drugs while in the womb.

An Uncertain Future

How badly are they damaged? In most cases, no one knows for sure. The question has sparked a fierce debate among doctors, social workers, educators and law-enforcement specialists. On one side are those who fear that most of the children are irredeemably harmed; on the other are those who firmly believe that with enough early treatment for babies and their mothers and special education, the large majority of crack kids can lead normal lives.

Among those who think the damage may be permanent is Kathy Kutschka, a director at the Speech and Language Development Center in Buena Park, Calif. Her department works with 45 crack kids, up to kindergarten age. When she observes them having trouble sitting in a chair or picking up a pencil, she despairs for their future. "Of the children we see," says Kutschka, "none will be able to function in a normal life-style without some kind of sheltered living arrangement."

An increasing number of medical experts, however, vehemently challenge the notion that most crack kids are doomed. In fact, they detest the term crack kids, charging that it unfairly brands the children and puts them all into a single dismal category. From this point of view, crack has become a convenient explanation for problems that are mainly caused by a bad environment. When a kindergartner from a broken home in an impoverished neighborhood misbehaves or seems slow, teachers may wrongly assume that crack is the chief reason, when other factors, like poor nutrition, are far more important.

Even when crack is responsible, the situation is rarely hopeless. "This is not a lost generation," says pediatrician Evelyn Davis of Harlem Hospital in New York City. "These children are not monsters. They are salvageable, capable of loving, of making good attachments. Yes, they present problems that we have not dealt with before, but they can be taught."

The Cost of Compassion

Help is possible if society will pay the price—a very big "if" in these days of tight budgets. Will taxpayers foot the bill to provide the best treatment and schooling to all the crack kids? In Boston a year of special education for a drug-exposed child can cost $13,000, compared with $5,000 spent per youngster at a regular school.

Experts agree that the most vital first step in helping crack kids is to get their mothers off the drug, preferably before birth. Yet only 11% of pregnant addicts get into treatment. Many detox programs do not accept the women because they are not equipped to deal with prenatal medical needs. And very few programs are designed to help drug-dependent women who already have children.

The failure to spend more money for early rehabilitation of crack addicts and their babies may be a social and financial disaster in the long run. Contends T. Berry Brazelton, the noted Harvard pediatrician: "If we worked with these infants from the first, it would cost us one-tenth or one-hundredth as much as it will cost us later. To educate them, to keep them off the streets, to keep them in prisons will cost us billions."

What the Drug Does

Cocaine causes blood vessels to constrict, thus reducing the vital flow of oxygen and other nutrients. Because fetal cells multiply swiftly in the first months, an embryo deprived of a proper blood supply by a mother's early and continuous use of cocaine is "dealt a small deck," says Zuckerman of Boston City Hospital.

Such babies look quite normal but are undersized, and the circumference of their heads tends to be unusually small, a trait associated with lower IQ scores. "Only the most intensive care after birth will give these babies a chance, but many won't receive it," Zuckerman points out.

Occasionally, heavy maternal cocaine use during the later months of pregnancy can lead to an embolism, or clot, that lodges in a fetal vessel and completely disrupts the blood supply to an organ or limb. The result: a shriveled arm or leg, a missing section of intestine or kidney, or other deformities. Such glaring defects, however, are extremely rare.

Cocaine exposure affects brain chemistry as well. The drug alters the action of neurotransmitters, the messengers that travel between nerve cells and help control a person's mood and responsiveness. Such changes may help explain the behavioral aberrations, including impulsiveness and moodiness, seen in some cocaine-exposed children as they mature.

Ultrasound studies of 82 drug-exposed infants by researchers at the University of California at San Diego revealed that about a third have lesions in the brain, usually in the deeper areas that govern learning and thinking. While a similar percentage of babies who are ill but have not been exposed to drugs have such lesions, only 5% of healthy newborns do. The long-term significance of this finding is uncertain, since the brain continues to develop during a baby's first year. If there is damage, it may not surface until a child takes on such complex tasks as learning to talk.

At birth, cocaine babies generally perform poorly on tests measuring their responsiveness. And at one month, some of the infants still do not perform at the level of normal two-day-olds. Cocaine-exposed babies are easily overstimulated. When that happens, some turn fussy for a while and then doze off; others tense up and squall for hours.

Caring for such infants is frustrating. "You don't do things that come naturally," notes Diane Carleson, a foster mother in San Mateo, Calif. "The more you bounce them and coo at them, the more they arch their backs to get away. Their poor mothers want so badly to make contact, yet they are headed for rejection unless they learn how not to overstimulate them."

Doctors at Harlem Hospital studied 70 such toddlers just under age 2 and found that almost all were slow in learning to talk and that more than half had impaired motor and social skills. An inability to distinguish between mothers and strangers is another hallmark of crack-exposed youngsters.

As the children reach school age, it becomes more difficult to separate the impact of drugs from the effects of upbringing and other influences. Yet many teachers think they can see the lingering legacy of crack. Beverly Beauzethier, a New York City kindergarten teacher, agonizes over some of her pupils. "They have trouble retaining basic things. They are not sure of colors or shapes or their names." Their behavior is also out of the ordinary. "Some are passive and cry a lot; sometimes they just sit in a heap in the corner," says Beauzethier. Even worse, "they can be very aggressive with the other children so that they are hard to stop, and I have to hold their arms," she says. "This is very scary. We don't know a lot about handling these children."

Helping Hands

Doctors and educators are only beginning to design the programs needed to help the crack kids. One notable pilot project is Zuckerman's Women and Infants Clinic at Boston City Hospital, which uses what Zuckerman calls the "one-stop shopping" technique. While pediatricians and child-development experts work with babies, addicted mothers get help in kicking their habits and learn how to care for their children. The first eight babies in the program, tested at age 1, all fell within the normal range on the Bayley scale of infant development; this means they can play pat-a-cake, walk unassisted, jabber expressively and turn pages in a book.

One of the leading organizations working to help older children is the Salvin Special Education Center in Los Angeles, which conducted a three-year pilot program with 50 drug-exposed kids, ages 3 to 5. Salvin's educators cite several elements of a successful school program: small classes (eight pupils to one teacher), fixed seat assignments and a rigid routine, and protection from loud noises and other disturbing stimulation. Activities are emphasized over paper-and-pencil exercises. "We'll read a story and bring it to life with hand puppets," explains school psychologist Valerie Wallace. Generous warmth and praise help youngsters achieve an emotional equilibrium. Of all Salvin's drug-exposed children, more than half have been able to transfer to regular school classes, with special tutoring and counseling.

Whether such success can be replicated on a large scale is

uncertain, but the evidence is encouraging. A study by Dr. Ira Chasnoff and his staff at Chicago-based NAPARE followed 300 cocaine-exposed babies who, along with their mothers, received intensive postnatal intervention. Of 90 children tested at age 3, 90% showed normal intelligence, 70% had no behavioral problems, and 60% did not need speech therapy.

That may be less than complete success, but considering the horrible blow these children suffered before birth, it is remarkable that so many can be helped so much. The studies suggest that early intervention can give the children a fighting chance of leading reasonably normal lives. Such a payback seems more than enough to justify a far greater investment in treatment and rehabilitation. Today's crack kids may be a troubled generation, but they do not have to be a lost generation—unless society abandons them.

SHOULD WE TAKE AWAY THEIR KIDS?[5]

Try, if you can, to imagine the pain and horror of Daniel Scott's last hours. The seven-month-old baby was found by police lying in a pool of blood next to his crib in a Bronx tenement. His mother, off on a six-day crack binge, had left him in the care of his father, who abandoned the child in his unlocked apartment without so much as a bottle of water. Emaciated, filthy, desperate, the infant had apparently hoisted himself out of the crib and tumbled onto the wood floor before finally dying of starvation and dehydration. Both parents—Jane Scott, 28, and Jose Valdez, 26—have been charged with manslaughter.

Confronted by such tragic chapters in the saga of crack, Americans tend to focus on questions of state intervention: At what point should authorities act to remove a child from the home of drug-abusing parents? At birth? When there is clear evidence of abuse or neglect? How about *before* birth?—the position of a growing number of people calling for mandatory birth control for female addicts. For Daniel Scott, intervention never came.

[5]Reprint of an article by James Willwerth, *Time* staffwriter. Reprinted by permission of *Time*, 137: 62–63. May 13 '91. Copyright © 1991 by Time Inc.

Around the country, prosecutors and state legislators have lost patience with what they regard as the softhearted and sometimes softheaded approach of social-service workers. Nineteen states now have laws that allow child-abuse charges to be pressed against any woman who gives birth to a child with illegal drugs in his bloodstream. In some cities local prosecutors have charged such mothers with a felony: delivering illegal drugs to a minor. The means of delivery: the umbilical cord. Floridian Jennifer Johnson, one of the first women convicted in such a case, was sentenced to mandatory drug treatment and 15 years of probation.

In Kansas, state representative Kerry Patrick wants to take the law a step further. He has introduced a bill that would require convicted female addicts to accept Norplant birth-control inserts, which prevent pregnancies for up to five years, if they wish to avoid jail. Under the proposed law, the state would pay for the $500 procedure, and also for its removal if the woman stays clean for a year. Says Patrick: "I've gotten a lot of support from nurses who deal with crack babies. Once you see one, you don't care about the rights of the mother."

Impatience with the niceties of civil liberties is also found among social-service experts. "Damn it, babies are dying out there!" says Dr. Michael Durfee, a child psychologist who tracks child-abuse cases for the Los Angeles County department of health. "You get someone with a terrible family history, stoned, no parenting skills—and we keep giving back her babies because we don't want to look racist or sexist."

Testimony from many of the addicts themselves seems to support Durfee's argument. Doreen Flaherty, 27, a recovering crack addict from Garden Grove, Calif., remembers spending a week in jail after being arrested for possession of cocaine. "I kept crying in jail because I wanted to see my little girl," she says. "That's all that mattered to me." After she made bail, Doreen did not return home to her daughter but sought out a drug dealer instead. When a girlfriend tracked her down at the crack house, Doreen told the dealer to say she was not there. "How could you do this to your daughter?" the girlfriend asked. "I'm sorry, I'm sorry!" Doreen wailed. "I just needed another hit."

But whisking a baby out of a troubled mother's arms does not ensure an end to the child's travails. Babies who become wards of the state have often wound up being boarded in hospitals for months, tended by ever-changing shifts of nurses. Such institutional care not only leads to emotional troubles down the road but

can also actually cause "failure to thrive," a medical term for a
condition in which infants do not gain enough weight and fail to
develop normally. It has been loosely translated as a loss of interest in life. Older children may be shuttled through a series of
foster homes, never learning to love or trust a soul. Staying at
home with an addicted mother who is actively participating in a
rehabilitation program can, in many cases, be the more promising
and safer route for the child. "Foster care is often so poor," says
Dr. Evelyn Lipper, director of child development at New York
Hospital–Cornell Medical Center. "Maybe these children are better off with their mothers."

Health officials point to another problem with the get-tough
approach. Throwing the book at female addicts for everything
from delivering drugs to a minor to child abuse makes it even less
likely that they will actively seek medical care when they are pregnant. And scaring them away from the clinic means even more
damaged babies.

The two U.S. cities with the biggest crack problems have
backed away from their initial seize-the-kids approach. Until
1986, Los Angeles County automatically took at least temporary
custody of drug-exposed newborns. Then the crack epidemic exploded. "If we took every child who came out with a positive tox
screen," says Gerhard Moland, a children's services administrator,
"it would overwhelm the system." Now social workers consider the
child's health and the mother's potential for rehabilitation when
making court recommendations. The biggest factor in determining whether or not the county takes custody: the presence of a
sober grandmother. Currently, grandmothers care for more than
half of the 1,000 high-risk babies in Moland's district.

New York City has also shifted strategies. In the mid-1980s,
under the administration of former Mayor Ed Koch, a single
positive toxicology report was enough for authorities to take a
newborn from its mother. But a series of cases of mistaken
charges of child abuse helped lead to a change of policy under
Mayor David Dinkins. In one notorious example, Brooklyn bank
clerk Judith Adams lost custody of her child for nearly two
months after the medication that doctors gave her during a cae-
sarean section resulted in a false-positive drug test. "Instead of
breast feeding my baby, I was looking for lawyers and going to
social workers' offices, trying to get him back," she recalls bitterly.

As in most such mishaps, the victim was a black woman at a
public hospital. The principal reason the Dinkins administration

abandoned the old approach was that it seemed discriminatory. Minority women giving birth in public hospitals are much more likely to be tested for drugs than are white women or patients in private hospitals. But the policy was also abandoned because it did not work. Explains Susan Demers, deputy commissioner and general counsel of the New York State department of social services: "It put the state in the position of destroying families as the quick-and-easy answer to the drug epidemic."

What does seem to work is a combination of the social-services carrot and the legal stick. The most successful programs for addicted mothers offer every kind of assistance, beginning with detoxification but extending to pediatric services for the child, psychological and job counseling for the mother, and extensive parenting classes. But all this is backed up with a none-too-subtle threat of legal intervention. The Women and Infants Clinic program at Boston City Hospital, for instance, takes this approach to helping addicted mothers. Women in the program must submit to random urine tests each week, and they are told that two unexplained absences in a row will trigger an immediate investigation for child neglect.

In many cities, a mother whose newborn tests positive for cocaine is given a choice: enter a treatment program or give up the child. This ultimatum can work surprisingly well, provided that a good program is available. Margaruite Custode was offered the choice between jail and treatment last June and picked the latter, figuring that she would dry out, get her baby back and get high again. Custode, a 30-year-old New Yorker, had been through detox before, and the treatment never stuck. She had lost custody of two previous children. But this time she entered a program at Daytop Village designed for mothers. To her amazement, she found that within a month she began to connect with other women in the program and to care about getting clean. "The fact that we are viewed as unfit mothers by society is one of the things that bonds us together," she says.

Drug-treatment experts have found that methods that work with men often backfire with women. "Women will not be spoken to harshly or in a condescending manner," says Eugene Williams, coordinator of a treatment program in East Palo Alto, Calif. "Nor is it profitable to accuse them of lying or not toeing the mark as we do in men's programs." Many women addicts turned to drugs because they were sexually abused or raped as children, and they need help repairing the damage. Says Custode of her sessions with other female addicts: "We share some sick secrets with each other that we wouldn't want to share with the opposite sex."

Two things are clear from the case of Margaruite Custode— and many others like hers. First, if it were not for the threat of losing legal custody, she would not have sought treatment for her drug habit. Second, if it were not for the all too rare opportunity for first-rate treatment, she would not be sober for nine months straight with a good chance of regaining custody of her child. Whether Custode will be a good parent is impossible to say, but both social-service workers and law-enforcement officials are finding that the best way to rescue a child is to rescue the mother as well.

IV. THE ISSUE OF LEGALIZING DRUGS

EDITOR'S INTRODUCTION

As article after article make clear, the verdict of many observers is in that the war on drugs has not been succeeding. Since increased interdiction efforts in South and Central America have failed to stem the flow of cocaine, heroin, and other drugs into the U.S., further escalation would seem to offer no more encouraging results. What then should our national response to the drug problem be? One response is that drugs should be legalized, a policy that would destroy the profits and power of the drug lords. But this proposal also carries the risk that the use of addictive drugs would vastly increase.

In the first article in this section, James Q. Wilson in *Commentary* argues that our present policy, regardless of its shortcomings, is preferable to the decriminalization of drugs. Speaking from his experience as chairman of the National Advisory Council for Drug Abuse Prevention in the 1970s, Wilson maintains that a policy of enforcement did contain the use of heroin. Had it been legal and readily available, there would have been no financial or medical reason to avoid heroin use. A moral issue also seems to him to be involved, for if drugs were legalized efforts to educate the public against their use would be rendered meaningless. Wilson's article is followed by a series of letters to the editor of *Commentary*, responding to his argument. Roman Foxbrunner maintains that if drugs should be illegal because they are harmful, so too should alcohol, cigarettes, and handguns. Stan Namovicz points out that although heroin use declined in the 1970s, it was only because cocaine took its place as the drug of choice of American users. And Ansley Hamid argues that the social costs of continued criminalization of drugs—in homelessness, unemployment, destabilized neighborhoods, and destroyed families—are too high a price to pay.

In an article in *Science*, Harold Kalant and Avram Goldstein are convinced that the legal sale of drugs would result in substantial increases of use and in the harmful consequences of heavy use. But they recommend a reduction of penalties for the possession of small amounts of drugs for personal use. Legislation mandating 5-year sentences for small-time users are unrealistic and ineffective. Chiefly, the authors urge a massive shift in the priorities of the drug war. The 71 percent of the federal budget now devoted to supply reduction should be redirected to prevention, education, treatment, and research.

In a following article in *U.S.A. Today* magazine, James Ostrowski comes out strongly in favor of legalization. Prohibition, he maintains, takes $10 billion a year from taxpayers to enforce, and enables organized crime to reap an $80 billion profit. Moreover, prohibition leads to widespread crime on the part of those who buy illicit drugs; creates an atmosphere of disrespect for the law; and destroys the economic viability of low-income neighborhoods. Ostrowski also maintains that experiments in decriminalizing drugs in other countries have not led to a surge in drug use. Instead, its use has remained constant or dramatically declined. Finally, in an article in *Foreign Policy*, Ethan Nadelmann compares the prohibition against drugs to the prohibition of alcohol earlier in the century. When Prohibition was repealed, alcohol use did not escalate but declined. The present policy of imposing draconic sentences for drug possession, he argues, is clogging the criminal justice system and imposing enormous costs in new prison construction and maintenance. An inter-American commission should be established, he asserts, to reassess the problem of drugs and to establish a rational and manageable policy concerning it.

AGAINST THE LEGALIZATION OF DRUGS[1]

In 1972, the President appointed me chairman of the National Advisory Council for Drug Abuse Prevention. Created by Congress, the Council was charged with providing guidance on how best to coordinate the national war on drugs. (Yes, we called it a war then, too.) In those days, the drug we were chiefly concerned with was heroin. When I took office, heroin use had been increas-

[1]Reprint of an article by James Q. Wilson, Collins Professor of management and public policy at UCLA. Reprinted by permission of *Commentary*, 89: 21–28. F '90. Copyright © 1990 by *Commentary*.

ing dramatically. Everybody was worried that this increase would continue. Such phrases as "heroin epidemic" were commonplace.

That same year, the eminent economist Milton Friedman published an essay in *Newsweek* in which he called for legalizing heroin. His argument was on two grounds: as a matter of ethics, the government has no right to tell people not to use heroin (or to drink or to commit suicide); as a matter of economics, the prohibition of drug use imposes costs on society that far exceed the benefits. Others, such as the psychoanalyst Thomas Szasz, made the same argument.

We did not take Friedman's advice. (Government commissions rarely do.) I do not recall that we even discussed legalizing heroin, though we did discuss (but did not take action on) legalizing a drug, cocaine, that many people then argued was benign. Our marching orders were to figure out how to win the war on heroin, not to run up the white flag of surrender.

That was 1972. Today, we have the same number of heroin addicts that we had then—half a million, give or take a few thousand. Having that many heroin addicts is no trivial matter; these people deserve our attention. But not having had an increase in that number for over fifteen years is also something that deserves our attention. What happened to the "heroin epidemic" that many people once thought would overwhelm us?

The facts are clear: a more or less stable pool of heroin addicts has been getting older, with relatively few new recruits. In 1976 the average age of heroin users who appeared in hospital emergency rooms was about twenty-seven; ten years later it was thirty-two. More than two-thirds of all heroin users appearing in emergency rooms are now over the age of thirty. Back in the early 1970's, when heroin got onto the national political agenda, the typical heroin addict was much younger, often a teenager. Household surveys show the same thing—the rate of opiate use (which includes heroin) has been flat for the better part of two decades. More fine-grained studies of inner-city neighborhoods confirm this. John Boyle and Ann Brunswick found that the percentage of young blacks in Harlem who used heroin fell from 8 percent in 1970–71 to about 3 percent in 1975–76.

Why did heroin lose its appeal for young people? When the young blacks in Harlem were asked why they stopped, more than half mentioned "trouble with the law" or "high cost" (and high cost is, of course, directly the result of law enforcement). Two-thirds said that heroin hurt their health; nearly all said they had

had a bad experience with it. We need not rely, however, simply on what they said. In New York City in 1973–75, the street price of heroin rose dramatically and its purity sharply declined, probably as a result of the heroin shortage caused by the success of the Turkish government in reducing the supply of opium base and of the French government in closing down heroin-processing laboratories located in and around Marseilles. These were short-lived gains for, just as Friedman predicted, alternative sources of supply—mostly in Mexico—quickly emerged. But the three-year heroin shortage interrupted the easy recruitment of new users.

Health and related problems were no doubt part of the reason for the reduced flow of recruits. Over the preceding years, Harlem youth had watched as more and more heroin users died of overdoses, were poisoned by adulterated doses, or acquired hepatitis from dirty needles. The word got around: heroin can kill you. By 1974 new hepatitis cases and drug-overdose deaths had dropped to a fraction of what they had been in 1970.

Alas, treatment did not seem to explain much of the cessation in drug use. Treatment programs can and do help heroin addicts, but treatment did not explain the drop in the number of *new* users (who by definition had never been in treatment) nor even much of the reduction in the number of experienced users.

No one knows how much of the decline to attribute to personal observation as opposed to high prices or reduced supply. But other evidence suggests strongly that price and supply played a large role. In 1972 the National Advisory Council was especially worried by the prospect that U.S. servicemen returning to this country from Vietnam would bring their heroin habits with them. Fortunately, a brilliant study by Lee Robins of Washington University in St. Louis put that fear to rest. She measured drug use of Vietnam veterans shortly after they had returned home. Though many had used heroin regularly while in Southeast Asia, most gave up the habit when back in the United States. The reason: here, heroin was less available and sanctions on its use were more pronounced. Of course, if a veteran had been willing to pay enough—which might have meant traveling to another city and would certainly have meant making an illegal contact with a disreputable dealer in a threatening neighborhood in order to acquire a (possibly) dangerous dose—he could have sustained his drug habit. Most veterans were unwilling to pay this price, and so their drug use declined or disappeared.

Reliving the Past

Suppose we had taken Friedman's advice in 1972. What would have happened? We cannot be entirely certain, but at a minimum we would have placed the young heroin addicts (and, above all, the prospective addicts) in a very different position from the one in which they actually found themselves. Heroin would have been legal. Its price would have been reduced by 95 percent (minus whatever we chose to recover in taxes.) Now that it could be sold by the same people who make aspirin, its quality would have been assured—no poisons, no adulterants. Sterile hypodermic needles would have been readily available at the neighborhood drugstore, probably at the same counter where the heroin was sold. No need to travel to big cities or unfamiliar neighborhoods—heroin could have been purchased anywhere, perhaps by mail order.

There would no longer have been any financial or medical reason to avoid heroin use. Anybody could have afforded it. We might have tried to prevent children from buying it, but as we have learned from our efforts to prevent minors from buying alcohol and tobacco, young people have a way of penetrating markets theoretically reserved for adults. Returning Vietnam veterans would have discovered that Omaha and Raleigh had been converted into the pharmaceutical equivalent of Saigon.

Under these circumstances, can we doubt for a moment that heroin use would have grown exponentially? Or that a vastly larger supply of new users would have been recruited? Professor Friedman is a Nobel Prize-winning economist whose understanding of market forces is profound. What did he think would happen to consumption under his legalized regime? Here are his words: "Legalizing drugs might increase the number of addicts, but it is not clear that it would. Forbidden fruit is attractive, particularly to the young."

Really? I suppose that we should expect no increase in Porsche sales if we cut the price by 95 percent, no increase in whiskey sales if we cut the price by a comparable amount— because young people only want fast cars and strong liquor when they are "forbidden." Perhaps Friedman's uncharacteristic lapse from the obvious implications of price theory can be explained by a misunderstanding of how drug users are recruited. In his 1972 essay he said that "drug addicts are deliberately made by pushers, who give likely prospects their first few doses free." If drugs were legal it would not pay anybody to produce addicts, because everybody would buy from the cheapest source. But as every drug expert knows, pushers do not produce addicts. Friends or acquaintances do. In fact, pushers are usually reluctant to deal with non-users because a non-user could be an undercover cop. Drug use spreads in the same way any fad or fashion spreads: somebody who is already a user urges his friends to try, or simply shows already-eager friends how to do it.

But we need not rely on speculation, however plausible, that lowered prices and more abundant supplies would have increased heroin usage. Great Britain once followed such a policy and with almost exactly those results. Until the mid-1960's, British physicians were allowed to prescribe heroin to certain classes of addicts. (Possessing these drugs without a doctor's prescription remained a criminal offense.) For many years this policy worked well enough because the addict patients were typically middle-class people who had become dependent on opiate painkillers while undergoing hospital treatment. There was no drug culture. The British system worked for many years, not because it prevented drug abuse, but because there was no problem of drug abuse that would test the system.

All that changed in the 1960's. A few unscrupulous doctors began passing out heroin in wholesale amounts. One doctor prescribed almost 600,000 heroin tablets—that is, over thirteen pounds—in just one year. A youthful drug culture emerged with a demand for drugs far different from that of the older addicts. As a result, the British government required doctors to refer users to government-run clinics to receive their heroin.

But the shift to clinics did not curtail the growth in heroin use. Throughout the 1960's the number of addicts increased—the late John Kaplan of Stanford estimated by fivefold—in part as a result of the diversion of heroin from clinic patients to new users on the streets. An addict would bargain with the clinic doctor over how big a dose he would receive. The patient wanted as much as he could get, the doctor wanted to give as little as was needed. The patient had an advantage in this conflict because the doctor could not be certain how much was really needed. Many patients would use some of their "maintenance" dose and sell the remaining part to friends, thereby recruiting new addicts. As the clinics learned of this, they began to shift their treatment away from heroin and toward methadone, an addictive drug that, when taken orally, does not produce a "high" but will block the withdrawal pains associated with heroin abstinence.

Whether what happened in England in the 1960's was a mini-epidemic or an epidemic depends on whether one looks at numbers or at rates of change. Compared to the United States, the numbers were small. In 1960 there were 68 heroin addicts known to the British government; by 1968 there were 2,000 in treatment and many more who refused treatment. (They would refuse in part because they did not want to get methadone at a clinic if they could get heroin on the street.) Richard Hartnoll estimates that the actual number of addicts in England is five times the number officially registered. At a minimum, the number of British addicts increased by thirtyfold in ten years; the actual increase may have been much larger.

In the early 1980's the numbers began to rise again, and this time nobody doubted that a real epidemic was at hand. The increase was estimated to be 40 percent a year. By 1982 there were thought to be 20,000 heroin users in London alone. Geoffrey Pearson reports that many cities—Glasgow, Liverpool, Manchester, and Sheffield among them—were now experiencing a drug problem that once had been largely confined to London. The problem, again, was supply. The country was being flooded with cheap, high-quality heroin, first from Iran and then from Southeast Asia.

The United States began the 1960's with a much larger number of heroin addicts and probably a bigger at-risk population than was the case in Great Britain. Even though it would be foolhardy to suppose that the British system, if installed here, would have worked the same way or with the same results, it would be equally foolhardy to suppose that a combination of heroin available from leaky clinics and from street dealers who faced only minimal law-enforcement risks would not have produced a much greater increase in heroin use than we actually experienced. My guess is that if we had allowed either doctors or clinics to prescribe heroin, we would have had far worse results than were produced in Britain, if for no other reason than the vastly larger number of addicts with which we began. We would have had to find some way to police thousands (not scores) of physicians and hundreds (not dozens) of clinics. If the British civil service found it difficult to keep heroin in the hands of addicts and out of the hands of recruits when it was dealing with a few hundred people, how well would the American civil service have accomplished the same tasks when dealing with tens of thousands of people?

Back to the Future

Now cocaine, especially in its potent form, crack, is the focus of attention. Now as in 1972 the government is trying to reduce its use. Now as then some people are advocating legalization. Is there any more reason to yield to those arguments today than there was almost two decades ago? [Footnote: I do not here take up the question of marijuana. For a variety of reasons—its widespread use and its lesser tendency to addict—it presents a different problem from cocaine or heroin. For a penetrating analysis, see Mark Kleiman, *Marijuana: Costs of Abuse, Costs of Control* (Greenwood Press, 217 pp., $37.95)]

I think not. If we had yielded in 1972 we almost certainly would have had today a permanent population of several million, not several hundred thousand, heroin addicts. If we yield now we will have a far more serious problem with cocaine.

Crack is worse than heroin by almost any measure. Heroin produces a pleasant drowsiness and, if hygienically administered, has only the physical side effects of constipation and sexual impotence. Regular heroin use incapacitates many users, especially poor ones, for any productive work or social responsibility. They will sit nodding on a street corner, helpless but at least harmless. By contrast, regular cocaine use leaves the user neither helpless nor harmless. When smoked (as with crack) or injected, cocaine produces instant, intense, and short-lived euphoria. The experience generates a powerful desire to repeat it. If the drug is readily available, repeat use will occur. Those people who progress to "bingeing" on cocaine become devoted to the drug and its effects to the exclusion of almost all other considerations—job, family, children, sleep, food, even sex. Dr. Frank Gawin at Yale and Dr. Everett Ellinwood at Duke report that a substantial percentage of all high-dose, binge users become uninhibited, impulsive, hypersexual, compulsive, irritable, and hyperactive. Their moods vacillate dramatically, leading at times to violence and homicide.

Women are much more likely to use crack than heroin, and if they are pregnant, the effects on their babies are tragic. Douglas Besharov, who has been following the effects of drugs on infants for twenty years, writes that nothing he learned about heroin prepared him for the devastation of cocaine. Cocaine harms the fetus and can lead to physical deformities or neurological damage. Some crack babies have for all practical purposes suffered a disabling stroke while still in the womb. The long-term consequences of this brain damage are lowered cognitive ability and the onset of mood disorders. Besharov estimates that about 30,000 to 50,000 such babies are born every year, about 7,000 in New York City alone. There may be ways to treat such infants, but from everything we now know the treatment will be long, difficult, and expensive. Worse, the mothers who are most likely to produce crack babies are precisely the ones who, because of poverty or temperament, are least able and willing to obtain such treatment. In fact, anecdotal evidence suggests that crack mothers are likely to abuse their infants.

The notion that abusing drugs such as cocaine is a "victimless crime" is not only absurd but dangerous. Even ignoring the fetal drug syndrome, crack-dependent people are, like heroin addicts, individuals who regularly victimize their children by neglect, their spouses by improvidence, their employers by lethargy, and their coworkers by carelessness. Society is not and could never be a collection of autonomous individuals. We all have a stake in ensuring that each of us displays a minimal level of dignity, responsibility, and empathy. We cannot, of course, coerce people into goodness, but we can and should insist that some standards must be met if society itself—on which the very existence of the human personality depends—is to persist. Drawing the line that defines those standards is difficult and contentious, but if crack and heroin use do not fall below it, what does?

The advocates of legalization will respond by suggesting that my picture is overdrawn. Ethan Nadelmann of Princeton argues that the risk of legalization is less than most people suppose. Over 20 million Americans between the ages of eighteen and twenty-five have tried cocaine (according to a government survey), but only a quarter million use it daily. From this Nadelmann concludes that at most 3 percent of all young people who try cocaine develop a problem with it. The implication is clear: make the drug legal and we only have to worry about 3 percent of our youth.

The implication rests on a logical fallacy and a factual error. The fallacy is this: the percentage of occasional cocaine users who become binge users *when the drug is illegal* (and thus expensive and hard to find) tells us nothing about the percentage who will become dependent when the drug is legal (and thus cheap and abundant). Drs. Gawin and Ellinwood report, in common with several other researchers, that controlled or occasional use of cocaine changes to compulsive and frequent use "when access to the drug increases" or when the user switches from snorting to smoking. More cocaine more potently administered alters, perhaps sharply, the proportion of "controlled" users who become heavy users.

The factual error is this: the federal survey Nadelmann quotes was done in 1985, *before* crack had become common. Thus the probability of becoming dependent on cocaine was derived from the responses of users who snorted the drug. The speed and potency of cocaine's action increases dramatically when it is smoked. We do not yet know how greatly the advent of crack increases the risk of dependency, but all the clinical evidence suggests that the increase is likely to be large.

It is possible that some people will not become heavy users even when the drug is readily available in its most potent form. So far there are no scientific grounds for predicting who will and who will not become dependent. Neither socioeconomic background nor personality traits differentiate between casual and intensive users. Thus, the only way to settle the question of who is correct about the effect of easy availability on drug use, Nadelmann or Gawin and Ellinwood, is to try it and see. But that social experiment is so risky as to be no experiment at all, for if cocaine is legalized and if the rate of its abusive use increases dramatically, there is no way to put the genie back in the bottle, and it is not a kindly genie.

Have We Lost?

Many people who agree that there are risks in legalizing cocaine or heroin still favor it because, they think, we have lost the war on drugs. "Nothing we have done has worked" and the current federal policy is just "more of the same." Whatever the costs of greater drug use, surely they would be less than the costs of our present, failed efforts.

That is exactly what I was told in 1972—and heroin is not quite as bad a drug as cocaine. We did not surrender and we did not lose. We did not win, either. What the nation accomplished then was what most efforts to save people from themselves accomplish: the problem was contained and the number of victims minimized, all at a considerable cost in law enforcement and increased crime. Was the cost worth it? I think so, but others may disagree. What are the lives of would-be addicts worth? I recall some people saying to me then, "Let them kill themselves." I was appalled. Happily, such views did not prevail.

Have we lost today? Not at all. High-rate cocaine use is not commonplace. The National Institute of Drug Abuse (NIDA) reports that less than 5 percent of high-school seniors used cocaine within the last thirty days. Of course this survey misses young people who have dropped out of school and miscounts those who lie on the questionnaire, but even if we inflate the NIDA estimate by some plausible percentage, it is still not much above 5 percent. Medical examiners reported in 1987 that about 1,500 died from cocaine use; hospital emergency rooms reported about 30,000 admissions related to cocaine abuse.

These are not small numbers, but neither are they evidence of a nationwide plague that threatens to engulf us all. Moreover, cities vary greatly in the proportion of people who are involved with cocaine. To get city-level data we need to turn to drug tests carried out on arrested persons, who obviously are more likely to be drug users than the average citizen. The National Institute of Justice, through its Drug Use Forecasting (DUF) project, collects urinalysis data on arrestees in 22 cities. As we have already seen, opiate (chiefly heroin) use has been flat or declining in most of these cities over the last decade. Cocaine use has gone up sharply, but with great variation among cities. New York, Philadelphia, and Washington, D.C., all report that two-thirds or more of their arrestees tested positive for cocaine, but in Portland, San Antonio, and Indianapolis the percentage was one-third or less.

In some neighborhoods, of course, matters have reached crisis proportions. Gangs control the streets, shootings terrorize residents, and drug-dealing occurs in plain view. The police seem barely able to contain matters. But in these neighborhoods—unlike at Palo Alto cocktail parties—the people are not calling for legalization, they are calling for help. And often not much help has come. Many cities are willing to do almost anything about the drug problem except spend more money on it. The federal government cannot change that; only local voters and politicians can. It is not clear that they will.

It took about ten years to contain heroin. We have had experience with crack for only about three or four years. Each year we spend perhaps $11 billion on law enforcement (and some of that goes to deal with marijuana) and perhaps $2 billion on treatment. Large sums, but not sums that should lead anyone to say, "We just can't afford this any more."

The illegality of drugs increases crime, partly because some users turn to crime to pay for their habits, partly because some users are stimulated by certain drugs (such as crack or PCP) to act more violently or ruthlessly than they otherwise would, and partly because criminal organizations seeking to control drug supplies use force to manage their markets. These also are serious costs, but no one knows how much they would be reduced if drugs were legalized. Addicts would no longer steal to pay black-market prices for drugs, a real gain. But some, perhaps a great deal, of that gain would be offset by the great increase in the number of addicts. These people, nodding on heroin or living in the delusion-ridden high of cocaine, would hardly be ideal employees. Many would steal simply to support themselves, since snatch-and-grab, opportunistic crime can be managed even by people unable to hold a regular job or plan an elaborate crime. Those British addicts who get their supplies from government clinics are not models of law-abiding decency. Most are in crime, and though their per-capita rate of criminality may be lower thanks to the cheapness of their drugs, the total volume of crime they produce may be quite large. Of course, society could decide to support all unemployable addicts on welfare, but that would mean that gains from lowered rates of crime would have to be offset by large increases in welfare budgets.

Proponents of legalization claim that the costs of having more addicts around would be largely if not entirely offset by having more money available with which to treat and care for them. The money would come from taxes levied on the sale of heroin and cocaine.

To obtain this fiscal dividend, however, legalization's supporters must first solve an economic dilemma. If they want to raise a lot of money to pay for welfare and treatment, the tax rate on the drugs will have to be quite high. Even if they themselves do not want a high rate, the politicians' love of "sin taxes" would probably guarantee that it would be high anyway. But the higher the tax, the higher the price of the drug, and the higher the price the greater the likelihood that addicts will turn to crime to find the money for it and that criminal organizations will be formed to sell tax-free drugs at below-market rates. If we managed to keep taxes (and thus prices) low, we would get that much less money to pay for welfare and treatment and more people could afford to become addicts. There may be an optimal tax rate for drugs that maximizes revenue while minimizing crime, bootlegging, and the recruitment of new addicts, but our experience with alcohol does not suggest that we know how to find it.

The Benefits of Illegality

The advocates of legalization find nothing to be said in favor of the current system except, possibly, that it keeps the number of addicts smaller than it would otherwise be. In fact, the benefits are more substantial than that.

First, treatment. All the talk about providing "treatment on demand" implies that there is a demand for treatment. That is not quite right. There are some drug-dependent people who genuinely want treatment and will remain in it if offered; they should receive it. But there are far more who want only short-term help after a bad crash; once stabilized and bathed, they are back on the street again, hustling. And even many of the addicts who enroll in a program honestly wanting help drop out after a short while when they discover that help takes time and commitment. Drug-dependent people have very short time horizons and a weak capacity for commitment. These two groups—those looking for a quick fix and those unable to stick with a long-term fix—are not easily helped. Even if we increase the number of treatment slots—as we should—we would have to do something to make treatment more effective.

One thing that can often make it more effective is compulsion. Douglas Anglin of UCLA, in common with many other researchers, has found that the longer one stays in a treatment program, the better the chances of a reduction in drug dependency. But he, again like most other researchers, has found that drop-out rates are high. He has also found, however, that patients who enter treatment under legal compulsion stay in the program longer than those not subject to such pressure. His research on the California civil-commitment program, for example, found that heroin users involved with its required drug-testing program had over the long term a lower rate of heroin use than similar addicts who were free of such constraints. If for many addicts compulsion is a useful component of treatment, it is not clear how compulsion could be achieved in a society in which purchasing, possessing, and using the drug were legal. It could be managed, I suppose, but I would not want to have to answer the challenge from the American Civil

Liberties Union that it is wrong to compel a person to undergo treatment for consuming a legal commodity.

Next, education. We are now investing substantially in drug-education programs in the schools. Though we do not yet know for certain what will work, there are some promising leads. But I wonder how credible such programs would be if they were aimed at dissuading children from doing something perfectly legal. We could, of course, treat drug education like smoking education: inhaling crack and inhaling tobacco are both legal, but you should not do it because it is bad for you. That tobacco is bad for you is easily shown; the Surgeon General has seen to that. But what do we say about crack? It is pleasurable, but devoting yourself to so much pleasure is not a good idea (though perfectly legal)? Unlike tobacco, cocaine will not give you cancer or emphysema, but it will lead you to neglect your duties to family, job, and neighborhood? Everybody is doing cocaine, but you should not?

Again, it might be possible under a legalized regime to have effective drug-prevention programs, but their effectiveness would depend heavily, I think, on first having decided that cocaine use, like tobacco use, is purely a matter of practical consequences; no fundamental moral significance attaches to either. But if we believe—as I do—that dependency on certain mind-altering drugs *is* a moral issue and that their illegality rests in part on their immorality, then legalizing them undercuts, if it does not eliminate altogether, the moral message.

That message is at the root of the distinction we now make between nicotine and cocaine. Both are highly addictive; both have harmful physical effects. But we treat the two drugs differently, not simply because nicotine is so widely used as to be beyond the reach of effective prohibition, but because its use does not destroy the user's essential humanity. Tobacco shortens one's life, cocaine debases it. Nicotine alters one's habits, cocaine alters one's soul. The heavy use of crack, unlike the heavy use of tobacco, corrodes those natural sentiments of sympathy and duty that constitute our human nature and make possible our social life. To say, as does Nadelmann, that distinguishing morally between tobacco and cocaine is "little more than a transient prejudice" is close to saying that morality itself is but a prejudice.

The Alcohol Problem

Now we have arrived where many arguments about legalizing drugs begin: is there any reason to treat heroin and cocaine differently from the way we treat alcohol?

There is no easy answer to that question because, as with so many human problems, one cannot decide simply on the basis either of moral principles or of individual consequences; one has to temper any policy by a common-sense judgment of what is possible. Alcohol, like heroin, cocaine, PCP, and marijuana, is a drug—that is, a mood-altering substance—and consumed to excess it certainly has harmful consequences: auto accidents, barroom fights, bedroom shootings. It is also, for some people, addictive. We cannot confidently compare the addictive powers of these drugs, but the best evidence suggests that crack and heroin are much more addictive than alcohol.

Many people, Nadelmann included, argue that since the health and financial costs of alcohol abuse are so much higher than those of cocaine or heroin abuse, it is hypocritical folly to devote our efforts to preventing cocaine or drug use. But as Mark Kleiman of Harvard has pointed out, this comparison is quite misleading. What Nadelmann is doing is showing that a *legalized* drug (alcohol) produces greater social harm than *illegal* ones (cocaine and heroin). But of course. Suppose that in the 1920's we had made heroin and cocaine legal and alcohol illegal. Can anyone doubt that Nadelmann would now be writing that it is folly to continue our ban on alcohol because cocaine and heroin are so much more harmful?

And let there be no doubt about it—widespread heroin and cocaine use are associated with all manner of ills. Thomas Bewley found that the mortality rate of British heroin addicts in 1968 was 28 times as high as the death rate of the same age group of non-addicts, even though in England at the time an addict could obtain free or low-cost heroin and clean needles from British clinics. Perform the following mental experiment: suppose we legalized heroin and cocaine in this country. In what proportion of auto fatalities would the state police report that the driver was nodding off on heroin or recklessly driving on a coke high? In what proportion of spouse-assault and child-abuse cases would the local police report that crack was involved? In what proportion of industrial accidents would safety investigators report that the forklift or drill-press operator was in a drug-induced stupor or frenzy? We do not know exactly what the proportion would be, but anyone who asserts that it would not be much higher than it is now would have to believe that these drugs have little appeal except when they are illegal. And that is nonsense.

An advocate of legalization might concede that social harm—perhaps harm equivalent to that already produced by alcohol—

would follow from making cocaine and heroin generally available. But at least, he might add, we would have the problem "out in the open" where it could be treated as a matter of "public health." That is well and good, *if* we knew how to treat—that is, cure— heroin and cocaine abuse. But we do not know how to do it for all the people who would need such help. We are having only limited success in coping with chronic alcoholics. Addictive behavior is immensely difficult to change, and the best methods for chang- ing it—living in drug-free therapeutic communities, becoming faithful members of Alcoholics Anonymous or Narcotics Anony- mous—require great personal commitment, a quality that is, alas, in short supply among the very persons—young people, disad- vantaged people—who are often most at risk for addiction.

Suppose that today we had, not 15 million alcohol abusers, but half a million. Suppose that we already knew what we have learned from our long experience with the widespread use of alcohol. Would we make whiskey legal? I do not know, but I suspect there would be a lively debate. The Surgeon General would remind us of the risks alcohol poses to pregnant women. The National Highway Traffic Safety Administration would point to the likelihood of more highway fatalities caused by drunk drivers. The Food and Drug Administration might find that there is a nontrivial increase in cancer associated with alcohol consumption. At the same time the police would report great difficulty in keeping illegal whiskey out of our cities, officers be- ing corrupted by bootleggers, and alcohol addicts often resorting to crime to feed their habit. Libertarians, for their part, would argue that every citizen has a right to drink anything he wishes and that drinking is, in any event, a "victimless crime."

However the debate might turn out, the central fact would be that the problem was still, at that point, a small one. The government cannot legislate away the addictive tendencies in all of us, nor can it remove completely even the most dangerous addictive substances. But it can cope with harms when the harms are still manageable.

Science and Addiction

One advantage of containing a problem while it is still con- tainable is that it buys time for science to learn more about it and perhaps to discover a cure. Almost unnoticed in the current de- bate over legalizing drugs is that basic science has made rapid strides in identifying the underlying neurological processes in- volved in some forms of addiction. Stimulants such as cocaine and amphetamines alter the way certain brain cells communicate with one another. That alteration is complex and not entirely understood, but in simplified form it involves modifying the way in which a neurotransmitter called dopamine sends signals from one cell to another.

When dopamine crosses the synapse between two cells, it is in effect carrying a message from the first cell to activate the second one. In certain parts of the brain that message is experienced as pleasure. After the message is delivered, the dopamine returns to the first cell. Cocaine apparently blocks this return, or "reuptake," so that the excited cell and others nearby continue to send pleasure messages. When the exaggerated high produced by cocaine-influenced dopamine finally ends, the brain cells may (in ways that are still a matter of dispute) suffer from an extreme lack of dopamine, thereby making the individual unable to experience any pleasure at all. This would explain why cocaine users often feel so depressed after enjoying the drug. Stimulants may also affect the way in which other neurotransmitters, such as serotonin and noradrenaline, operate.

Whatever the exact mechanism may be, once it is identified it becomes possible to use drugs to block either the effect of cocaine or its tendency to produce dependency. There have already been experiments using desipramine, imipramine, bromocriptine, carbamazepine, and other chemicals. There are some promising results.

Tragically, we spend very little on such research, and the agencies funding it have not in the past occupied very influential or visible posts in the federal bureaucracy. If there is one aspect of the "war on drugs" metaphor that I dislike, it is its tendency to focus attention almost exclusively on the troops in the trenches, whether engaged in enforcement or treatment, and away from the research-and-development efforts back on the home front where the war may ultimately be decided.

I believe that the prospects of scientists in controlling addiction will be strongly influenced by the size and character of the problem they face. If the problem is a few hundred thousand chronic, high-dose users of an illegal product, the chances of making a difference at a reasonable cost will be much greater than if the problem is a few million chronic users of legal substances. Once a drug is legal, not only will its use increase but many of those who then use it will prefer the drug to the treatment: they will want the pleasure, whatever the cost to themselves or their families, and they will resist—probably successfully—any effort to wean them away from experiencing the high that comes from inhaling a legal substance.

If I Am Wrong . . .

No one can know what our society would be like if we changed the law to make access to cocaine, heroin, and PCP easier. I believe, for reasons given, that the result would be a sharp increase in use, a more widespread degradation of the human personality, and a greater rate of accidents and violence.

I may be wrong. If I am, then we will needlessly have incurred heavy costs in law enforcement and some forms of criminality. But if I am right, and the legalizers prevail anyway, then we will have consigned millions of people, hundreds of thousands of infants, and hundreds of neighborhoods to a life of oblivion and disease. To the lives and families destroyed by alcohol we will have added countless more destroyed by cocaine, heroin, PCP, and whatever else a basement scientist can invent.

Human character is formed by society; indeed, human character is inconceivable without society, and good character is less likely in a bad society. Will we, in the name of an abstract doctrine of radical individualism, and with the false comfort of suspect predictions, decide to take the chance that somehow individual decency can survive amid a more general level of degradation?

I think not. The American people are too wise for that, whatever the academic essayists and cocktail-party pundits may say. But if Americans today are less wise than I suppose, then Americans at some future time will look back on us now and wonder, what kind of people were they that they could have done such a thing?

ON THE LEGALIZATION OF DRUGS, ROUND 2[2]

To the Editor of *Commentary*:
    . . . After many columns of rambling argumentation, James Q. Wilson in "Against the Legalization of Drugs" [February], states

[2]Reprint of letters to the editor in response to James Q. Wilson's preceding article in F '90 issue of *Commentary* (with a rebuttal by the author). Reprinted by permission of *Commentary*, 89: 8–11. Je '90. Copyright © by *Commentary*.

his premise in the next to last paragraph of his article: "Human character is formed by society; indeed, human character is inconceivable without society."

Every argument in the article depends on this premise, which is unprovable because it is undefinable. What is human character? That which is formed by society. What is society? That which forms human character. People sympathetic to Mr. Wilson's view "just know" what human character is and what society is. Others don't count; they're on the wrong side of the war.

Personally, I think my character is formed by me, and society consists of the interactions I choose. Since the responsibility for my life thus falls entirely on me, I wouldn't dream of clouding my mind with poisonous drugs—it's the only one I've got. But if Mr. Wilson is right, and it's not my responsibility but William J. Bennett's, then what the heck, I might as well try just one little snort. . . .

JAMES SEDGWICK
Oakland, California

To the Editor of *Commentary*:

James Q. Wilson's moral distinction between cocaine and nicotine is bizarre. His antiseptic characterization of tobacco, that it (merely) shortens one's life but does not destroy one's "essential humanity," suggests that Mr. Wilson has never comforted an addict through the nervous unravelings of nicotine withdrawal or one devastated by respiratory cancer or its treatments. Cocaine, he says, debases one's life and "alters one's soul." . . .

Let us say we were to legalize cocaine and outlaw tobacco. The mass media would soon be sensationalizing the horrors of cighouses and butt dealers. They would turn their cameras and microphones on the most desperate addicts, creating the illusion that they were typical users, inevitable products of fateful first puffs. . . . Public-affairs reports would treat the public to the most graphic gore of carcinomas, interviews via tracheotomy, inner-city maternity wards bursting with "tar babies," and the inevitable gang mayhem (all the while the Royale Coke Smokes cowboy would be riding satisfied into endless sunsets, trailing a surgeon general's warning, of course). In other words, stack the deck of public perception the other way, and I am sure most people would soon perceive tobacco as dehumanizing and cocaine as merely inadvisable. The morality of drug prohibition is a social fiction manufactured by mass-media managers driven by market shares and by politicians looking for enemies against whom to rail and rally the electorate.

While moralizing about illegal drug use, Mr. Wilson takes a pragmatic view of alcohol and tobacco. He says "nicotine is so widely used as to be beyond the reach of effective prohibition," and about alcohol that "one has to temper any policy by a common-sense judgment of what is possible." But is tolerance of the inebriant that flows at the country club coupled with intolerance of the one that burns in the ghetto "a common-sense judgment" or simply bigotry? . . . It would be refreshing to hear someone in the mass media address the probability that the only reason punitive measures are not proposed against casual alcohol and tobacco consumers is that too many of them are middle-class whites.

Mr. Wilson spends a lot of ink arguing that present heroin-usage levels demonstrate the wisdom of the war against heroin during the 1970's. . . . But even Mr. Wilson must admit that the war on drugs today is fundamentally different in character from the anti-heroin campaign of the 1970's. By adopting the tactics of historical purges and pogroms waged against unpopular minorities, today's drug war has taken on an ominous and menacing character that never was present during the campaigns of the 1970's. . . .

How can a government deal with members of unpopular minorities? Well, "We can take away their assets, their money, their privileges and possessions. Let us take away their fancy homes and cars and jeopardize their professional licenses." Those words belong not to Adolf Hitler, . . . but to Minnesota Attorney General Hubert H. Humphrey III. The Attorney General was speaking to members of the Criminal Justice Institute about drug users. Here in Minnesota, newly enacted legislation empowers the state to confiscate and auction the property of suspected drug users, whether they are convicted or acquitted; whether, in fact, they even go to trial! If the lessons of history are applicable, these steps seem to constitute enabling measures for a narcocide. . . .

Mr. Wilson's accusation that cocaine alters the soul suggests that narcs are not actually law-enforcement officers but exorcists, and that the Drug Enforcement Agency is not a secular administrative agency but a national church. . . . The drug war may be a holy war in the minds of its perpetrators, but to outsiders it has the feel of a new Inquisition. . . .

KENNETH JOPP
St. Paul, Minnesota

To the Editor of *Commentary:*

Like most discussions of the subject, James Q. Wilson's argument against legalizing drugs overlooks the fundamental question, namely, what is the primary legitimate purpose of democratic government? If, as Jefferson maintains, it is to secure its citizens' right to pursue happiness freely without (directly) injuring others, then they should be free to make themselves temporarily happy by taking drugs. Similarly, if, as Locke maintains, it is to protect its citizens' persons and property, these would be far more secure for the majority (who are nonusers) if drugs were legalized.

But if the primary legitimate purpose of democratic government is to promote the material or moral or physical or spiritual welfare of its citizens, then drugs should remain illegal, cigarettes and handguns should become illegal, and alcohol consumption should be carefully controlled. The hairsplitting distinctions Mr. Wilson and others make among them are essentially *ex-post-facto* rationalizations for a status quo that is easier to defend than to change.

A second and related oversight in this otherwise excellent article is its failure to consider the virtual absence of drug use among religiously oriented communities like Orthodox Jews. What distinguishes these communities is their tacit rejection of the natural-rights doctrine on which modern democratic government is based and their concomitant ability to imbue their youth with a sense of purpose in life that centers not on the self and its right to pursue happiness or secure property, but on service to God, benefit to others, and the duty to pursue virtue.

ROMAN A. FOXBRUNNER
Brookline, Massachusetts

To the Editor of *Commentary:*

James Q. Wilson makes a better defense of our national drug policy than does drug czar William J. Bennett. Nonetheless, it is a weak defense. He claims credit for a strategy that succeeded in maintaining zero-growth in heroin use during the last fifteen-plus years, but during that same time, cocaine was supplanting heroin as the users' drug of choice! This would have been a Pyrrhic victory even if there had been a measurable decline in heroin use, let alone a mere holding of the line. . . .

Those of us who favor legalization of drugs are not seeking to raise the "white flag of surrender." Rather, we are trying to focus the nation's batteries on drug abuse, the real enemy. But the war is being led by generals like Mr. Wilson who consider any use of a mind-altering drug (other than alcohol) to be morally unacceptable. In their futile attempts to ban all drug use, they succeed only in making drugs available to anybody who wants them, without regulation and without regard to age. Then we exacerbate the dangers of use by adding criminal sanctions. . . .

Just as Mr. Wilson chose to define the war against drugs as a war against heroin, so does the current leadership wage its war against crack. And already we are reading about the increasing popularity of "ice." A few years ago we were attacking relatively benign cocaine powder, which was replaced by the cheaper and more dangerous crack, and no doubt some of your older readers can remember when marijuana was receiving the same kind of scare publicity that crack now gets. We tend to "buy" this publicity uncritically. For example, the plight of the crack babies makes very effective drug-war propaganda—as though these babies born of miserably poor and malnourished women and girls would have been healthy, bouncing infants absent the demon crack!

Surely, James Q. Wilson, a writer on crime, knows better than to imply that the use of illicit drugs is a significant causative factor in violent crime, other than those daily turf-war murders that are an integral part of a multibillion-dollar market in illegal goods. The crimes that are "caused" by drugs are the crimes of using and selling the drugs—crimes that offend only those to whom the use of psychoactive drugs, other than alcohol, is a "moral issue."

There are some drug-war tactics that are effective, but they would be even more effective under a policy of legalization and regulation. For example, the barrage of publicity about the dangers of drug use does have some beneficent impact. But that publicity would (and should) be continued, let us hope with greater honesty, when drugs are made legal. There are better, more persuasive reasons for steering clear of drug use than simple fear of, or respect for, an arbitrary law. . . .

STAN NAMOVICZ
Takoma Park, Maryland

To the Editor of *Commentary:*

James Q. Wilson's article seeks to establish the view that increased and vigilant law enforcement effectively contains drug use, abuse, and distribution. . . .

In fact, the history of drug use in the United States proves quite another theorem. The threat of arrest and incarceration does little to discourage use. Instead, illegality turns benign and moderate patterns of use into their opposites, replaces safe routes of administration by riskier ones, encourages experimentation with many drugs or polydrug use, introduces into distribution features which redound to use in malign ways—adulteration of the product, distrust and conflict among distributors, and between them and their clienteles—and draws successively larger increments of innocents into use.

In sum, illegality has brought a lack of regulation to all drug-related behaviors. In particular, the criminalization of heroin in 1914 may be seen as the direct cause of today's crack epidemic. . . .

Heroin was sniffed or taken in pill form for several decades in the United States before it became illegal. For most of a few million users, use was benign, and was encouraged by factory owner and physician alike. When heroin became illegal, users were reduced in number to about half-a-million, but they had become injectors—injecting being a route of administration which gave more "high" for the (now) expensive drug. Injecting invited infection, and made the user more vulnerable to adulterants. In that it also became compulsive, injecting made the user unusually dependent upon distributors, and upon the circumstances of greed, distrust, and conflict in which illegality obliged the latter to operate.

It was primarily as youth-gang members drawn into the quick cash of criminal distribution that the age cohort of users (1964–72) Mr. Wilson discusses became involved with heroin . . . By the end of the decade, heroin use was widespread in minority, inner-city neighborhoods.

It is disheartening to learn that Mr. Wilson refused to discuss the legalization of heroin in 1972. By that date, inner-city youths had become quite fed up with heroin use. Veins had collapsed, bodies had become gaunt and covered with sores, general health was extremely poor, and, in distribution, habits precluded profits. Had heroin been legalized at this time, they still would have been unwilling (or unable, given the condition of veins) to inject. Indeed, many did seek medical care. Upon recuperation, they could have been encouraged by medical personnel to sniff moderate amounts of heroin, or to inhale it in cigarettes. . . .

Tiring of heroin injecting and seeking medical attention in

the 1970's, . . . heroin users were very receptive to the newly available, medically-monitored, legal drug, methadone. But they soon discovered that methadone would not give them the "high" its government sponsors had advertised. . . . Users were led next to cocaine, a drug which was being snorted contentedly and without remark by a small, satisfied following. . . . When former heroin injectors or persons maintained on methadone began injecting cocaine, they diffused this practice to cocaine snorters too. The pool of IV drug users was therefore increased.

The enlarged pool of injectors soon began to complain about the adverse effects of cocaine injecting. It "froze" their veins, making them difficult to pierce. Their whole bodies felt "frozen," so that they feared that they were unable to bleed. This dissatisfaction . . . persuaded users to experiment with smoking cocaine. . . .

Arrival at a smokeable form of cocaine now brought that drug to the attention of a much larger population of drug smokers— 100 million cigarette smokers, and more especially 45 million marijuana smokers. In 1981, the latter had begun to experience the consequences of intensified enforcement of the laws against their drug of choice. Crop eradication and interdiction had made marijuana scarce, and in South America its cultivators were diverted to coca cultivation.

In the U.S., marijuana distributors, who had often made substantial and extensive reinvestments in local-level, community self-renewal, were harassed by street-level law enforcement, and found themselves hard-pressed to find marijuana to retail in their marijuana-selling locations, the backbone of this community work. Seeking another medium of exchange, they were drawn, very reluctantly and guiltily, into experimentation with the use and distribution of the smokeable cocaine which other law-frustrated drug users had unearthed, as described, and eventually they and their successors, through (criminal) marketing exigencies, brought many millions to crack.

Frustration with crack is currently reintroducing heroin to these many millions, since it affords the crack user a few hours of "nodding out" before the far brisker craving for crack can reassert itself. It may even lead them to ice (smokeable metamphetamine) in the near future. If it does, I expect that a lot of "pill-poppers" . . . may become users. By successively larger increments of population, therefore, illegality will have brought us from the benign use of drugs (which was restricted to a few million, medically supervised users in 1914) to a completely and adversely drug-affected America.

The American experience of alcohol demonstrates clearly that legalization is the context in which good sense in the matter of drugs is expected to prevail. In the fifty years since Prohibition, average per-capita consumption of alcohol has fallen to its lowest level since the discovery of America. . . . In the context of legality, tobacco consumption has also been reduced. . . .

It is frightening to observe how rapidly opponents of legalization resort in the end to ill-founded moral sentiments to strengthen the case of intensified law enforcement. . . . An efficient corrective to this sort of thinking might be an actual meeting with crack users in the low-income minority neighborhoods where crack causes the most trouble. Here Mr. Wilson would discover that crack use is subjected to different degrees of control; and that crack users, human beings with quite unaltered souls, assign very different values to the drug, with corresponding variation in behavioral outcomes. . . . Whole blocks of abandoned buildings and empty or rubbish-strewn lots would give him clues to the contexts of crack use, and to the factors which turn crack against its local users.

The hope of legalization is that these real problems (homelessness, unemployment, destabilized neighborhoods, destroyed families, etc.) will no longer be obscured by scapegoating drugs or drug users' characters; and that a "drug peace dividend" will earmark substantial resources toward their solution.

ANSLEY HAMID
Department of Anthropology
John Jay College of Criminal Justice
New York City

To the Editor of *Commentary:*

. . . I must admit that when I first picked up James Q. Wilson's article, I was ready to ridicule anything he might have to say against legalizing drugs. Not that I am a drug user, but I have always thought that legalization would help more people than it would hurt. Most importantly, it would get drugs out of the schools.

I expected Mr. Wilson's article to be very one-sided, giving only his point of view on the situation, but to my surprise, the article was very fair to the opposing view. Both sides of the argument were given and every point and counter-point was supported with evidence, even though in the end the argument for keeping drugs illegal prevailed. . . .

While reading the article, I kept asking myself, what about alcohol? I have always felt that drugs and alcohol should be treated in the same way, since alcohol causes as many fatalities, if not more, than drugs. Yet even as I was asking myself the question, I turned the page and Mr. Wilson surprised me again. . . . His section on alcohol answered all my arguments and gave good reasons why they were not the right ones. . . .

On a few points I still disagree with James Q. Wilson. As a criminal-justice major, I still believe that legalization might save money and might save some lives by eliminating drug-pushers. But the article has basically changed my mind on this topic, and I hope many others' minds have also been changed. . . .

E. J. Mazzei
Winona, Minnesota

James Q. Wilson writes:

James Sedgwick is not only a libertarian, he is a mightily confused one: "I think my character is formed by me, and society consists of the interactions I choose." I hope he will tell us what "interactions" he "chose" when he was two years old and explain to us how society is formed by those choices. Meanwhile, please read Aristotle before you write another line.

Kenneth Jopp thinks the only difference between nicotine and cocaine is that we have waged propaganda against cocaine and protected nicotine in the country clubs. He thus reveals that he is a lousy chemist; if any dean of a medical school reads this, please don't admit Mr. Jopp as a student. (To describe the current anti-drug effort as a "pogrom" suggests that he isn't much of a historian, either.)

Stan Namovicz accuses me of having taken credit for stopping heroin; I did nothing of the kind. When he turns to crack, he puts its awful effects down to scare publicity. Babies born to crack mothers would have been miserable even without the cocaine in their placentas. Oh? I hope the medical-school dean also keeps an eye out for this fellow.

Roman A. Foxbrunner wants consistency at any expense. I want consistency—up to a point. I have no real quarrel with him, however; I just hope he and Mr. Jopp can get together to talk over the advantages of banning cigarettes.

Ansley Hamid blames drug abuse on the fact that drugs are illegal. If they weren't, there would be less abuse. How does he know this? Because we had less before 1914. I only wish he had bothered to list *all* of the ways the world has changed since 1914 (another unpromising recruit for a history department). But I think his real agenda is revealed, not by his truncated history, but by the sentences in which he sketches the benign statesmanship of drug dealers. In case the reader missed them, let me quote:

[M]arijuana distributors, who had often made substantial and extensive reinvestments in local-level, community self-renewal, were harassed by street-level law enforcement, and found themselves hard-pressed to find marijuana to retail in their marijuana-selling locations, the backbone of this community work. Seeking another medium of exchange, they were drawn, very reluctantly and guiltily, into experimentation with the use and distribution of . . . smokeable cocaine.

If chemistry and history have been mishandled by my correspondents, anthropology has been stood on its head. A drug dealer is a latter-day Jane Addams or Saul Alinsky, eagerly promoting community renewal while reluctantly agreeing to sell cocaine just to keep his charitable activities alive? I am speechless.

Finally, I would like to thank E. J. Mazzei for his generous letter. To have changed one person's mind through the agency of prose is a rare honor indeed.

DRUG POLICY: STRIKING THE RIGHT BALANCE[3]

Psychoactive drugs obviously provide pleasure or relief to millions of users, but also can do enormous individual and social harm. The recurring debate about legalizing illicit drugs arises from different perceptions of the degree of harm caused by their prohibition, relative to the harm caused by the drugs themselves. At one extreme are libertarians who advocate removal of criminal sanctions from all drugs. At the other extreme are governments that apply the death penalty for even minor levels of trafficking. The status quo in most of the world consists of different degrees

[3]Reprint of an article by Harold Kalant, professor of pharmacology at the University of Toronto, and Avram Goldstein, professor of pharmacology, emeritus, at Stanford University. Reprinted by permission of *Science*, 249: 1513–21. S 28 '90. Copyright © 1990 by *Science*.

of regulation for different psychoactive drugs, only caffeine being available without restriction. Accordingly, the debate is not about the oversimplified dichotomy, legalization versus prohibition, but rather about the specifics of regulatory policies for each drug.

An ideal policy for each drug would strike the best balance among all the costs and benefits. The right to enjoy the pleasurable effects of drugs and freedom from state interference in citizens' private lives must be weighed against the benefits of governmental measures to protect the well-being of drug users, people around them, and society at large. The harm produced by excessive drug use must be weighed against the costs, both monetary and social, of enforcing whatever degree of regulation is imposed. Every cost-benefit analysis carries an implicit bias, which reflects the ethical, social, religious, and political views of those doing the analysis. Our bias is toward a humane and democratic society that provides maximum individual freedom, but the exercise of such freedom must be consistent with the rights of others and the harmonious functioning of the community. All laws have potentially harmful effects, but policy recommendations based only on considering harm caused by the law would be just as unbalanced as those based only on considering harm caused by the drugs themselves.

All drugs can be dangerous; even when they are pure and are used on prescription to treat disease, they often have adverse effects. Most governments are required, by public consensus and demand, to protect citizens against numerous avoidable hazards and not merely to warn them of possible dangers. The U.S. Pure Food and Drug Laws, enacted in 1906, set up the technical machinery, the Food and Drug Administration (FDA), for assessing drug hazards, forbidding over-the-counter sale of the more dangerous drugs, requiring manufacturers to report on unanticipated adverse reactions, and exercising legal control over drug distribution. This legislation grew out of the recognition that innocent people, without the technical expertise needed to assess the risks, were being hurt by drugs with unacceptably high risk-to-benefit ratios.

The use of drugs for nonmedical purposes carries risks not only for the user, but for society as well. A compassionate society ultimately pays the costs, not only of injury to nonusers, but even of self-inflicted injuries to users themselves. Society pays the costs of all acute and chronic toxicity through loss of productivity and by subsidizing medical care, providing welfare assistance to users' families and dealing with the special educational needs of children whose brains were damaged in utero. Thus, drug abuse is rarely a victimless crime. We think that society has a right to take the costs into account in formulating its drug policies.

We shall argue here that (i) psychoactive drugs are, to varying degrees, dangerous to users and to society, (ii) drug consumption is strongly influenced by availability, (iii) availability can be modified, not only by outright prohibition, but in many ways short of prohibition, (iv) although supply reduction is a desirable goal, demand reduction is the real key to lasting amelioration of the drug problem, and (v) rational drug policy ought to be tailored to the dangers presented by each psychoactive drug to users and to society.

Psychoactive Drugs Are Dangerous

Legalizing and regulating drugs that are now illicit would, through quality control measures, eliminate harmful effects due to unknown and variable potencies, adulterants (such as particulates responsible for embolism after intravenous injection), toxic byproducts of illicit manufacture, and bacterial or viral contamination. All other adverse effects, however, are due to intrinsic properties of each drug and thus are independent of legal status. Harm to the user may occur immediately or only after chronic use and may be due to behavioral effects of the drug or to toxic actions on organ systems.

An example of a significant threat to both the user and society is the paranoid psychosis, sometimes accompanied by violence, that can result from repeated use of amphetamines or cocaine. In classic experiments administration of amphetamine or cocaine to normal human volunteers on a regular dosage schedule produced paranoid psychotic behavior. Such studies showed that no previous psychopathology was required and that paranoid reactions to drugs of this class by addicts cannot be attributed to fear of law enforcement but are due to direct drug effects on the brain. Another example is the possibility of lasting brain damage from alcohol, volatile solvents, cocaine, phencyclidine (PCP), marijuana, and 3,4-methylenedioxy-methamphetamine (MDMA, which is also known as ecstasy).

The addicting drugs have two special characteristics with policy implications. First, repeated long-term administration produces a state of physical dependence, so that neurochemical brain function is disturbed (withdrawal syndrome) if the drug is suddenly discontinued. This dependence occurs in animals as well as in humans. The pattern of dependence and the intensity of the withdrawal syndrome differ among drugs and among users. Dependence accounts, in part, for the compulsion to continue use of an addicting drug, and it complicates the treatment of addicts. However, there are effective medical procedures for ameliorating withdrawal distress during detoxification.

The second special characteristic, tolerance, which is typically associated with the development of physical dependence, is manifested by a tendency to escalate dosage because the same dose is no longer as effective as it was before. As with physical dependence, the degree of tolerance differs among drugs and among users. An extreme form of dosage escalation is seen with heroin and cocaine under both experimental and real-life conditions. Dosage escalation complicates schemes for providing addicts with their favorite drugs free or at low prices; when this was tried in the British clinics for heroin addicts, the black market was resorted to for supplemental supplies when the dosage ceiling (high though it was) had been reached.

Many people are able to use addictive drugs in moderation. There are coffee drinkers who take only a cup or two a day, occasional smokers who use only a few cigarettes a day, social drinkers who consume no more than a couple of drinks a day, and marijuana users who smoke a "joint" once in a while. Some people (at least for some period of time) can restrict their use of heroin to weekends, or of cocaine to an occasional party. Others, in contrast, are vulnerable to becoming compulsive heavy users, then stopping only with great difficulty if at all, and relapsing readily. There is no sharp separation between so-called social users and addicted users, but rather a continuum of increasing levels of use and increasing levels of risk.

The compulsive quality of drug addiction presents a special danger because for most drugs there is no way to predict who is at greatest risk. People who become addicted usually believe, at the outset, that they will be able to maintain control. After the compulsion takes control, addicts persist in using high doses, often by dangerous routes of administration. As the heavy users constitute the heart of the drug problem, there is an urgent need for more research to explain why they doggedly persist in a self-destructive activity despite full knowledge of its consequences.

A part of the explanation is in the pharmacology of the drugs themselves. Despite the acknowledged importance of peer group pressures, fads, personal and social stresses, price, and numerous other factors that affect drug use by humans, one cannot ignore the psychoactive drug actions, which are sought by the users. Experiments with rats, monkeys, and other species have shown that an animal fitted with an indwelling venous cannula, through which it can obtain an injection by pressing a lever, will establish a regular rhythm of lever-pressing if (and only if) the injection contains one of the known addicting drugs. One measure of the addictiveness of a drug is how hard the animal will work (that is, how many lever-presses it will make) for each injection. Another measure is the extent to which the animal engages in drug self-administration to the exclusion of normal activities such as eating, drinking, exploratory behavior, grooming, or sex. Yet another measure is the rapidity of relapse after a period of enforced abstinence. By these criteria cocaine is the most addictive drug known. Monkeys with unrestricted access in this laboratory procedure will actually kill themselves with cocaine by cardiovascular collapse, starvation, dehydration, or skin infections due to self-mutilation.

Cognitive factors have a role in moderating the behavior of humans who try psychoactive drugs but do not become addicted. Nevertheless, single-minded preoccupation of many cocaine, heroin, nicotine, and alcohol addicts with obtaining and using their respective drugs is disturbingly reminiscent of the animal experiments and reflects a major role of direct drug effects in driving addictive behavior. Research has begun to reveal where the addicting drugs act in the brain to produce the rewarding effects that give rise to self-administration behavior. We are far from understanding fully how and where each psychoactive drug acts on these reward pathways, but the emerging picture suggests the following. Reward systems have developed over the course of evolution to reinforce useful behaviors and extinguish harmful ones and to maintain and adaptively regulate a fine-tuned set of drives related to pleasure and pain, emotional and sexual satisfaction, hunger, thirst, and satiety. Addicting drugs act on these same systems by substituting for the natural neurotransmitters that act at different points in the circuitry, thus producing an artificial state of reward (euphoria), a powerful compulsion to sustain that state, and possibly irreversible (or long persistent) dysfunctions of the reward mechanisms.

Availability Affects Consumption

As would be expected, the ease of obtaining a drug affects its consumption. Contrary to the prevalent view that prohibition failed, there is substantial evidence that it reduced alcohol consumption substantially, albeit at the price of bootlegging, gangsterism, violence, and disrespect for the law among some segments of society. De facto prohibition of alcohol was introduced in the United States around 1916 and continued as a wartime restriction, at a time when the temperance movement (and then the war effort) enjoyed a wide public support. A prompt fall occurred in the death rate from liver cirrhosis, which is a good index of the prevalence of alcoholism in the population and which correlates well with the mean per capita consumption of alcohol. The decrease in cirrhosis deaths from about 12 per 100,000 in 1916 to less than 7 in 1920 corresponds to a 50% fall in alcohol use.

Conversely, lowering of the legal drinking age in a number of states and provinces led to an immediate increase in alcohol-related driving accidents contributed by those under 21. Thus, although drinking by those under 21 had, no doubt, gone on previously, it increased sharply when the law permitted it. The potential effectiveness of legal restraints is also indicated by the ending of the Japanese methamphetamine epidemic through stringent enforcement by the police, backed by an anti-drug consensus among the general population.

An example of how availability affects drug use is provided by the experience of physicians, dentists, and nurses, who have easy (though illegal) personal access to psychoactive drugs that are forbidden to the general public. Despite the risk of heavy sanctions, such as loss of professional license and possible criminal prosecution, the per capita prevalence of addiction to opiates and other drugs was found to be much higher than in a matched control population.

Injudicious prescribing practices may allow diversion of a medically approved drug into the illicit market. In New York State, the simple step of imposing a triplicate prescription system for benzodiazepines, to permit accurate record keeping by the authorities, produced a dramatic drop in consumption (especially of Valium) and a steep increase in the street price of these widely abused drugs.

From the standpoint of the consumer, a rise in price is tantamount to decreased availability and vice versa. Thus, price affects drug use. The mean per capita consumption of alcohol in Ontario between 1928 and 1974 varied inversely with the unit price of alcohol in constant dollars, in almost perfect mirror-image fashion, and a similar relationship has been shown for several European countries. The cirrhosis death rate also varied inversely with price, indicating that alcoholics as well as social drinkers are affected by price changes. This price elasticity of alcohol use by alcoholics has even been demonstrated experimentally. Similarly, smoking has varied inversely with the level of taxation on cigarettes. The sudden large increase in the use of cocaine in North American cities following the introduction of crack, a crude form of cocaine free base, has been attributed to the lower price of crack than of cocaine salt preparations, as well as to the easier and more effective method of administration by smoking. These data suggest that anything making drugs less expensive, such as legal sale at lower prices, would result in substantial increases in use and in the harmful consequences of heavy use.

Finally, education, fashion, and social consensus contribute to the shaping of public attitudes and practices with respect to drugs. Alcohol in western societies, cannabis in the Moslem world, and hallucinogens in Native American religions illustrate how socially accepted psychoactive drugs are incorporated into the traditions, values, and practices of a society. Social incorporation of a drug rests on a consensus with respect to the circumstances, amounts, and patterns of use that are considered acceptable. There is therefore an important difference between behaviors with respect to a long-acculturated drug and a newly introduced one, especially in a society undergoing rapid change. Illustrative are the current difficulties with cocaine in some American and Canadian cities in contrast to the stable or even declining use of longer established drugs in both countries.

Policy Options: The Polar Extremes

The pharmacologic, toxicologic, social, and historical factors noted above provide a basis for predicting the consequences of various options for reducing drug availability. One option would be an even more Draconian enforcement of current drug prohibition laws. However, greater expenditure on measures of the kind now being used seems unlikely; political difficulties would arise if funds were diverted massively from other high-priority programs. Consequently, a more militant antidrug policy might well take the form of new measures that do not cost more but increase police powers by infringement of civil liberties, such as search without warrant, prolonged detention for interrogation without formal charges, or further dramatic increases in the severity of penalties.

Stern measures have, indeed, been credited with ending major drug problems. It is claimed that the serious opium problem in China was ended by stern measures, including the death penalty, after the Communists came to power. The Japanese methamphetamine epidemic was stamped out by less brutal but nonetheless forceful measures. However, the cost, if democratic governments were to adopt similar measures, would be a significant change in the character of the society. In addition, the explicit constitutional guarantees of the U.S. Bill of Rights and Canadian Charter of Rights would pose formidable obstacles to such a drastic course.

The antithesis of this approach, the legalization of psychoactive drugs, has been proposed as a possible way to reduce the high costs of enforcing existing prohibitions. Not only would the police, courts, and prisons no longer have to deal with the huge load of drug cases with which they are now burdened, but also the legal sale of drugs of known purity at moderate prices would, it is argued, drive the illicit traffic out of existence. In addition, licit businesses and governments would allegedly earn huge revenues that now find their way into drug traffickers' bank accounts.

On the cost side, however, would be the consequences of increased use and abuse of the drugs themselves. Even the proponents of legalization acknowledge some risk of increased drug use with its attendant problems, but they argue that the extent of such increase would be small. However, as an editorial in *The New York Times* remarked, ". . . there is little evidence to support so stupendous a contradiction of common sense"; indeed, past experience suggests that the increase in use would be very large.

This common-sense expectation is generally confirmed by historical evidence. Alcohol and tobacco, which are now so freely available, are also the most widely abused drugs, but—as noted earlier—alcohol consumption was much lower when the drug was less readily available. Social custom made cigarettes effectively unavailable to women until after World War I; then consumption increased steadily as it became more acceptable for women to smoke, and the lung cancer rate for females eventually matched that for males. Opiates and cocaine were legal and freely available before passage of the Harrison Act in 1914. Despite the absence of sound nationwide surveys, there is evidence to suggest that this availability had given rise to widespread and serious misuse. According to an epidemiologic study conducted in 1913, the percentage of adults addicted to these drugs appears to have been not very different from the percentage addicted to alcohol in present-day North America.

The history of alcohol provides some basis for predicting what might be expected from the removal of all drug prohibitions. The key question is whether legalization of opiates and cocaine would result in levels of addiction comparable to those seen currently among the users of alcohol and tobacco. Opiates and cocaine are certainly not less addictive than alcohol or nicotine by any criterion. And although the intravenous route might never become widely popular, smoking (especially of crack) would be the route of choice for the millions. There is no reason to doubt that the increased costs to society would rival those now attributable to alcohol. In that case the economic savings that might be achieved, even if it were possible to eliminate all the costs of drug law enforcement, might well be offset by the additional costs resulting from the consequences of increased drug use.

If the government were to attempt to prevent large increases in consumption by raising the prices for drugs sold through licit outlets, as suggested by some proponents of legalization, prices of illicit drugs could then be competitive, and drug traffickers could continue in business. Government would be in the unhappy position of having to choose between raising prices to discourage excessive use, thus allowing the illicit traffic to continue, and lowering prices enough to drive out the illicit trade, thus increasing consumption.

It has been argued that legalizing and taxing drugs would provide financial resources for treatment of those who become addicted, but in Canada in 1984 the total social costs of alcohol were double the revenues generated from alcohol at all levels of government. In the United States in 1983 this ratio exceeded 10 to 1.

A further inevitable consequence of legalization would be the impact on public attitudes toward psychoactive drugs. The recent decline in drug use among high school students in the United States and Canada probably reflects a gradual acceptance of medical evidence that has been part of the justification for the continued illegal status of some drugs. Removal of the legal restrictions would risk conveying the message that drug use is not really as harmful as the students had come to believe and thus would weaken an important influence tending to keep consumption levels low.

The right balance, we believe, lies somewhere between these policy extremes. The specific recommendations offered in the next section embody a variety of intermediate options based on two goals: (i) to reduce the recruitment of new addicts by making it more difficult and more expensive to obtain psychoactive drugs and by strengthening an anti-drug consensus through education; and (ii) to ameliorate the circumstances of those already addicted by regarding them as victims of a life-threatening disease (as indeed they are) requiring compassionate treatment.

Current Extent of the Problem

The "War on Drugs" may be a useful metaphor, in the sense that war mobilizes social forces, sets priorities, marshals extraordinary resources, and embodies shared societal goals. But, as with so many medical and social dysfunctions, total victory is an illusory goal. Psychoactive drugs have always been with us and probably always will be. The practical aim of drug policy should be to minimize the extent of use, and thus to minimize the harm. How best to do this is often uncertain, so budgets established in drug legislation should routinely mandate sufficient funds for evaluation. And inasmuch as behavior change comes slowly, it is important, as the elements of an improved drug policy are put in place, to be patient and give them time to work; this may well prove the most difficult of our recommendations to implement.

The first step toward a more rational and more effective drug policy is for the media, the public, and governments to see the drug problem in correct perspective. The current degree of concern about illicit drug use, bordering on hysteria, is at variance with the actual data on the magnitude of the problem. As to how this distorted perception came about, one is reminded of Lincoln Steffens's description of how newspapers, in his day, created "crime waves."

What is the magnitude of the problem? Regular sources of national U.S. data are the National Household Survey and the High School Seniors Survey, DAWN [the Drug Abuse Warning Network for emergency room drug mentions], and surveys of military personnel. These are supplemented by ad hoc and local epidemiologic studies. In Ontario, surveys of students in grades 7 through 13 and of the adult general population have been carried out biennially since 1972. The most recent estimates show that our most serious problem drugs by far are alcohol and nicotine (tobacco), whether assessed by damage to users, harm to society, or numbers of addicts.

[Data indicates] . . . (though not sensationalized by the media) that drug use, overall, has been declining—in all sections of the population, all parts of North America, and for all psychoactive drugs whether licit or illicit. The exception to this encouraging trend has been the recent increase in the number of people who use crack daily. This number is still relatively small, but it is of concern because of the peculiarly seductive quality of this form of cocaine and because of the concentration of sales and associated violence in the inner cities.

Recommendations

Concerning supply reduction and the appropriate degrees of regulation. Ideally, one would wish to match the degree of regulation and the effort expended in enforcement to the real dangers posed by each drug to the user and to society. This would respond effectively to the criticism that our present laws are hypocritical, in that dangerous addicting drugs like alcohol and nicotine are freely available and even advertised, whereas marijuana, which is less dangerous than cocaine or heroin (but by no means harmless), is under stringent legal controls.

One way to use technical expertise instead of politics to formulate more rational policies would be to apply the model of the FDA, whose mission, with respect to therapeutic agents, is to match the degree of regulation to the actual danger each presents. Congress could delegate regulation of the nonmedical use of psychoactive drugs to the existing Alcohol, Drug Abuse, and Mental Health Administration (ADAMHA) with its three component institutes, the National Institute on Drug Abuse (NIDA), the National Institute on Alcohol Abuse and Alcoholism (NIAAA), and the National Institute on Mental Health (NIMH), much as it has delegated the regulation of therapeutic agents to the FDA. Under such a system, law enforcement responsibilities would remain with the Department of Justice. If removing the drug problem from politics is not yet feasible, the legislature should at least be guided, on a routine ongoing basis, by the best factual information from nongovernmental experts on psychoactive self-administered drugs, representing such fields as pharmacology, toxicology, medicine, psychology, psychiatry, criminology, law enforcement, and education.

Whatever degree of regulation is deemed, on balance, to be desirable for each drug, enforcement is essential for credibility and as a concrete expression of social disapproval. Enforcement has the desirable consequence of raising the black-market price of illicit drugs and making such drugs more difficult to obtain. The present situation, in which drug bazaars operate in full view of the police, seems intolerable in a society that claims to be ruled by law. It is unclear in such cases whether the police are corrupt or only demoralized, but it is noteworthy that corruption cuts through all strata of our governmental and private sectors, as numerous recent scandals have revealed. Thus, dealing effectively with the drug problem has broad implications for the rule of law in a democratic society.

Enforcement should be directed primarily at the higher levels of the distribution chain, but grandiose attempts to achieve a total interdiction of drug entry from abroad are a relatively poor investment. Advances in pharmaceutical chemistry are such that highly potent psychoactive drugs of every kind can be synthesized readily in clandestine laboratories, so the illicit market would adjust quickly even to a complete sealing of our borders, were that possible. A modest level of highly visible interdiction activities should probably be continued, if only for their symbolic value. But a massive shift of available funds is called for, from supply reduction to demand reduction (prevention education, treatment, and research). The federal drug war budget would be more cost-effective if the presently proposed ratio of supply reduction to demand reduction—71% to 29%—were reversed.

Enforcement will be most effective if coupled to community action, originating locally but supported by adequate governmental funding and other forms of assistance. Especially in some inner-city, ethnic minority communities, enforcement is presently weakened by a widespread perception that the police apparatus behaves as a hostile, alien, and often racist force invading the community.

We advise retaining, for the present—and enforcing—the legal prohibitions on the importation, manufacture, distribution, and sale of opiates, amphetamines, cocaine, marijuana, and dangerous hallucinogens like PCP. At the same time we suggest reducing the penalties for possession of small amounts of these drugs for personal use. Other differential enforcement options should be explored; without rewriting the laws, some laws could be enforced more strictly than others, according to the dangers of the particular drugs and the individual circumstances, as has been done for marijuana in some jurisdictions. Unfortunately, recent U.S. legislation compels judges to inflict minimum 5-year sentences even for small-time users who sell or share small amounts of drugs. We believe that criminalizing drug use per se is not productive, and we recommend that humane and constructive sentencing options be restored in drug cases.

It is sometimes argued that as marijuana seems to be the least harmful of the psychoactive drugs (excepting only caffeine), it could be legalized safely. However, the scientific evidence is still insufficient as to the potential magnitude of long-term harm, whereas the acute disturbance of psychomotor behavior is clearly dangerous under certain circumstances. It is not possible to predict with confidence what the result would be of vast expansion of the user goals, and public attitudes and other nonlegal controls over cannabis use become strong enough, it might eventually be possible to loosen the regulatory controls without risk of a major increase in use and the likely attendant problems. The experience of states like Oregon and Alaska, which have experimented with relaxing total prohibition, should be studied carefully with a view to understanding the effects on consumption. The much-vaunted Dutch system deserves study; however, it was not a sweeping drug legalization, but rather a specific reduction of penalties for use of cannabis, while penalties on trafficking in other drugs were made more severe.

We advise increased taxation on tobacco and alcohol—as is already being done in some jurisdictions—inasmuch as this is known to be an effective means of discouraging consumption. However, the resulting price increases must not be so great as to make an illicit market profitable. Uniformity of taxation across the country will be essential to avoid providing an incentive for interstate smuggling. One problem is preventing tax revenues from becoming incentives for government agencies to promote increased consumption. In the government monopoly retail sales model (another means of discouraging consumption), sales revenues themselves have this potential. Therefore, tax revenues (or sales profits) should go only to drug-related research, education, and treatment, not into the general treasury.

The degree of regulation on tobacco should be increased. Social pressures are reducing consumption, especially in the adult middle-class population, but sales to minors are still a problem. Federal and state laws abolishing cigarette vending machines would have a significant beneficial impact; with such machines accessible, laws forbidding sale to minors are completely ineffective, as shown in a recent study in the Washington, D.C., metropolitan area. Regulation on alcohol should also be increased. As with tobacco, there are many options short of total prohibition that would decrease consumption without stimulating a black market and associated criminal activities.

In principle, routine or random drug testing is justifiable for people in sensitive jobs, whose use of psychoactive drugs (whether licit or illicit) could endanger public safety. As the role of alcohol and other drugs in highway accidents is well documented, we believe that on-the-highway testing of drivers for alcohol on a nondiscriminatory basis at road blocks is justified as a protection for the innocent, and the U.S. Supreme Court has ruled that such tests are not unreasonable searches as specified in the U.S. Constitution. Moreover, lowering of the permissible legal limit (currently 0.10% in many jurisdictions) to 0.08% or 0.06% could have significant beneficial effects on highway safety. However, although urine testing for other drugs has improved greatly in accuracy, a significant problem in inferring psychomotor impairment from test results is that whereas breath or blood tests give a real-time result, urine tests provide only a record of past use and therefore cannot determine whether a person is under the influence of a drug at the time the sample is obtained. Further research is needed for the development of noninvasive analytical methods for estimating concentrations of psychoactive drugs in blood.

The North American demand for drugs is the driving force that creates major socioeconomic and political stress for the producer countries, especially in Latin America. The United States and Canada should assist these countries in reducing their economic dependence on drug exports. We should recognize and acknowledge that U.S. export of tobacco (especially to developing countries) undercuts any principled opposition to coca or opium export by other countries. A trade deficit does not justify our continuing in the role of major world supplier of a highly toxic and addictive substance.

Concerning demand reduction through prevention education, treatment, and research. All kinds of prevention efforts should be expanded as part of a broad strategy of demand reduction. Perhaps the most effective single factor in achieving this goal would be a social consensus on the appropriate circumstances and amounts of drug use. To change attitudes, beliefs, and values at all levels of a society in order to achieve the desired consensus requires carefully planned, internally consistent, and sustained long-term programs of education aimed at different ages, cultures, and socioeconomic groups.

The time is long overdue to recognize officially, publicize, and incorporate into common speech and legislation the fact that tobacco (nicotine) and alcohol are potentially hazardous addicting drugs. We need to expunge from the language the phrases "alcohol and drugs" and "tobacco and drugs." This is not mere semantic nitpicking; language influences the way we think.

The ban on TV advertising of cigarettes should be strengthened to prevent its circumvention by the prominent, supposedly incidental, display of cigarette product names during TV coverage of sports and other public events. Current U.S. and Canadian policies forbidding advertisements for distilled spirits on television were a useful first step, but there is not yet a well-founded policy on alcohol advertising in either country. A flood of beer advertisements has appeared, appealing primarily to youth, and linking beer to sports and sexual interests; and international comparisons show that alcoholism can occur just as readily in predominantly beer- or wine-drinking as in spirit-drinking countries. To date, scientific studies have failed either to prove or to exclude a short-term effect of alcohol advertising on consumption. This is not surprising, given the ubiquity of drinking in films, TV, and print media, which probably have a greater impact on attitudes and behavioral norms than commercial advertising does. Nevertheless, we regard a progressive restriction of the right to advertise addictive drugs as an important and desirable first step in a long-term process of altering the present public perception of these substances as ordinary consumer products.

Ideally, classroom programs should not be drug-specific but should deal more broadly with the hazards of using psychoactive drugs. Integrated prevention efforts involving both the schools and the community are desirable. Finally, effective education is honest education; the educational message has to be the real dangers of each drug to the user and to society. It is useless to merely warn of the dangers of being caught, and health personnel (not law officers) should carry the drug message into the classrooms.

For specific populations with exceptionally severe drug problems, such as American Indian communities, or low-income African-American or Hispanic groups in major urban centers, effective prevention may be impossible without creating opportunities for economic advancement within a licit social framework and for enhanced self-respect through reinforcement of traditional social and cultural values.

Treatment should be available to all who desire it; long waiting lists are counterproductive. Having enough clinics to meet the demand will require very large investments, but these could be cost-effective in the long run. Adequate funding should be furnished for treatment research to test innovative therapeutic approaches, provided the research design will permit rigorous evaluation. Programs should be developed for making humane contact with addicts as a first step to treatment; needle exchanges may serve a useful purpose in this regard.

We should consider developing and testing treatment programs that incorporate an initial phase in which the addict's drug of choice is made available. This approach might serve as a lure to bring some alienated users of heroin or cocaine into contact with health personnel, but it must be in the context of a genuine treatment and rehabilitation program. Many formidable practical difficulties would have to be overcome, not the least of which is to work out reliable methods of preventing the clinic itself from becoming a recruiting ground for new addicts.

A different medical approach is illustrated by methadone maintenance, in which opiate addicts are stabilized on a long-lasting, orally administered opiate. Many methadone programs—provided they employ adequate dosages—have achieved the successful social rehabilitation of a considerable fraction of addicts (about one-half to two-thirds), some of them continuing to take methadone, some eventually becoming opiate-free. Reduction of street crime by addicts enrolled in methadone programs is well documented. Experts agree that methadone maintenance should not be the sole treatment for heroin addicts, but this treatment modality is well enough established to warrant expansion to meet the need.

Some heroin addicts unquestionably benefit from drug-free residential environments (halfway houses). Extensive follow-up data show that some treatment is better than no treatment, but that a variety of therapeutic modalities is probably required to meet the needs of all heroin addicts. Although treatment programs of all types have achieved beneficial and humane results, there have also been practical difficulties, not the least of which is the relatively small proportion of addicts (especially to drugs other than opiates) who are treated during any given year. In addition, although some lessons can undoubtedly be learned from treatment experiences with heroin addicts, there is no agreement yet on appropriate treatment strategies for cocaine addicts.

The funding should be increased for basic and applied research on all aspects of the drug problem. We predict that neuro-chemical and neurobiologic research will yield new understandings about the mechanisms of the drug addictions. In the future, as in the past, such knowledge can be counted on to produce novel diagnostic, predictive, and therapeutic interventions. Specifically, learning more about the neurobiology and pharmacology of reward will lay a sounder basis for therapy. Testing for genetic vulnerability might permit better targeting of prevention efforts to those who are most vulnerable. Novel pharmacologic treatments that need to be developed include a long-acting agonist to supplant cocaine (analogous to methadone in opiate addiction), long-acting antagonists or immunization procedures, and drugs to facilitate detoxification and suppress craving. Finally, we need the patience to fund and carry out very long-term studies on the effectiveness of prevention education strategies; to do these studies well will be very expensive.

Concluding Remarks

An atmosphere of desperation, which seems to prevail today in the War on Drugs, is not conducive to sound policy decisions or effective legislation. Until calm and reason can prevail, it may be better to do nothing than to take actions rashly that will make matters worse. If we strike the right balance in drug policies, as we have suggested here, it should be possible to bring about a reduction in the demand for psychoactive drugs. A reduced demand for drugs offers the only real hope of eventually achieving, not a drug-free society, but one with substantially less drug abuse.

HAS THE TIME COME TO LEGALIZE
DRUGS?[4]

Most of the serious problems that the public tends to associate with illegal drug use in reality are caused directly or indirectly by drug prohibition. Let's assume the war on drugs was given up as the misguided enterprise it is. What would happen? The day after legalization went into effect, the streets of America would be safer. The drug dealers would be gone. The shootouts between drug dealers would end. Innocent bystanders no longer would be murdered. Hundreds of thousands of drug "addicts" would stop roaming the streets, shoplifting, mugging, breaking into homes in the middle of the night to steal, and dealing violently with those who happened to wake up. One year after prohibition was repealed, 1,600 innocent people who otherwise would have been dead at the hands of drug criminals would be alive.

Within days of prohibition repeal, thousands of judges, prosecutors, and police would be freed to catch, try, and imprison violent career criminals who commit 50 to 100 serious crimes per year when on the loose, including robbery, rape, and murder. For the first time in years, our overcrowded prisons would have room for them. Ultimately, repeal of prohibition would open up 75,000 jail cells. The day after repeal, organized crime would get a big pay cut—$80,000,000,000 a year.

How about those drug dealers who are the new role models for the youth of inner cities, with their designer clothes and Mercedes convertibles, always wearing a broad, smug smile that says crime pays? They snicker at the honest kids going to school or to work at the minimum wage. The day after repeal, the honest kids will have the last laugh. The dealers will be out of a job. The day after repeal, real drug education can begin and, for the first time in history, it can be honest. There will be no more need to prop up the failed war on drugs.

The year before repeal, 500,000 Americans would have died from illnesses related to overeating and lack of exercise, 390,000 from smoking, and 150,000 from drinking alcohol. About 3,000

[4]Reprint of an article by James Ostrowski, vice chairman of the New York County Lawyers Association Committee on Law Reform. Reprinted from *USA Today Magazine*, 119: 27–30. Jl. '90. Copyright © 1990 by the Society for the Advancement of Education.

would have died from cocaine, heroin, and marijuana combined, with many of these deaths the result of the lack of quality control in the black market. The day after repeal, cocaine, heroin, and marijuana, by and large, would do no harm to those who chose not to consume them. In contrast, the day before prohibition repeal, all Americans, whether or not they elected to use illegal drugs, were forced to endure the violence, street crime, erosion of civil liberties, corruption, and social and economic decay triggered by illegal drug use.

Today's war on drugs is immoral as well as impractical. It imposes enormous costs on large numbers of non-drug-abusing citizens in the failed attempt to save a relatively small group of hard-core drug abusers from themselves. It is immoral and absurd to force some people to bear costs so that others might be prevented from choosing to do harm to themselves. This crucial utilitarian sacrifice—so at odds with traditional American values—never has been, and never can be, justified. That is why the war on drugs must end and why it *will* be ended once the public comes to understand the truth about this destructive policy.

What about the economic impact of prohibition? First, take a common estimate of annual black market drug sales—$80,000,000,000. Because the black market price of drugs is inflated, at the very least, 10-fold over what the legal price would likely be, 90%, or about $70,000,000,000, constitutes an economic loss caused by prohibition. That is, the drug user and his dependents are deprived of the purchasing power of 90% of the money he spends on illegal drugs without any *net* benefit accruing to the economy as a whole. The added expenditure by the drug user pays for the dramatically increased costs of producing and selling illegal drugs. Large amounts of land, labor, and capital, not required in the legal drug market, are utilized in the illicit one. The high prices users pay for illegal drugs compensate dealers for their expenditure of these resources, as well as for the risk of violence and imprisonment they face. In a world of scarce prison resources, sending a drug offender to prison for one year is equivalent to freeing a violent criminal to commit 40 robberies, seven assaults, 110 burglaries, and 25 auto thefts.

Ironically, the economic loss to users under prohibition frequently is cited as a justification for prohibition. However, this harm is a major cost of prohibition, to be held against it in the debate over legalization. The total cost of drug-related law enforcement—courts, police, prisons, on all levels of government—

is about $10,000,000,000 each year. In a sense, each dollar spent on drug enforcement yields seven dollars in economic *loss*. That is, prohibition takes $10,000,000,000 from taxpayers and uses it to raise $80,000,000,000 for organized crime and drug dealers, impoverishing many users in the process. To pay for expensive black market drugs, poor users then victimize the taxpayers again by stealing $7,500,000,000 from them.

This $80,000,000,000 figure does not include a number of other negative economic consequences of prohibition that are difficult to estimate, such as the lost productivity of those who die as a result of prohibition, those in prison on drug convictions, and users who must "hustle" all day to pay for their drugs; the costs imposed by organized crime activities funded by narcotics profits; government and private funds spent on prohibition-related illnesses such as AIDS, hepatitis, and accidental overdose; and the funds spent on private security to fight drug-related crime.

Another financial toll merits special mention—the negative impact of prohibition on the economic viability of inner cities and their inhabitants. Prohibition-related violence and property crime raise costs, make loans and insurance difficult or impossible to secure, and make it difficult to attract skilled workers. Prohibition lures some workers away from legitimate businesses and into the black market, where salaries are astronomically higher. As long as a black market in illegal drugs thrives in the inner cities, it is difficult to see how they ever can become economically viable.

The fatal flaw in the policy of prohibition is that those who need to be protected most—hard-core users—are those least likely to be deterred by laws against drugs. For these individuals, drug use is one of the highest values in life. They will take great risks, pay exorbitant prices, and violate the law in pursuit of drugs. Further, it is naive to think that prohibition relieves prospective or even moderate drug users of the need to make responsible decisions with respect to illegal drugs. It is too easy and inexpensive to obtain a few batches of crack or heroin to claim that prohibition obviates individual choice. Consumer preference—not law enforcement—is the likely explanation for the existence of 20,000,000 marijuana smokers, but only 500,000 heroin users. If 20,000,000 people sought heroin, the black market would meet that demand, perhaps with synthetic substitutes, just as it met the enormous demand for alcohol in the 1920's. Prohibition is a comforting illusion at best.

Perhaps the most telling indicator of the ineffectiveness of U.S. drug laws is their failure to reduce the over-all use of illegal substances. On a per capita basis, the use of narcotics was no more prevalent before prohibition than it is today, and the use of cocaine is more widespread than when it was legally available. In 1915, the year the first national control laws became effective, there were about 200,000 regular narcotics users and only 20,000 regular cocaine users. Today, there are about 500,000 regular heroin users and 2,000,000 regular cocaine users. (Opium and morphine essentially have been driven out of circulation by the more profitable heroin. Prohibition has not reduced use, but it has made narcotics more powerful.) Thus, with a population more than twice what it was in 1915, the percentage of Americans using narcotics has remained the same, while cocaine use has increased by more than 4,000%. Seventy years of intensive law enforcement efforts have failed to reduce drug use measurably.

The failure of drug control should not be surprising. During Prohibition, drinkers switched from beer and wine to hard liquor, often of dubious quality, resulting in a drastic increase in deaths from alcohol poisoning. Whether Prohibition actually reduced total consumption is disputed, but it *is* known that its repeal did not lead to an explosive increase in drinking. More recently, in those states that have decriminalized marijuana, no substantial increase in use has occurred. When the Netherlands decriminalized marijuana in 1978, use actually declined.

Common sense indicates that illegal drugs always will be readily available. Prison wardens can not keep drugs out of their own institutions—an important lesson for those who would turn this country into a prison to stop drug use. Police officers regularly are caught using, selling, and *stealing* drugs. How are these people going to lead a war on drugs?

Drug money corrupts law enforcement officials. Corruption is a major problem in drug enforcement because drug agents are given tremendous power over desperate people in possession of large amounts of cash. Drug corruption charges have been leveled against FBI agents, police officers, prison guards, U.S. Customs inspectors, even prosecutors. In 1986, in New York City's 77th Precinct, 12 police officers were arrested for stealing and selling drugs. Miami's problem is worse. In June, 1986, seven officers there were indicted for using their jobs to run a drug operation that used murders, threats, and bribery. Add to that two dozen other cases of corruption in the last three years in

Miami alone. We must question a policy that so frequently turns police officers into criminals.

Civil Liberties Threatened

Drug hysteria also has created an atmosphere in which long-cherished rights are discarded whenever narcotics are concerned. Urine-testing, roadblocks, routine strip searches, school locker searches without probable cause, preventive detention, and non-judicial forfeiture of property are routine weapons in the war on drugs. These governmental intrusions into our most personal activities are the natural and necessary consequence of drug prohibition. It is no accident that a law review article entitled "Crackdown: The Emerging 'Drug Exception' to the Bill of Rights" was published in a law journal in 1987. Explaining why drug prohibition, by its very nature, threatens civil liberties, law professor Randy Barnett notes that drug offenses differ from violent crimes in that there rarely is a complaining witness to a drug transaction. Because sales are illegal, but their participants are willing, the transactions are hidden from police view. Thus, to be at all effective, drug agents must intrude into the innermost private lives of *suspected* drug criminals.

Dangerous precedents are tolerated in the war on drugs, but they represent a permanent increase in government power for all purposes. The tragedy is how cheaply our rights have been sold. Our society was once one in which the very thought of men and women being strip-searched and forced to urinate in the presence of witnesses was revolting. That now seems like a long time ago. All of this stems from a policy that simply does not work, since it is prohibition itself that causes the very problems that make these extreme measures seem necessary to a befuddled public.

In spite of the greatest anti-drug enforcement effort in U.S. history, the drug problem is worse than ever. What should be done now—get tougher in the war on drugs, imprison middle-class drug users, use the military, impose the death penalty for drug dealing, shoot down unmarked planes entering the U.S.? The *status quo* is intolerable, as everyone agrees. However, there are only two alternatives—further escalate the war on drugs or legalize them. Once the public grasps the consequences of escalation, legalization may win out by default.

Escalating the war on drugs is doomed to fail, as it did under Pres. Richard M. Nixon, Gov. Nelson A. Rockefeller in New York, and Pres. Ronald Reagan. It is confronted by a host of seemingly intractable problems: lack of funds, prison space, and political will to put middle-class users in jail, and the sheer impossibility of preventing consenting adults in a free society from engaging in extremely profitable transactions involving tiny amounts of illegal drugs.

Yet, none of these factors ultimately explains why escalating the war on drugs wouldn't work. Failure is guaranteed because the black market thrives on the war on drugs and benefits from any intensification of it. At best, increased enforcement simply boosts the black market price, encouraging suppliers to supply more drugs. The publicized conviction of a dealer, by instantly creating a vacancy in the lucrative drug business, has the same effect as hanging up a help-wanted sign saying, "Drug dealer needed—$5,000 a week to start—exciting work."

Furthermore, there is a real danger that escalating the war on drugs would squander much of the nation's wealth and freedom, causing enormous social disruption. No limit is yet in sight to the amount of money and new enforcement powers that committed advocates of prohibition will demand before giving up on that approach.

As author Thomas Sowell writes, "policies are judged by their consequences, but crusades are judged by how good they make the crusaders feel." So, the question must be: do drug laws cause more harm than good? Drug laws greatly increase the price of illegal substances, often forcing users to steal to get the money to obtain them. Although difficult to estimate, the black market prices of heroin and cocaine appear to be about 100 times greater than their pharmaceutical prices. For example, a hospital-dispensed dose of morphine, a drug from which heroin is derived relatively easily, costs only pennies; legal cocaine costs about $20 per ounce. It frequently is estimated that at least 40% of all property crime in the U.S. is committed by drug users so they can maintain their habits. That amounts to about 4,000,000 crimes per year and $7,500,000,000 in stolen property.

Supporters of prohibition traditionally have used drug-related crime as a simplistic argument for enforcement: stop drug use to halt such criminal acts. They even have exaggerated the amount of such crime in the hopes of demonstrating a need for larger budgets and greater powers. In recent years, however, the more astute prohibitionists have noticed that drug-related crime is, in fact, drug-*law*-related. Thus, in many cases, they have begun to argue that, even if drugs were legal and thus relatively inexpensive, users still would commit crimes simply because they are criminals at heart. The fact is, while some researchers have questioned the causal connection between illegal drugs and street crime, many studies over a long period have confirmed what every inner-city dweller already knows: users steal to get the money to buy expensive illegal drugs. Moreover, prohibition also stimulates crime by criminalizing users of illegal drugs, thus creating disrespect for the law; forcing users into daily contact with professional criminals, which often leads to arrest and prison records that make legitimate employment difficult to obtain; discouraging legitimate employment because of the need to "hustle" for drug money; encouraging young people to become criminals by creating an extremely lucrative black market in drugs; destroying, through drug crime, the economic viability of low-income neighborhoods, leaving young people fewer alternatives to working in the black market; and removing the settling of drug-related disputes from the legal process, creating a context of violence for the buying and selling of narcotics.

In addition, every property crime committed by a drug user is potentially a violent one. Many victims are beaten and severely injured, and 1,600 are murdered each year. In 1988, a 16-year-old boy murdered 39-year-old Eli Wald of Brooklyn, father of a baby girl, taking $200 to buy crack. Another New York City crack user murdered five people in an eight-day period to get the money to buy crack.

Prohibition also causes what the media and police misname "drug-related violence." This is really *prohibition*-related violence, and includes all the random shootings and murders associated with black market transactions—rip-offs, eliminating the competition, and killing informers and suspected informers. The President's Commission on Organized Crime estimates a total of about 70 drug-market murders yearly in Miami alone. Based on that figure and FBI data, a reasonable nationwide estimate would be at least 750 such murders each year. Recent estimates from New York and Washington suggest an even higher figure. Those who doubt that prohibition is responsible for this violence need only note the absence of violence in the legal drug market. For example, there is no violence associated with the production, distribution, and sale of alcohol. Such violence was ended by the repeal of Prohibition.

Health and Social Consequences

Because there is no quality control in the black market, prohibition also kills by making drug use more dangerous. Illegal drugs contain poisons, are of uncertain potency, and are injected with dirty needles. Many deaths are caused by infections, accidental overdoses, and poisoning. At least 3,500 people each year will die from AIDS caused by using unsterile needles, a greater number than the combined death toll from cocaine and heroin. These casualties include the sexual partners and children of intravenous drug users. Drug-related AIDS is almost exclusively the result of drug prohibition. Users inject drugs rather than taking them in tablet form because tablets are expensive; go to "shooting galleries" to avoid arrests for possessing drugs and needles; and share needles because these implements are illegal and thus difficult to obtain. In Hong Kong, where needles are legal, there are *no* cases of drug-related AIDS.

As many as 2,400 of the 3,000 deaths attributed to heroin and cocaine use each year—80%—actually are caused by black market factors. For example, many heroin deaths are the result of an allergic reaction to the street mixture of the drug, while 30% are caused by infections. The attempt to protect users from themselves has backfired, as it did during Prohibition. The drug laws have succeeded only in making use much more dangerous and in driving it underground, out of the reach of moderating social and medical influences.

Drug prohibition has had devastating effects on inner-city minority communities. A poorly educated young person in the inner city now has three choices—welfare, a low-wage job, or the glamorous and high-profit drug business. It is no wonder that large numbers of ghetto youth have gone into drug dealing. How can a mother maintain authority over a 16-year-old son who pays the rent out of his petty cash? How can a teacher persuade students to study hard, when dropouts drive BMW's? The profits from prohibition make a mockery of the work ethic and of family authority.

A related problem is that prohibition also forces users to come into contact with people of real criminal intent. For all the harm that alcohol and tobacco do, one does not have to deal with criminals to use those substances. Prohibition drags the drug user into a criminal culture. Once accustomed to breaking the law by using drugs and to dealing with criminals, it is hard for the user, and especially the dealer, to maintain respect for other laws. Honesty, respect for private property, and similar marks of a law-abiding community are further casualties. When the huge illicit profits and violence of the illegal-drug business permeate a neighborhood, it ceases to be a functioning community. The consequences range from the discouraging of legitimate businesses to disdain for education and violence that makes mail carriers and ambulance drivers afraid to enter housing complexes.

Drug switching is another issue that any regime of control must face. What is the point of attempting to limit access to certain drugs, when the user merely turns to other, more dangerous ones? For example, opium use in China may or may not have been reduced vastly, but tranquilizers and sedative pills have been used widely in China, and they are easily available on the market. Furthermore, two-thirds of all Chinese men now smoke cigarettes. Examples of drug switching abound. When narcotics first were outlawed, many middle-class users switched to barbiturates and later to sedatives and tranquilizers. The laws did nothing to terminate this group of addicts—they simply changed the drug to which the users were addicted. Marijuana smoking first became popular as a replacement for alcohol during Prohibition. Similarly, it is common for alcoholics trying to stay sober to take up smoking instead. Recently, it has been reported that some intravenous heroin users have switched to smoking crack to avoid the risk of AIDS.

In both America and England, narcotics use peaked and then declined long before national prohibition was adopted. Today, in spite of the availability of alcohol, problem drinkers are considered to compose only about 10% of the population. In spite of the fact that marijuana can be purchased on virtually any street corner in some cities, only about 10% of the population has done so in the last month, according to the National Institute on Drug Abuse. Significantly, the figures for cocaine are quite similar, despite the drug's reputation for addictiveness. About 20,000,000 have tried the drug, but only 25% of that number have used it in the last month and only about 10% are considered addicts. It bears remembering that, for cocaine, the sample population is drawn from that segment of the population already interested enough in drugs to break the law to obtain them. Thus, an even lower percentage of repeat users could be expected from the over-all population under legalization. These numbers support Stanton Peele's claim in the *Journal of Drug Issues* that "cocaine use is now described [incorrectly] as presenting the same kind of lurid monomania that pharmacologists once claimed only heroin could produce."

Drugs have a direct, powerful effect on human consciousness

and emotions. Drug laws, on the other hand, have only an occasional impact on the user. For the many users who continue to take drugs even after being penalized by law, the subjective benefits of drugs outweigh the costs of criminal penalties.

Even without criminal sanctions, many users continue to take drugs despite the severe physical penalties these substances impose on their bodies. Again, they simply consider the psychic benefit of drug use more important than the physical harm. The fact is, drugs motivate some people—those who most need protection from them—more than any penalties a civilized society can impose, and even more than what some less-than-civilized societies have imposed. The undeniable seductiveness of drugs, usually considered a justification for prohibition, thus actually argues for legalization. The law simply can not deter millions of people deeply attracted to drugs; it only can increase the social costs of drug use greatly.

As for drug sellers, they are simply more highly motivated than those who are paid to stop them. They make enormous profits—much more than they could make at legal jobs—and are willing to risk death and long prison terms to do so. They are professionals, on the job 24 hours a day, and able to pour huge amounts of capital into their enterprises. They are willing to murder competitors, informers, and police as needed.

Drug dealers have 10 times as much money to work with as do those attempting to stop them. Drug enforcement suffers from all the inefficiencies of bureaucracies, while dealers are entrepreneurs, unrestrained by arbitrary bureaucratic rules and procedures. They do what needs to be done based on their own judgment and, unlike drug enforcers, are not restrained by the law. The public has the false impression that drug enforcers are highly innovative, continually devising new schemes to catch dealers. Actually, the reverse is true. The dealers, like successful businessmen, are usually one step ahead of the "competition."

Legalization has been justified on both philosophical and pragmatic grounds. Some argue that it is no business of government what individuals do with their bodies and minds. I take no position on this philosophical issue. Rather, I argue on purely practical grounds that drug prohibition has been an extremely costly failure. I challenge advocates of prohibition to rise above the level of platitudes and good intentions and to present hard evidence that prohibition, *in actual practice*, does more good than harm.

U.S. DRUG POLICY: A BAD EXPORT[5]

Almost everyone seems to agree that the "drug problem" is now a major international issue. U.S. relations with several Latin American countries are seriously strained because of these countries' inability to control the drug trade. Political leaders across the spectrum are advocating U.S. military involvement in suppression efforts; U.S. troops have even been deployed abroad in an effort to disrupt the production and export of cocaine from Bolivia.

At home political figures endorse increasingly repressive measures to try to stamp out drug use. There are calls for more widespread drug testing, increasingly powerful investigative tools for drug enforcement agencies, and greater expenditures on all aspects of drug enforcement.

The political tide is now so strong that drug policy, perhaps more than any other domain of public policy, has been captured by its own rhetoric and effectively immunized from critical examination. Clearly the time has come for a more rational discussion of the drug problem—one that attempts to distinguish the problems of drug abuse, on the one hand, from the problems that result from drug prohibition policies, on the other.

Obsessed with the need to control drug trafficking, governments have enacted and enforced increasingly harsh criminal penalties regulating virtually every aspect of drug use with little regard for the costs imposed by these laws. These costs can be measured not just in tax dollars, but also in individual lives, personal liberties, political stability, social welfare, and moral well-being. Federal and state governments spend several billion dollars each year to enforce the increasingly repressive laws inside the United States. And U.S. diplomats press governments around the world to follow the American lead and enact their own harsh measures against drug use and trafficking. Meanwhile, there is no indication that the magnitude of the worldwide drug abuse problem is declining. Indeed, there is good reason to believe that the

[5]Reprint of an article by Ethan A. Nadelmann, assistant professor of politics and public affairs at the Woodrow Wilson School of Public and International Affairs at Princeton University. Reprinted by permission of *Foreign Policy*, 70: 83–108. Sp '88. Copyright © 1988 by *Foreign Policy*.

current American approach actually may be exacerbating most aspects of what is commonly identified as the drug problem.

Sixty years ago, most Americans demonstrated a clear ability to distinguish between the problems of alcoholism and alcohol abuse and the costs imposed by the prohibition laws. The debate between proponents and opponents of Prohibition ultimately revolved around conflicting interpretations of what both sides regarded as a cost-benefit analysis. Unfortunately, today few Americans demonstrate any aptitude for distinguishing between the problems of drug abuse and those occasioned by the drug prohibition laws. Yet so much of what Americans typically identify as part and parcel of the drug problem falls within the latter, not the former, category.

No doubt most people resist thinking about the drug problem in terms of the Prohibition analogy because the notion of repealing the current drug laws is not regarded as a viable policy option. Indeed, the very suggestion of such a possibility quickly conjures up images of an America transformed into a modern-day Sodom and Gomorrah. Yet there are powerful reasons to at least attempt a reasoned analysis of the costs and benefits of current drug policies. First, an optimal drug policy must aim to minimize not just drug abuse but also the costs to society imposed by drug control measures. Second, there are numerous alternatives to current policies, among which the libertarian vision of unrestricted access to all drugs is only one and certainly the most radical. Third, there is good reason to believe that repealing many of the current drug laws would not lead to a dramatic rise in drug abuse, especially if intelligent alternative measures were implemented.

All public policies create beneficiaries and victims, both intended and unintended. When a policy results in a disproportionate magnitude of unintended victims, there is good reason to reevaluate its assumptions. In the case of drug prohibition policies, the intended beneficiaries are those individuals who would become drug abusers but for the existence and enforcement of the drug laws. The intended victims are those who traffic in illicit drugs and suffer the legal consequences. The unintended beneficiaries, conversely, are the drug producers and traffickers who profit handsomely from the illegality of the market while avoiding arrest by the authorities and violence by other criminals. Each of these three categories is readily recognizable. The unintended victims of drug prohibition policies, however, are rarely recognized as such. Indeed, they are most typically portrayed as the victims of the unintended beneficiaries—that is, the drug traffickers—when in fact the drug prohibition policies are the principal cause of their victimization.

In certain respects, the Latin American countries are among the principal unintended beneficiaries of U.S. drug policies. The international demand for illegal drugs such as marijuana and cocaine has proved to be an economic boon for Latin America. This has been especially true for the main source countries— Bolivia, Colombia, and Peru. Much, but by no means all, of the economic benefit has derived from the market's illegality. Government repression of the market has had the same effect as a huge tax except that the revenue is collected not by governments but by illicit sellers. Hundreds of thousands of farm families, primarily in Bolivia, Colombia, and Peru, have earned far more from growing coca, the agricultural raw material for cocaine, than they would have from growing any other crop. The same is true of tens of thousands of marijuana growers in Belize, Colombia, Jamaica, and Mexico. Others involved in refining, transporting, or protecting the illegal product have supplemented or replaced meager incomes earned in the legitimate economy. Countless corrupt officials likewise have pocketed money from the illicit trade. In addition to these groups that benefit directly, significant sectors of the population in several Latin American countries have benefited indirectly from the trickle-down effects of the trade.

Because the market is illicit, it is impossible to offer any but the most speculative estimates of its total value to Latin Americans. The Bolivian government has estimated that the cocaine trade brings about $600 million per year into its economy, a figure equal to the country's total legal export income. Peru, which produces about the same amount of cocaine, probably earns a similar amount although it accounts for a lesser proportion of its total exports. In both these countries, a large proportion of the coca money is distributed among the growers and other low-level participants in the market. In Colombia, there are fewer growers but more people involved in support areas of the business such as transport and security. All told, cocaine and marijuana exports probably generate a minimum of $2 billion a year in foreign currency for Latin Americans—excluding the additional billions invested outside the continent.

If it is fair to say that some Latin Americans are the unintended economic beneficiaries of U.S. and international drug prohibition policies, it is equally valid to identify others as the unintended political and social victims of those policies. The recent dramatic increases in cocaine smoking among the youth of Bolivia, Colombia, and Peru are one consequence. Even more ominous, the drug market's huge size, combined with its illegality, has generated tremendous corruption, lawlessness, and violence throughout Latin America. It is not that these evils did not exist before the boom in drug trafficking, but that they have mushroomed in scope and magnitude. Government officials ranging from common police officers to judges to cabinet ministers have been offered bribes many times their annual government salaries, and often for doing nothing more than looking the other way. Inducing cooperation has been the threat of violence if the bribes are not accepted. In addition, the limits on what can be bought with corruption have evaporated. Supreme court judges, high-ranking police and military officials, and cabinet ministers are no longer above such things.

The ultimate degree of corruption is when government officials take the initiative in perpetrating crimes. This also has happened throughout much of Latin America. Police officers no longer just accept bribes or extort from traffickers but engage in trafficking themselves. Provincial mayors and governors enter into partnerships with full-time drug traffickers. And even military officers, who in at least a few countries traditionally have shunned drug corruption, have succumbed to the temptation of cocaine dollars. This has occurred not just in the major drug-producing countries but throughout the continent as well. No country, from Cuba to Chile, seems to be immune.

Perhaps even worse than the corruption of governments has been the growth in the power of criminal groups. The two cannot be disentangled from one another, of course, but they are distinct. In many Latin American countries drug-trafficking organizations, rather than the government, now represent the ultimate power in portions of a country if not the country as a whole. Government officials who oppose this extralegal power know that ultimately the government cannot protect them or their families. In the United States, only one federal judge has been killed in a hundred years, and it is almost unheard of for a federal prosecutor to be killed. Even police rarely need to fear the vengeance of those they arrest. In Latin America, however, not just police but also prosecutors and judges have been killed by the dozens. In Colombia, drug traffickers have killed a minister of justice, a

Supreme Court justice, an attorney general, and a chief of the narcotics police. In the final analysis, the monumental scope of the illicit drug traffic, created largely by U.S. demand and the illegality of the market, has eroded the ultimate authority of the state as a symbol and enforcer of law and order in many Latin American countries.

What can Latin American countries do? From their perspective, the most sensible solution to drug-related corruption and criminal activity would be international legalization of the marijuana and cocaine markets. Their drug problems, after all, stem almost entirely from the illegality of the market. If it were legal, it would function not unlike the international markets in legal substances such as liquor, coffee, and tobacco. It would be regulated to varying degrees by the governments of both producing and consuming countries; the individual and corporate participants in the market would pay taxes and duties; consumers would have available more accurate information on the products themselves; and the governments would spare themselves the exorbitant costs of trying to enforce the drug prohibition laws. No doubt companies already specializing in the production and marketing of alcohol, coffee, and tobacco would play a major role in this business as well. There probably would be some market adjustment. For example, foreign suppliers, especially of marijuana, might yield a sizable share of their market to new suppliers within the United States. And there undoubtedly would also be a certain amount of smuggling, largely to avoid duties and other customs regulations. But its incentives and scale probably would be most similar to those that attend the legal substance markets today.

The social and political benefits would be critical. Levels of corruption, violence, and lawlessness would decline dramatically. Latin American governments no longer would be placed in the awkward situation of trying to destroy the livelihoods of hundreds of thousands of campesinos. Radical guerrilla groups such as Peru's Sendero Luminoso (Shining Path), which have gained political support from their attacks on U.S.-sponsored antidrug programs, would lose some of their appeal. Other guerrilla and terrorist groups, such as Colombia's FARC (Colombian Revolutionary Armed Forces) and M-19, which have profited from their involvement in the illicit drug trade, would lose a major source of funding. And governments would be able to reassert some degree of control over regions of their countries that are now dominated by powerful *narcotraficantes*.

Today many drug specialists, including Drug Enforcement Administration chief John Lawn, concede that stopping the flow of drugs is impossible. They know that whenever drug control efforts succeed in cracking down on one source country or disrupting one major trafficking route, another soon emerges in its place. International drug enforcement efforts are thus justified on the grounds that they are essential in limiting consumption by keeping the retail street price of the substances as high as possible. But the price is, in fact, influenced little, if at all, by changes in drug enforcement efforts in the supplying countries. In 1987, for instance, average-grade marijuana reportedly was selling for $6–$11 per pound at Colombian beaches and airstrips. On arrival in the United States, its worth increased approximately ninetyfold, to $550–$990 per pound. With respect to cocaine, the markup from Colombian airstrip to Miami wholesaler was only fivefold, from $3,600–$4,400 to $17,000–$22,000 per kilo. But unlike marijuana, which increases only three or four times in value from wholesale to retail, the ultimate value of a kilo of cocaine is $80,000–$120,000, for as much as a sevenfold markup.

Although the tremendous range in drug prices renders precise calculations impossible, estimated average prices indicate that the foreign price of marijuana is only slightly more than 1 per cent of its U.S. wholesale price and .5 per cent of the retail price paid by the U.S. consumer. The foreign price of cocaine is 20 per cent of the U.S. wholesale price but only about 4 per cent of the ultimate retail price. Consequently, even if substantial enforcement efforts were to quadruple or quintuple the foreign prices of these substances, there would be almost no price effect on the American consumer—and only in the case of cocaine would wholesalers be much affected. With respect to heroin, the irrelevance of source control efforts to the retail street price in the United States is even greater.

Limitations on the ultimate success of the international regime to control drug trafficking are best comprehended by comparing the drug regime with other international law enforcement regimes. In certain important respects the drug regime resembles other international law enforcement regimes, such as those that nearly eradicated piracy and slavery during the previous century or those established more recently that deal with counterfeit currency and airplane hijacking. In each case, the vast majority of governments ultimately recognized a mutual interest in not participating, directly or indirectly, in such illegal acts and in cooperating in their suppression. Moreover, each act has come to be regarded in international law as in some sense an international crime.

However, the drug regime differs from other international law enforcement regimes in at least two significant respects. First, despite rhetoric to the contrary, it lacks a deeply rooted moral consensus that the activity in question is wrong. Second, crimes that require limited resources and no particular expertise to commit, that are easily concealable, and that create no victims with an interest in notifying authorities are most likely to resist enforcement efforts. Each of these characteristics describes drug trafficking. For instance, unlike counterfeiting, no particular expertise is required to become a drug smuggler. Even in the United States, marijuana is grown profitably by tens of thousands of people with no more training than can be acquired in a local library. In the less developed countries where opium poppies, coca, and cannabis for foreign markets are grown and refined, hundreds of thousands of poorly educated farmers participate in the market. Nor does it require any special expertise to be a drug courier. The potential number of successful counterfeiters is an extremely small number; the potential number of successful drug traffickers is virtually infinite.

Most aspects of drug trafficking are easily concealable. The crops are often grown in inaccessible hinterlands and camouflaged with legitimate crops. Their transport to the United States is also exceedingly difficult to detect. The approximately 100 tons of cocaine exported from Latin America during each of the past few years constitute a small percentage of the total volume of exports. The private aircraft in which large shipments are typically transported are exceedingly difficult to interdict. There also are tremendous economic incentives to smuggle even very small amounts. An average profit for smuggling just 1, easily concealed, kilo of cocaine, after all, is $15,000. With temptation such as this, there is almost no limit to the number of individuals willing to transport 1 or 2 kilos on commercial aircraft.

Although the international slave trade, like the drug traffic, was driven by the prospect of higher profits than could be attained in legitimate commerce, it was a far more visible trade. Ships carrying slaves from Africa usually could be identified far more readily than the vessels that transport marijuana and cocaine today. Even more important, the purchasers of slaves had much more difficulty concealing their illegal "property" than do the ultimate customers of illicit drugs.

Finally, the victims of slavery, piracy, counterfeiting, and hi-

jacking are eager to have others know of their plight. But the
willing "victims" of the drug trade have no intention of notifying
the authorities. Drug trafficking, which involves willing buyers
and sellers, unlike the other targets of international law enforcement regimes, is an entirely consensual activity.

It can be argued, of course, that drug trafficking also creates
its own victims—in particular those who become dependent upon
the drugs and, less directly, those who suffer as a consequence of
others' abuse of drugs. The great difference, however, is that the
immediate victims of drug trafficking, unlike the victims of other
international crimes, are self-chosen in that their initial steps on
the road to victimization are consensual ones.

In the case of each successful international law enforcement
regime, the activity could not be effectively suppressed until a
broad consensus had developed across diverse societies that
viewed the activity as morally noxious. Such a consensus in regard
to the immorality of piracy developed throughout much of the
world during the 18th century. A similar consensus evolved with
respect to slavery during the 19th century. The reason these and
subsequent consensuses underlying other international law enforcement regimes evolved was essentially the same: the activity
itself directly victimized innocents. The basic problem of the antidrug regime, and for that matter of the efforts in the early part of
this century to create antialcohol and antiprostitution regimes,
has been the absence of just such a consensus. For all the undeniable victims of these vices, many others involved in the activities
were not, and did not perceive themselves as, victims. Thus despite the efforts of the United States and some other governments
to create the veneer of an international moral consensus on the
drug issue, a true consensus does not exist—and will not be
attained—either within the United States or around the world.

Comparing Risks

The case for legalization is particularly convincing when the
risks inherent in alcohol and tobacco use are compared with those
associated with illicit drug use. Both in Latin America and in the
United States, the health costs exacted by illicit drug use pale in
comparison with those associated with tobacco and alcohol use. In
September 1986, the Department of Health and Human Services
reported that in the United States, alcohol was a contributing
factor in 10 per cent of work-related injuries, 40 per cent of

suicide attempts, and also 40 per cent of the approximately 46,000 traffic deaths in 1983. That same year the total cost of alcohol abuse to American society was estimated at more than $100 billion. An estimated 18 million Americans are currently reported to be either alcoholics or alcohol abusers. Alcohol has been identified as the direct cause of 80,000 to 100,000 deaths annually and as a contributing factor in an additional 100,000 deaths. The health costs of tobacco use in the United States and elsewhere are different but of similar magnitude. In the United States alone in 1984, more than 320,000 deaths were attributed to tobacco consumption. All of the health costs of marijuana, cocaine, and heroin combined amount to only a fraction of those of either of the two licit substances.

According to the National Council on Alcoholism, only 3,562 people were known to have died in 1985 from use of all illegal drugs combined. Logic would dictate that, if any substances warrant criminal sanction for health reasons, they are alcohol and tobacco, which are used by 140,000,000 and 50,000,000 people respectively. However, most people seem to believe that there is something fundamentally different about alcohol and tobacco that legitimates the legal distinction between those two substances and the illicit ones. The most common distinction is based on the assumption that the illicit drugs are more dangerous than the licit ones. Cocaine, heroin, the various hallucinogens, and, to a lesser extent, marijuana, are widely perceived as, in the words of the President's Commission on Organized Crime, "inherently destructive to mind and body." They are also believed to be more addictive and more likely to cause dangerous and violent behavior than are alcohol and tobacco. All use of illicit drugs is typically equated with drug abuse. In short, the distinction between use and abuse of psychoactive substances that most people recognize with respect to alcohol is not regarded as relevant in the case of illicit substances.

Many Americans also make the fallacious assumption that the government would not criminalize certain psychoactive substances if they were not in fact dangerous. They then jump to the conclusion that any use of those substances is a form of abuse. The government, in its efforts to discourage people from using illicit drugs, has encouraged and perpetuated these misconceptions not just in its rhetoric but also in its purportedly educational materials. Only by reading between the lines can the fact be discerned that the vast majority of Americans who have used illicit drugs have done so in moderation, that relatively few have suffered negative short-term consequences, and given available evidence, that few are likely to suffer long-term harm.

The evidence is most persuasive with respect to marijuana. The National Narcotics Intelligence Consumers Committee, an interagency body that coordinates drug-related intelligence, did not include marijuana-related deaths in its June 1987 report, apparently because so few occur. Nor is marijuana strongly identified as a dependence-causing substance. The dangers associated with cocaine, heroin, and hallucinogens certainly are greater, but not nearly as great as most people seem to think. Consider the case of cocaine. In 1986 the National Institute on Drug Abuse (NIDA) reported that more than 20 million Americans had tried cocaine in 1985, that 12.2 million had consumed it at least once during that year, and that nearly 5.8 million had used it within the past month. It should be noted that the NIDA survey did not include persons residing in military or student dormitories, prison inmates, or the homeless.

Although a figure for weekly cocaine consumption among the entire survey population is unavailable, NIDA has compiled such information with regard to 18–25-year-olds: 250,000 had used it on the average weekly; 2.5 million had used it within the past month; 5.3 million had used it within the past year; and 8.2 million Americans in this age group had ever used cocaine. It could be inferred from these figures that a quarter of a million young Americans were potential problem users. It could also be determined that only 3 per cent of those 18–25-year-olds who had ever tried the drug fell into that category, and that only 10 per cent of those who had used cocaine monthly were at risk.

All of this is not to say that cocaine is not a potentially dangerous drug, especially when it is injected or smoked in the form of "crack." But there is also evidence that most cocaine users do not get into trouble with the drug. So much of the media attention has focused on the small percentage of cocaine users who become addicted that the popular perception of how most people use cocaine has become badly distorted. In one survey of high school seniors' drug use, the researchers questioned those who had used cocaine recently as to whether they had ever tried to stop using cocaine and found that they could not. Only 3.8 per cent responded affirmatively, in contrast with the almost 7 per cent of marijuana smokers who said they had tried to stop and found they could not and the 18 per cent of cigarette smokers who answered similarly. Although a survey of adult users probably would reveal a higher proportion of cocaine addicts, evidence such as this suggests that only a small percentage of people who use cocaine end up having a problem with it. In this respect, most Americans differ from monkeys, who have demonstrated in tests that they will starve themselves to death if provided with unlimited cocaine.

With respect to the hallucinogens such as LSD and psilocybin, their potential for addiction is virtually nil. The dangers arise primarily from using them irresponsibly on individual occasions. Although many of those who have used one or another of the hallucinogens have experienced "bad trips," far more have reported positive experiences and very few have suffered any long-term harm.

Perhaps no drugs are regarded with as much horror as the opiates, and in particular heroin, which is a more concentrated form of morphine. There is no question that heroin is potentially highly addictive. But despite the popular association of heroin use with the most down-and-out inhabitants of urban ghettos, heroin causes relatively little physical harm to the human body and certainly far less than alcohol and tobacco. That is one reason many American doctors in the 19th and early 20th centuries saw opiate addiction as preferable to alcoholism and prescribed the former as treatment for the latter when abstinence did not seem a realistic option. It is both insightful and important to think about the illicit drugs in the same way as alcohol and tobacco. Like tobacco, many of the illicit substances are highly addictive, but many people can consume them on a regular basis for decades without any demonstrable harm. Like alcohol, most of the substances can be, and are, used by most consumers in moderation with little in the way of harmful effects; but like alcohol they also lend themselves to abuse by a minority of users who become addicted or otherwise harm themselves or others as a consequence. And like both the legal substances, the psychoactive effects of each of the illegal drugs vary greatly from one person to another. To be sure, the pharmacology of the substance is important, as is its purity and the manner in which it is consumed. But much also depends upon not just the physiology and psychology of the consumers but their expectations of the drug, their social milieu, and the broader cultural environment—what the Harvard University psychiatrist Norman Zinberg has called the "set and setting" of the drug. These factors might change dramatically, albeit in indeterminate ways, were the illicit drugs made legally available.

Clearly, then, there is no valid basis for distinguishing between alcohol and tobacco, on the one hand, and most of the illicit substances, on the other, as far as their relative dangers are concerned. However, even many of those who acknowledge this fact insist that there is another distinction, a moral one, that justifies the different legal treatments of the various drugs. But when this distinction is subjected to reasoned analysis, it also quickly disintegrates. Once the fact that there is nothing immoral about drinking alcohol or smoking tobacco for nonmedicinal reasons is acknowledged, it becomes difficult to condemn on moral grounds consumption of marijuana, cocaine, and other substances. The "moral" condemnation of some substances and not others is revealed as little more than a prejudice in favor of some drugs and against others. It could be argued, of course, that morality is really nothing more than the prejudices of the majority. But to the extent that it is defined as something more than that, there can be no legitimate reason for distinguishing on moral grounds between alcohol and tobacco use and the use of illicit substances.

The same false distinction is drawn even more severely when it comes to those who provide the psychoactive substances to users and abusers alike. If degrees of immorality were measured by the levels of harm caused by a dealer's products, the "traffickers" in tobacco and alcohol would be vilified as the most evil of all substance purveyors. That they are perceived instead as respectable, even important, members of the community while providers of the no more dangerous illicit substances are punished with long prison sentences says much about the prejudices of most Americans with respect to psychoactive substances but little about the morality or immorality of their activities.

Although a direct moral distinction cannot be drawn between the licit and the illicit psychoactive substances, it is possible to point to a different kind of moral justification for the drug laws. Those laws can be viewed as embodying a paternalistic obligation to protect those who cannot protect themselves from succumbing to their own weaknesses. If the illegal drugs were legally available, most people would either abstain from using them or else use them responsibly and in moderation. A small minority who lacked sufficient self-restraint, however, would end up harming themselves if the substances were more readily available. Therefore, it is argued, the majority has a moral obligation to deny its members legal access to certain substances because of the foibles of the minority. This obligation presumably applies most strongly when children are included among the minority.

This argument, at least in principle, seems to provide the strongest moral justification for the drug laws. But ultimately the moral quality of laws must be judged not by how those laws are intended to work in principle but by how they function in fact. When laws intended to reflect a moral obligation cause new harms of a different kind, arguably even greater in impact, there is a need to re-evaluate them and inquire whether those laws have become in some sense immoral.

Drug-Policy Alternatives

There are those who acknowledge the greater harms caused by alcohol and tobacco but who justify the criminalization of other substances on the ground that two wrongs do not make a third wrong right. The logic of their argument, however, ultimately crumbles when the costs of the drug laws are considered. There is little question that if the production, sale, and possession of alcohol and tobacco were criminalized, the health costs associated with their use and abuse could be reduced. But most Americans do not believe that criminalizing the alcohol and tobacco markets would be a good idea. Their opposition stems largely from two beliefs: that adult Americans have the right to choose what substances they will consume and what risks they will take, and that the economic costs of trying to coerce so many Americans into abstaining from those substances would be enormous and the social costs disastrous.

An assessment of the costs and benefits of current drug control policies in the United States requires some sense of what the alternatives would be. When Prohibition's proponents and opponents debated the merits of the 18th Amendment, they were able to draw on their recent memories. The difficulty in contemplating the alternatives to drug prohibition is that few people can remember when heroin, cocaine, and even marijuana were legally available. The first federal legislation severely restricting the sale of cocaine and the opiates was the 1914 Harrison Act. Marijuana did not become the subject of federal legislation until 1937, when Congress passed the Marijuana Tax Act. In both cases, however, state legislatures around the country already had imposed their own restrictions on the availability of these drugs, motivated in good part by the popular association of these substances with feared minorities—the opiates with the Chinese immigrants; cocaine with blacks; and marijuana with blacks and Hispanics. Even so, the late 19th century and the first years of the 20th century could be described as a period in which most of today's illicit drugs were more or less legally available to those who wanted them. The United States at that time had a drug abuse problem of roughly similar magnitude to today's problem, but it was perceived almost entirely as a public and private health issue. Crime and law enforcement played little role in the nature, perception, and handling of the problem.

In 1987 direct expenditures on drug interdiction incurred by the military, which markedly underestimate actual costs, increased significantly from almost nothing in 1981 to about $165 million. Expenditures in this area by the three principal intelligence agencies—the CIA, the Defense Intelligence Agency, and the National Security Agency—also have increased dramatically. The Drug Enforcement Administration's budget has risen from about $200 million in 1980 to a projected $500 million in 1988, and almost all of the other federal law enforcement agencies—in particular, the FBI and the U.S. Customs Service—have increased dramatically the proportion of their resources devoted to drug enforcement activities. In an August 1987 study prepared for the U.S. Customs Service by Wharton Econometrics, state and local police were estimated to have devoted about one-fifth of their total budgets, or close to $5 billion, to drug-law enforcement in 1986. This represented a 19 per cent increase over the previous year's expenditures. All told, 1987 expenditures on all aspects of drug enforcement, from drug eradication in foreign countries to imprisonment of drug users and dealers in the United States, probably totaled at least $8 billion.

Even more significant than the actual expenditures has been the diversion of limited resources—including experienced and talented judges and prosecutors and law enforcement agents, as well as scarce prison space—from enforcement against criminal activities that harm far more innocent victims than do violators of the drug laws. Drug-law violators account for approximately one-tenth of the roughly 800,000 inmates in state prisons and local jails and more than one-third of the 44,000 federal prison inmates, according to U.S. Department of Justice statistics. These proportions are expected to increase in coming years even as total prison populations continue to rise dramatically. Largely as a consequence of the Anti-Drug Abuse Act passed by Congress in 1986, the proportion of federal inmates incarcerated for drug violations is expected to rise from one-third of the 44,000 prisoners currently sentenced to federal prisons to one-half of the 100,000–150,000 federal prisoners anticipated in 15 years. The direct cost of building and maintaining enough state and federal prisons to house this growing population is rising at an astronomical rate. The opportunity costs in terms of alternative social expenditures forgone and other types of criminals not imprisoned are perhaps even more severe.

FBI figures show that during each of the last few years, about 750,000 people were arrested on drug charges. Slightly more than three-fourths of these arrests were not for manufacturing or dealing drugs but solely for possessing an illicit drug, typically marijuana. (Those arrested, it is worth noting, represented less than 3 per cent of the 30 million Americans estimated to have consumed an illegal drug during the past year.) Criminal justice systems in many cities are clogged. In New York City, 41 per cent of all felony indictments during the first 3 months of 1987 were for drug offenses.

Other costs are equally great but somewhat harder to evaluate: the governmental corruption that inevitably attends enforcement of the drug laws; the effects of labeling the tens of millions who use drugs illicitly as criminals, subjecting them to the risks of criminal sanction and obliging many of those same people to enter into relationships with drug dealers—who may be criminals in many more senses of the word—to purchase their drugs; the cynicism that such laws generate toward other laws and the law in general; and the sense of hostility and suspicion that many otherwise law-abiding individuals feel toward law enforcement officials. It was costs like these that strongly influenced many of Prohibition's more conservative opponents. As John D. Rockefeller, Jr., wrote in explaining why he was withdrawing as a leading supporter of Prohibition and calling for its repeal:

That a vast array of lawbreakers has been recruited and financed on a colossal scale; that many of our best citizens, piqued at what they regarded as an infringement of their private rights, have openly and unabashedly disregarded the Eighteenth Amendment; that as an inevitable result respect for all law has been greatly lessened; that crime has increased to an unprecedented degree—I have slowly and reluctantly come to believe.

The unintended beneficiaries of the drug laws, as in Latin America, have been the organized and unorganized criminals who thwart the law to their great profit. A report issued by the President's Commission on Organized Crime identified the sale of illicit drugs as the leading source of revenue for organized crime in 1986, with the marijuana and heroin business each providing more than \$7 billion and the cocaine business more than \$13 billion. By contrast, revenues from cigarette bootlegging were estimated at \$290,000,000. If the marijuana, cocaine, and heroin markets were legal, state and federal governments would collect billions of dollars annually in tax revenues. Instead they expend billions.

During Prohibition, violent struggles between bootlegging gangs and hijackings of liquor-laden trucks and sea vessels were frequent and notorious occurrences. Today's equivalents are the booby traps that surround some marijuana fields, the Caribbean pirates looking to plunder drug-laden vessels en route to U.S. shores, and the machine-gun battles and executions of the more sordid drug mafias—all of which occasionally kill innocent people. Most law enforcement authorities agree that the dramatic increases in urban murder rates during the past few years can be explained almost entirely by the rise in drug-dealer killings, mainly of one another.

Perhaps the most unfortunate victims of the drug prohibition policies have been the law-abiding residents of America's ghettos. These policies account for much of what ghetto residents identify as the drug problem. In many neighborhoods, it often seems to be the aggressive, gun-toting drug dealers who upset residents far more than the addicts nodding in doorways. As in Medellín, Colombia, and Rio de Janeiro, Brazil, the drug dealers are widely perceived as heroes and successful role models. In impoverished neighborhoods, they often stand out as symbols of success to children who see no other options. At the same time, the increasingly harsh criminal penalties imposed on adult drug dealers have led to the widespread recruitment of juveniles by drug traffickers. Where once children started dealing drugs only after they had been using them for a few years, today the sequence is often reversed. Many children start to use illegal drugs now only after they have worked for older drug dealers for a while. And the juvenile justice system offers no realistic options for dealing with this growing problem.

Among the most difficult costs to evaluate are those created by the high price of most illicit drugs, notably cocaine and heroin. Whereas drug laws and their enforcement seek to make the drugs so prohibitive in price that people cannot or will not pay for them, there are vast costs involved in making drugs so expensive. In particular, many of those who desire or become addicted to the illicit substances not only divert substantial portions of their incomes to drug purchases but often end up committing crimes to fund their drug needs. Unlike the millions of alcoholics who can support their habits for relatively modest amounts, many cocaine and heroin addicts are reported to spend hundreds and even thousands of dollars per week. If those drugs were dramatically cheaper, which would be the case either if they were legalized or if the drug laws were no longer enforced, the number of crimes committed by drug addicts to pay for their habits would obviously decline dramatically. So would the profits, power, and incentives of the drug traffickers.

The drug prohibition laws pose additional problems for the millions of drug users who have not been deterred from using illicit drugs in the first place. Nothing resembling an underground Food and Drug Administration has arisen to impose quality control on the illegal drug market. Many marijuana smokers are worse off for having smoked cannabis that was grown with dangerous fertilizers, sprayed with the herbicide paraquat, or mixed with more dangerous substances. Consumers of heroin and the various synthetic substances sold on the street face even severer consequences, including fatal overdoses and poisonings from unexpectedly potent or impure drug supplies. Many advocates of current policies argue, probably correctly, that the unreliable quality of illicit drugs serves as an important deterrent to more widespread use. The question that few ask, however, is whether the costs of that deterrent factor outweigh the benefits.

In fact, intravenous drug users accounted for more than 50 per cent of all deaths related to acquired immune deficiency syndrome (AIDS) in New York City from 1981 to 1986. Reports have emerged that drug dealers are beginning to provide clean needles along with their illegal drugs. But even as other local governments around the world actively attempt to limit the spread of AIDS by and among drug users by making treatment programs more readily available and instituting free needle-exchange programs, state and municipal governments in the United States resist following suit. Only in January 1988 did New York City approve such a program on a very limited and experimental basis. The thought cannot help coming to mind that government policy in this area is motivated in part by the unspoken assumption that

AIDS will resolve the heroin problem in a way the criminal justice system never can.

Another cost of current drug prohibition policies, caused largely by the government's enthusiasm for demonizing the drugs that are illegal, are the restrictions on using the illicit drugs for legitimate medical purposes. For example, marijuana has been found to be useful in treating glaucoma and as an anticonvulsant for some victims of cerebral palsy and multiple sclerosis, and it is particularly effective in reducing the nausea that accompanies chemotherapy. And research indicates that psychedelic drugs, such as LSD, peyote, and MDMA (known as Ecstasy), may be helpful in psychotherapy and in reducing tension, depression, pain, and fear of death in the terminally ill. Similarly, heroin has proved more effective than other painkillers in helping some patients deal with acute pain. But current drug prohibition laws make it difficult, if not impossible, for doctors to prescribe these drugs, and they severely hamper the efforts of researchers to investigate these and other potential medical uses of the illegal drugs.

Perhaps the most intangible costs of the drug prohibition policies stem from the ways in which they are enforced. Because violations of the drug laws involve consensual activities and create no victims with an interest in reporting the crime to the police, law enforcement authorities are particularly dependent upon the most invasive and noxious investigative techniques to detect criminal violations. Drug enforcement agents rely heavily on informants drawn from the criminal milieu, on undercover operations, and on electronic surveillance. These techniques are certainly indispensable to effective law enforcement, but they are also among the least desirable of the tools available to police. And there are good reasons for requiring that they be used sparingly. Certainly a country committed to many of the values reflected in the U.S. Constitution should find it hard to admire the notion of police spying on citizens and paying others to do the same.

Voices for Legalization

Despite the soaring costs—economic, political, and social—associated with drug prohibition policies, little popular support can be found for repealing the drug laws. The percentage of Americans supporting legalization even of marijuana has dropped markedly since the late 1970s. Liberal politicians tend to

choose the drug issue as the most profitable one on which to
abandon their liberal principles and prove their tough-on-crime
credentials. Even the civil liberties unions shy away from this
issue, limiting their input primarily to the drug-testing debate.
The minority communities in the ghetto, for whom repeal of the
drug laws promises the greatest benefits, fail to recognize the
costs of the drug prohibition policies for what they are. And
typical middle-class Americans, who hope only that their children
will not succumb to drug abuse, tend to favor any measures that
they believe will make illegal drugs less accessible to them.

The few scholars who have spoken out in favor of repeal are
primarily from the conservative end of the political spectrum: the
economists Milton Friedman and Gary Becker, the criminologist
Ernest van den Haag, and the magazine editor William F. Buckley, Jr. However, there is also a significant silent constituency in
favor of repeal found among the criminal justice officials and
scholars, intelligence analysts, and military interdicters who have
spent the most time thinking about the problem. More often than
not, job-security considerations combined with an awareness that
they can do little to change official policies ensure that their views
remain discreet and off the record.

Among Latin American officials, the need for discretion in
advocating repeal of some or all of the drug prohibition laws is
only slightly less than in the United States. During the late 1970s,
the Colombian National Association of Financial Institutions lob-
bied for the legalization of marijuana. More recently, numerous
high-level Colombians, including a former justice minister, a former attorney general, and the current president of an appointed
advisory group, the Council of State, Samuel Buitrago Hurtado,
have spoken publicly in favor of legalizing and taxing the illicit
drug industries. And in a potentially significant development, the
Inter-American Dialogue, a group composed of prominent politicians, scholars, business leaders, and former high-level government officials from the United States, Latin America, and the
Caribbean, has called for serious study of "selective legalization"
as one approach for dealing with the inter-American drug problem.

There can be no guarantee, of course, that legalization would
lead to better and healthier societies in either the short or the
long run. Indeed, the possibility cannot be excluded that drug
abuse would become more widespread than it is now. But that
prospect is by no means a certainty. At the same time, it is certain

that most of the costs of current drug policies would be reduced dramatically in both North and South America. If the objective of American and international drug control policy is to consider the costs not just of drug abuse but also of drug control measures, then it is essential to consider the legalization option.

Of course, there is no single legalization option. Legalization can mean a free market, or one closely regulated by the government, or even a government monopoly. Just consider the range of regulatory regimes for the control of alcohol that state and even municipal governments have devised. Nor does legalization imply an end to law enforcement, as the Bureau of Alcohol, Tobacco and Firearms can attest. Legalization under almost any regime, however, does promise many advantages over the current approach. Government expenditures on drug-law enforcement would drop dramatically. So would organized crime revenues. Between reduced expenditures on drug-law enforcement and increased revenues raised by taxing drug consumers and producers, the net benefit to government treasuries in the United States would easily be many billions of dollars per year. In Latin America, the net benefits would be smaller in terms of dollars, perhaps only a few billion, but far greater in terms of social gains—less corruption, more law and order, and a strengthening of the role of government in society.

It is troubling to note the opposite trends in the purity of legal and illegal substances. The average tar content of cigarettes is declining as smokers seek relatively safer products. Similarly, alcohol drinkers are shifting away from hard liquor and toward wine and beer, motivated in good part by health concerns. During the same period, conversely, the average amount of THC, the primary psychoactive ingredient of marijuana, has increased significantly; the average purity of cocaine has risen from 12 per cent to 60 per cent; and smoking crack has become far more widespread. In addition, the spread of high-potency "black tar" heroin from Mexico has contributed to an increase in the drug's average purity. Government law enforcement efforts help explain these trends in that they place a premium on minimizing the bulk of the illicit product to avoid detection. But the increasing purity is also an indication of the failure of law enforcement efforts. Under a legal drug regime, government regulators could establish relatively low purity levels, thus reducing the potential for drug abuse and addiction. They also could ensure quality and provide warnings as to the potential dangers of the licit substances. A black market still would exist for higher purity and even more dangerous substances, but it would be a fraction of its current size. Given the option of obtaining reliable supplies from government-regulated vendors, few drug users would have much to gain by resorting to the black market. And the government could set drug prices at a level high enough to discourage consumption but low enough to minimize black market opportunities.

Of all the drugs that are currently illicit, marijuana perhaps presents the easiest case for repeal of the prohibition laws, in good part because it presents relatively few serious risks to users and is less dangerous in most respects than both alcohol and tobacco. Moreover, the available evidence indicates no apparent increase in marijuana use following the decriminalization of marijuana possession in about a dozen states during the late 1970s. In the Netherlands, which went even further during the 1970s in relaxing enforcement of marijuana laws, some studies indicate use of the drug has actually declined. Marijuana arrests may not account for most of the drug offenders in U.S. federal and state prisons, but they do account for most of the drug arrests as well as for a large portion of the money spent on local drug enforcement by municipal criminal justice systems and on interdiction by the Coast Guard and the military.

Cocaine, heroin, and the various amphetamines, barbiturates, and tranquilizers that people consume illegally present much tougher policy problems. If they were legally available at reasonable prices, would millions more Americans use and abuse them? Drawing comparisons with other countries and historical periods provides clues but no definitive answers for the simple reason that culture and personality often prove to be the most important determinants of how drugs are used in a society. Availability and price play important roles, but not as important as cultural variables. There is good reason to assume that even if all the illegal drugs were made legally available, the same cultural restraints that now keep most Americans from becoming drug abusers would persist and perhaps even strengthen.

No progress can be expected, however, until more people and governments realize the extent of the costs exacted by current drug control policies. Every once in a while, a commission appointed to study a public-policy problem actually makes a difference. One such example was the Wickersham commission appointed by President Herbert Hoover in 1929 to evaluate the state of law

enforcement and especially Prohibition in the United States. Its
report played an important role in educating Americans about
the limits and costs of Prohibition and helped shape the national
debate that preceded the repeal of the 18th Amendment.

A similar commission, composed of North and South Americans, could evaluate the costs and benefits, as well as the potential
and limits, of the international drug control regime. Unlike the
recently created White House Conference for a Drug Free America, this commission could examine the entire range of options
for reducing not just drug abuse but also the costs of drug prohibition policies. It would not begin its investigation, as the White
House Conference has, with the unquestioned assumption that
any use of illicit drugs is by definition drug abuse. Nor would it
automatically assume that increased law enforcement and increasingly harsh criminal sanctions can produce a more effective
drug control strategy. Rather, its mandate would include intensive
scrutiny of the very assumptions that underlie current drug policies. For instance, the commission could make recommendations
on how to deal more effectively with the violence, crime, and
corruption that stem in good part from current drug prohibition
strategies. In short, it would be an inter-American commission
mandated to evaluate the value and effectiveness of current drug
control strategies and to consider any and all alternatives.

In the final analysis, the drug problem remains an international problem that needs international solutions. Latin American governments realize the consequences for their countries of
the U.S.-inspired policies, but they are unable to offer alternatives. They are hampered not only by their historical incapacity
for concerted action but also by their recognition that the drug
issue is one on which the U.S. government is liable to act impul-
sively, and even irrationally, to the detriment of everyone's interests. So rather than seek more effective and less costly drug policies, the Latin American governments find themselves torn
between trying to appease their powerful neighbor to the north
and trying to minimize the harmful consequences of a problem
that lies beyond their control. Publicly they proclaim their adher-
ence to the chimerical objectives of eliminating illicit drug production and use. But in practice they pursue "drug control" policies that really are nothing more than damage-limitation
strategies designed to keep the drug traffickers from taking over
their countries and the U.S. government from striking out at or
abandoning them.

One of the most important steps the U.S. government could take, therefore, would be to let the Latin Americans evaluate their own best interests independent of U.S. demands. If they determine that their overall interests are best served by policies designed not to suppress but to control and regulate the production of marijuana and cocaine, then the U.S. government should be willing to consider policy alternatives that acknowledge those interests. Indeed, it is far from certain that the interests of the United States in this regard necessarily conflict with those of Latin America. For U.S. interests lie not only in reducing the costs of drug prohibition policies abroad but also in developing alternatives to a drug control policy that has proved both largely unsuccessful and increasingly costly at home.

BIBLIOGRAPHY

BOOKS AND PAMPHLETS

Abadinsky, Howard. Drug abuse: an introduction. Nelson-Hall. '89.

Alexander, Bruce K. Peaceful measures: Canada's way out of the 'war on drugs.' University of Toronto Press. '90.

Allen, David F. The cocaine crisis. Plenum. '87.

Andrulis, Dennis P. Crisis at the frontline. Unwin Hyman. '89.

Argeriou, Milton & McCarty, Dennis, eds. Treating alcoholism and drug abuse among homeless men and women. Haworth. '90.

Arrington, Stephen. Journey into darkness. Huntington. '92.

Auraham, Dennis P. The downside of drugs. Chelsea House. '88.

Bach, Julie, ed. Drug abuse: opposing viewpoints. Greenhaven. '88.

Bakalar, James B. & Grinspoon, Lester. Drug control in a free society. Cambridge University Press. '89.

Balfour, D. J. Psychotropic drugs of abuse. Pergamon. '90.

Benjamin, Daniel K. & Miller, Roger L. Undoing drugs: beyond legalization. Basic. '91.

Berger, Gilda & Berger, Melvin. Drug abuse A-Z. Enslow. '90.

Bernards, Neal, ed. The war on drugs: opposing viewpoints. Greenhaven. '90.

Berridge, Virginia. Drugs research and policy in Britain: a review of the 1980s. Ashgate. '90.

Botero, Cecilia. Drugs and Latin America: a bibliography. Vance. '90.

Brownstein, Paul J., et al. Substance use and delinquency among inner city adolescent males. Urban Institute Press. '90.

Clifford, J. Stephen. Cocaine addiction: the challenge of a modern epidemic. Edgehill. '90.

Cook, Paddy. Alcohol, tobacco, and other drugs may harm the unborn. U.S. Department of Health and Human Services. '90.

Coombs, Robert H. The family context of adolescent drug use. Haworth. '88.

Currie, Elliott. Reckoning: drugs, the cities and the American future. Hill & Wang. '93.

Dorn, Nicholas & Smith, Nigel, eds. A land fit for heroin? St. Martin's Press. '87.

Dorn, Nicholas, et al. Trafficking: drug markets and law enforcement. Routledge. '91.

Douglass, Joseph D. Red cocaine: the drugging of America. Clarion. '90.

Drug abuse and drug abuse research: the third triennial report to congress. Department of Health and Human Services. U.S. Government Printing Office. '91.

Dryfoos, Joy G. Adolescents at risk: prevalence and prevention. Oxford University Press. '90.

Eddy, Paul. Cocaine wars. Bantam. '89.

Eisenach, Jeffrey A., ed. Winning the drug war: new challenges for the 1990s. Heritage Foundation. '91.

Evans, Rod L. & Berent, Irwin M., eds. Drug legalization: for and against. Open Court. '92.

Falco, Mathea. The making of a drug-free America. Times Books. '93.

Flewelling, Robert L. Socioeconomic and demographic correlates of drug and alcohol use: findings in the 1988 and 1990 national household surveys on drug use. National Institute on Drug Abuse. '92.

Girdano, Daniel A. & Dusek, Dorothy E. Drug education: content and methods. Random House. '88.

Glassner, Barry. Drugs in adolescent worlds: burnouts to straights. St. Martin's Press. '87.

Goode, Lamond. Drugs in American society. McGraw. '88.

Gugliotta, Guy & Leen, Jeff. Kings of cocaine. Harper Collins. '90.

Hard-core cocaine addicts: measuring—and fighting—the epidemic: a staff report. Senate Committee on the Judiciary. U.S. Government Printing Office. '90.

Horton, Lowell. Developing effective drug education. Phi Delta Kappan Educational Foundation. '92.

Hubbard, Robert L. Drug abuse treatment: a national study of effectiveness. University of North Carolina Press. '89.

Johanson, Chris-Ellyn. Cocaine: a new epidemic. Chelsea House. '92.

Kirkpatrick, Sidney D. & Abrahams, Peter. Turning the tide: one man against the Medellin cartel. NAL-Dutton. '92.

Lee, Martin A. Acid dreams: the complete social history of LSD. Grove Weidenfeld. '92.

Lee, Rensselaer. The white labyrinth: cocaine and political power. Transaction. '89.

Legalization of illicit drugs: impact and feasibility. Select Committee on Narcotics Abuse and Control. 101st Congress. U.S. Government Printing Office. '89.

Long, Robert Emmet, ed. Drugs and American society. H. W. Wilson. '86.

Lyman, Michael D. Drugs in society. Anderson. '91.

Mabray, Donald J. The Latin American narcotics trade and U.S. national security. Greenwood. '89.

MacDonald, Dave & Patterson, Vicky. A handbook of drug training: learning about drugs and working with drug users. Routledge. '91.

Macdonald, Scott B. Dancing on a volcano: the Latin American drug trade. Praeger. '88.

Macdonald, Scott B. Mountain high, white avalanche: cocaine and power in Andean states and Panama. Praeger. '89.

MacGregor, Felipe E., ed. Coca and cocaine: an Andean perspective. Greenwood. '93.

MacGregor, Suzanne. Drugs and British society. Routledge. '89.

Malamud-Goti, Jaime. Smoke and mirrors: the drug wars in Bolivia. Westview. '92.

Mansfield, Wendy. Public school principal survey on safe, disciplined, and drug-free schools. U.S. Department of Education. '92.

Martin, John M. & Romano, Anne. Multinational crime: the challenge of terrorism, espionage, drugs & arms trafficking. Sage. '92.

McCoy, Alfred W. The politics of heroin: CIA complicity in the global drug war. L. Hill. '91.

Melville, Keith. The drug crisis: public strategies for breaking the habit. Kendall-Hunt. '89.

Miller, Richard. The case for legalizing drugs. Praeger. '91.

Mitchell, Chester N. The drug solution. Carleton University Press. '90.

Monkkonen, Eric H. Prostitution, drugs, gambling, and organized crime. K. G. Saur. '92.

Morales, Edmundo. Cocaine: white gold rush in Peru. University of Arizona Press. '89.

Moser, Leslie E. Crack, cocaine, methamphetamine. Multi-Media. '90.

Musta, Donald F. The American disease: origins of narcotics control. Oxford University Press. '89.

Nahas, Gabriel G. Cocaine: the great white plague. Erickson. '89.

National AIDS Demonstration Project. Community-based AIDS prevention: studies of intravenous drug users and their sexual partners. U.S. Department of Health and Human Services. '91.

National Issues Forum Staff. The drug crisis. Kendall-Hunt. '89.

Nordquist, Joan. Substance abuse: a bibliography. Reference and Research Services. '89.

Ottomanelli, Gennaro. HIV infection and intravenous drug use. Greenwood. '92.

Padilla, Felice M. The gang as an American enterprise. Rutgers University Press. '92.

Pearson, Geoffrey. The new heroin users. Blackwell. '87.

Peluso, Emanuel. Women and drugs. CompCare Publications. '88.

Powis, Robert E. The money launderers. Probus. '92.

Reitz, Raymond J., ed. Drug abuse. Phi Delta Kappan Center on Evaluation, Development, and Research. '87.

Reuter, Peter, Crawford, Gordon, & Cave, Jonathan. Sealing the borders. Rand Corporation. '88.

Rice, Dorothy P. The economic costs of alcohol & drug abuse and mental health. U.S. Department of Health and Human Services. '90.

Ricketts, Max & Bien, Edward. The great anxiety escape. Matulungi. '90.

Roth, Paula, ed. Alcohol and drugs are women's issues. Scarecrow. '91.

Rucker, R. D. Drug addiction & drug dealing. Vantage. '91.

Santos, Michael G. Drugs and money. Galleria. '90.

Scott, Peter D. & Marshall, Jonathan. Cocaine politics: drugs, armies, and the CIA in Central America. University of California Press. '91.

Segal, Bernard. Drug-taking behavior among school-aged youth: the Alaska experience & comparisons with lower-48 states. Haworth. '90.

Shulman, Jeffrey. Focus on cocaine and crack. Twenty-first Century Books. '90.

Simpson, Opioid. Addiction and treatment. Krieger. '90.

Staley, Sam. Drug policy and the decline of the American city. Transaction. '92.

Stamper, Laura. When the drug war hits home. Deaconess Press. '91.

Stephens, Richard C. The street addict role: a theory of heroin addiction. State University of New York Press. '91.

Stevens, Jay. Storming heaven: LSD and the American dream. Atlantic Monthly Press. '87.

Stimmel, Barry. The facts about drug use. Consumer Report Books. '91.

Stuck, Mary Frances. Adolescent worlds: drug use and athletic activity. Praeger. '90.

Swisher, Karin, ed. Drug trafficking. Greenhaven. '91.

Trebach, Arnold S. The great drug war. Macmillan. '87.

Trebach, Arnold S. & Zeese, Kevin B., eds. Drug prohibition and the conscience of nations. Drug Policy Foundation. '90.

Tullis, Karin, ed. Drug Trafficking. Greenhaven. '91.

Washton, Arnold & Boundy, Donna. Cocaine and crack; what you need to know. Enslow. '89.

Watson, Ronald, ed. Drug and alcohol abuse prevention. Humana. '91.

What American users spend on illegal drugs. Office of National Drug Control Policy. '91.

Wisotsky, Steven. Beyond the war on drugs: overcoming a failed public policy. Prometheus Books. '90.

ADDITIONAL PERIODICAL ARTICLES WITH ABSTRACTS

For those who wish to read more widely on the subject of drugs in America, this section contains abstracts of additional articles that bear on the topic. Readers who require a comprehensive list of materials are advised to consult the *Reader's Guide to Periodical Literature* and other Wilson indexes.

Medellín's new generation James Ring Adams *The American Spectator* 24:22–5 D '91

The younger generation of Colombia's Medellín drug cartel may be more ruthless than the kingpins of the older generation, many of whom have been jailed. The U.S. Drug Enforcement Administration claims that the Cali cartel is the new menace, but the Medellín is regrouping under a more sophisticated leadership that may prove to be more effective and more deadly than that of the Cali.

The organization of the man likely to emerge as the new cartel boss, the elusive Gerardo Moncada, claims privately to ship more than 4 tons of cocaine a month into New York City. A university graduate and an industrial engineer, Moncada was able to evade the Colombian government's crackdown on other cartel leaders and a U.S. Customs Service sting that exposed the Bank of Credit and Commerce International, which laundered money for Moncada. Moncada's ability to escape notice and capture testifies to the need for more effective intelligence in the war on drugs.

Germany's brash new import: dirty money Igor Reichlin *Business Week* 44 Ap 6 '92

Germany is now the largest European financial center where money laundering is not illegal. Since Switzerland tightened its disclosure policies last year, Germany has become a new mecca for global narcotics funds. German authorities estimate that since 1991, up to $50 billion—much of it from Colombian, Turkish, and Italian drug cartels—has flowed into the country. The money is used to buy securities, gold, or real estate and companies in east Germany and Eastern Europe. Because of bitter memories of the Nazi years, lawmakers are reluctant to draft rules on taking property, even if criminal activity is involved. As a result, German curbs on money laundering are loose at best, and investigators are finding more and more links between German banks and international drug operators. The U.S. Drug Enforcement Agency and the European Community are pressuring Germany to impose laws against money laundering, but banks and several politicians oppose such measures.

Dispatches from the drug war Gerry Fitzgerald *Common Cause Magazine* 16:13–19 Ja/F '90

The federal government has turned to mandatory minimum sentences with no possibility of parole in its war on drugs. The tough new laws are supposed to lower drug use and drug dealing by increasing the certainty of punishment, but similar laws enacted in New York in the early 1970s proved ineffective. In addition, such laws undermine basic liberties. Nationwide, mandatory minimum sentences are likely to result in overburdened prisons and courts and insufficient resources to counsel people on drugs and to treat addiction. Critics also charge that mandatory minimum sentences and current law-enforcement tactics tend to result in the imprisonment mostly of people who are minor dealers or only marginally involved in the drug trade, while the major traffickers are able to trade information for lighter penalties or freedom. Mandatory minimum sentences are representative of the government's tendency to seek simple solutions to complex problems.

Colombia at the crossroads John D. Martz *Current History* 90:69–72+ F '91

New Colombian president Cesar Gaviria has assumed power at a time when his country is approaching a historic crossroads. Popular demands for democratization and political reform are on the rise, and the traditional two-party monopoly on government has been weakened. In response to Colombia's economic problems, Gaviria has announced a program that calls for opening the economy to foreign investors, offering incentives for exports, and privatizing state enterprises. He has adopted a flexible approach in dealing with the narcotics industry, offering drug traffickers alternatives to extradition to the United States. Colombia's endemic violence constitutes a problem that extends far beyond the drug war, however.

Don't fry your brain Joshua Levine *Forbes* 147:116–17 F 4 '91

The Partnership for a Drug-Free America, a coalition of advertising agencies and others in the industry, has undertaken a mammoth campaign to get and keep America's youngsters off drugs. Over the past three years, the campaign has used nearly $800 million of donated media time and space, making it second only to McDonald's in advertising clout. The effort has featured such images as frying eggs, loaded guns, and screaming ambulances to remove the glamour from marijuana, cocaine, and crack use. Its success is difficult to measure, but some statistics show that drug consumption is declining. The campaign initially targeted trendsetters and youths with the goal of eliminating any cachet that drug use possessed, but some of the coalition's members are now wondering if the ads should focus on the more or less ignored hardcore drug users. According to Partnership president Thomas Hedrick, the coalition wants to avoid stigmatizing drug users and may reexamine its tactics.

Two black-and-white drug issues Sol Gordon, Joey Tranchina *The Humanist* 51:37–8 My/Je '91

The war on drugs has given rise to certain policies that are plainly irrational. It makes no sense, for example, to inhibit the therapeutic use of marijuana, a drug that can relieve the severe side effects of chemotherapy and prevent some glaucoma sufferers from going blind. It is also tragically counterproductive to block needle exchange programs, which would permit intravenous drug users to protect themselves and their sexual partners from the spread of HIV, the virus that causes AIDS.

Children of the damned Edward Barnes *Life* 13:30–6+ Je '90

In crack-ridden North Philadelphia, childhood has ceased to exist. The biggest problem facing the children who live there is not random violence but their position in the drug trade. Children as young as 8 enter the drug business, which is more dependent on child labor than any 19th-century factory. These children must grind out profits on a shift, protect their bundles of crack, handle thousands of dollars in cash and drugs, and try to stay alive. They fear the street bosses but have a strong desire to emulate them. Once they become involved, they will never know security, never trust anyone, and never escape the twisted values of the drug world. A 12-year-old who buys his mother crack, a 13-year-old small-time drug dealer, a woman who started dealing drugs so that she could raise her grandchildren, and a top drug dealer are profiled.

Just say whoa David Beers *Mother Jones* 16:36–43+ Jl/Ag '91

Part of a special section on the drug war. Harm reduction, the drug control approach taken by the Netherlands and by Liverpool, England, stops short of full legalization but challenges the basic premises of the drug war. Fifty-two Dutch cities have syringe-exchange programs, and the country spends most of its drug budget not on law enforcement but on prevention, treatment, research, and a school curriculum that teaches children the risks of all intoxicants and the need to take responsibility for their actions. According to Leo Zaal, the chief superintendent of Amsterdam's narcotics squad, the real keys to limiting drug abuse are employment, social programs, and education. Meanwhile, in Liverpool, the Maryland Center offers syringes to addicts, and psychiatrist John Marks prescribes heroin on a regular basis to users. The HIV infection rate among injectors in Liverpool is only 1.6 percent, and drug related crime has reportedly dropped for three straight years.

Justice's war on drug treatment David Corn *The Nation* 250:659–62 My 14 '90

Despite the Justice Department's tough talk about eliminating crime and illegal drug use, the department has cut funding for a program that demonstrably reduces the number of substance abusers and criminals. Stay'n Out, a prison drug rehabilitation program, provides convicts who have histories of drug abuse with counseling sessions, seminars on values, and strict rules that prohibit alcohol, drugs, fighting, and lying. A study shows that three-quarters of Stay'n Out alumni stayed off drugs and were not arrested during their parole periods. Nevertheless, the Bureau of Justice Assistance allocated no money for jailhouse drug rehabilitation in its $49.6 million discretionary budget this year. Criminal justice administrators prefer to build more prisons and believe, according to one insider, that treatment programs represent coddling.

Villa Narco Bill Berkeley *The New Republic* 205:10+ N 11 '91

The city of San Francisco de Macoris is a symbol of the Dominican Republic's new prominence in the distribution network for crack and powder cocaine. Dominicans in New York have emerged as the preeminent distributors of Colombian cocaine, and police are only now realizing that nearly three-quarters of the young Dominicans arrested on drug charges are recent arrivals from San Francisco de Macoris and its surrounding towns. Mostly illiterate peasants unable to speak English, young Dominicans are lured to New York by friends or relatives. Those who avoid arrest or addiction often travel back and forth between the United States and the Dominican Republic, where their money enables them to build mansions and live in luxury in San Francisco de Macoris. Local prosecutor Francisco Antonio Gaton estimates that 60 percent of the local economy is somehow connected to drugs sold in New York.

Out there William Finnegan *The New Yorker* 66:51–2+ S 10 '90

New Haven, Connecticut, one of the poorest big cities in the United States, is in the midst of a major illegal drug boom. The city's loosely organized drug trade revolves around numerous small gangs, each more or less affiliated with a neighborhood-based federation known as a posse, that deal primarily in cocaine. Most posse members are black teenage boys, many of them without other prospects for employment, who endure enormous risks for the sake of highly lucrative work in the drug trade. The New Haven chief of police now estimates that 80 percent of all crime in the city is drug-related, and drug abuse and drug-related crime were two of the three worst city problems cited in a recent opinion poll conducted by the New Haven Register. The black community has unquestionably been hardest hit both by drug use and by the violence that it has spawned. A black New Haven family's involvement in the drug culture is discussed.

In the cocaine war. . . the jungle is winning Michael Massing *The New York Times Magazine* 26–7+ Mr 4 '90

The U.S. government has taken its harshest stand on drugs in Peru's Upper Huallaga Valley, a major source of the coca that feeds the U.S.

cocaine habit, but a State Department official notes that the war on drugs will have to escalate if cocaine is to be controlled. Drug Enforcement Administration agents are stationed in Peru, and the United States is expanding its intelligence presence there. In addition, the State Department's Special Project for Control and Eradication of Coca in the Upper Huallaga (Corah) employs 400 workers who aim to destroy more than 2,500 acres of coca each month. The program has suffered setbacks, however. Since 1982, almost 40 Corah workers have been killed by the Sendero Luminoso, a guerrilla group that protects the growers. Nearly all of the area's peasants grow coca, and the farmers resent the destruction of their fields. Peru's economy is so poor that the war on cocaine is a low priority to government officials.

D.C.'s war on drugs: why Bennett is losing Michael Massing *The New York Times Magazine* 36–7+ S 23 '90

William J. Bennett, director of the Office of National Drug Control Policy, is losing the battle against drug abuse in Washington, D.C. Bennett selected the District of Columbia as the centerpiece of his antidrug campaign, and he initiated a plan for the city that cost nearly $100 million. Since the plan's implementation, the percentage of adults arrested in Washington testing positive for cocaine has dropped, but cocaine and crack remain widely available and drug-related violence shows few signs of abating. Bennett acknowledges the lack of progress in the District, but he places the blame on local officials. In fact, Bennett excluded local officials from his efforts. Moreover, some of the most effective antidrug measures have been local ones that emphasize community involvement in conjunction with police actions.

The Canadian connection Harry F. Waters *Newsweek* 115:60 Ja 8 '90

South American drug merchants appear to be responding to the antismuggling pressure along the United States' southern border by taking advantage of the largely unpatrolled 5,500-mile U.S.-Canadian border. The Canadian province of New Brunswick, which has an extensive sheltered coastline, 136 isolated airstrips, and many logging roads, seems to be the newest outpost in the drug war. In November, two Colombian pilots were sentenced to lengthy prison terms after they landed on a remote New Brunswick airstrip with $215 million worth of cocaine, which was apparently en route to the United States. Four other Colombians were later sentenced for conspiring to break the pilots out of jail, and Tito Sanchez Ruiz, who refused to plead guilty to the escape charges, will soon be tried. Although authorities have made a number of major drug seizures in eastern Canada, they believe that they have intercepted only a small percentage of the drugs coming through the country.

Busting the mayor *Newsweek* 115:24–30 Ja 29 '90

A cover story examines the arrest of Washington, D.C., mayor Marion Barry on drug charges. After years of rumors, leaks, and official denials concerning Barry's alleged drug use, the mayor was caught in an FBI sting operation. The probe, which was launched following a December 1988 incident involving Barry and former city employee Charles Lewis, culminated recently when the mayor was invited to a downtown hotel by a woman said to be his longtime friend and lover. There, FBI agents videotaped him buying and smoking crack cocaine and arrested him. He subsequently relinquished control over city government. Since then, attention has focused on his and the city's political future and on whether Barry is the victim of the white establishment. Articles examine the racial and ethical aspects of the case, the possibility of a Jesse Jackson mayoral campaign this year, and the failure of antidrug efforts in Washington.

Uncivil liberties? Tom Morganthau *Newsweek* 115:18–20 Ap 23 '90

Concern is growing that drug war tactics may be jeopardizing civil liberties. In the nation's cities, SWAT-team raids, stop-and-frisk tactics, and a wide variety of aggressive surveillance techniques have become the hallmarks of the war against drugs. In suburban schools, in the workplace, and throughout the electronic banking system, the government is steadily broadening its monitoring of the affairs of private citizens. Many Americans, convinced that drugs and drug-related crime pose a danger to the nation, believe that such measures may be the price of civil order, but some civil libertarians are alarmed over the erosion of constitutional safeguards. Among the issues that worry them are the increased use of drug testing at work and in schools, the use of drug-courier profiles based on looks and behavior rather than on reasonable suspicion, and housing project sweeps intended to evict drug dealers, sometimes at the expense of due process.

The walled cities of L.A. Eloise Salholz *Newsweek* 115:24–5 My 14 '90

Violent crime in Newton, a south-central neighborhood of Los Angeles, has fallen almost 90 percent since the police declared its 30 square blocks a Narcotics Enforcement Area. In February, Los Angeles police erected concrete barriers and off-limits signs around the drug-infested area, which had become a war zone for rival gangs. Patrol officers have developed close relationships with Newton residents and have routinely stopped and frisked suspected gang members. By the end of April, crime within the barricaded area had dropped significantly and drive-by shootings had dropped quite dramatically. Critics charge that the program, known as Operation Cul-de-Sac, has created a walled city and note that drug traffickers traditionally move elsewhere in times of police crack-

downs. Newton residents support the barricades, however, and have begun to wonder and worry about what will happen to their neighborhood
if the program ends.

The widening drug war Tom Morganthau *Newsweek* 118:32–4 Jl
1 '91

President George Bush's Andean drug offensive seems to be falling apart.
Colombian kingpin Pablo Escobar, the reputed godfather of the Medellin
cartel, recently surrendered to the Colombian government. Many U.S.
officials, however, believe that Colombian president Cesar Gaviria has
capitulated to the traffickers by agreeing to end the extradition of Colombian criminal suspects. No one knows if Gaviria has given up the war
against trafficking in return for an end to the violence that has racked the
country for seven years. Also, since Bush announced his Andean strategy
16 months ago, the cartels have begun to move their smuggling and
cocaine-processing operations out of Colombia and into nearly a dozen
other Latin American countries. The U.S.-backed war against drugs is
also faltering in Bolivia and Peru. These countries, which have long been
the prime source of raw coca for the drug syndicates, are rapidly becoming producers of finished cocaine as well.

Less bang-bang for the buck Reuben M. Greenberg *Policy Review*
59:56–60 Wint '92

The police chief of Charleston, South Carolina, describes the success of
his market-based approach to combating drug dealing: Street level drug
dealing was reduced by assigning uniformed officers to stand in drug
dealing areas, thereby scaring away customers. Prisoners were brought
out of jail to pick up trash in such neighborhoods and make them appear
more safe. Crime was reduced in public housing by screening the people
who sought to live in the units to exclude convicted felons, by evicting
anyone who engaged in illegal activities, and by allowing in only visitors
who had permission from a tenant. The result was a 40 percent drop in
the city crime rate from 1982 to 1989. Public housing, in which 8 percent
of the city's population lives, became one of the safest places to be. These
successes were accomplished without a massive increase in resources or
overburdening the criminal justice system.

Troops, not talks, in Bolivia Jo Ann Kawell *The Progressive* 55:27–
9 Jl '91

Part of a cover story on the failure of America's war on drugs. The U.S.
policy of involving the Bolivian military in drug control could touch off a
spiral of violence in that country, with Bolivia's military just as likely to
provoke the violence as to control it. Bolivia is a fragile democracy whose
recent history is fraught with coups and cocaine profits. Unfortunately,

Bolivian president Jaime Paz Zamora seems to have forgotten the military-backed violence in his country's past and has agreed to let the armed forces take part in drug control in exchange for a U.S. promise of some $35 million in military aid. A better way to control drugs in Bolivia would be to establish an alternative national economy there that does not depend on coca dollars. It is unlikely, however, that the United States and other drug consuming countries would be willing to provide the billions of dollars that are needed to carry out such a transformation.

The CIA connection Alfred W. McCoy *The Progressive* 55:20–6 Jl '91

Part of a cover story on the failure of America's war on drugs. An article adapted from The Politics of Heroin: CIA Complicity in the Global Drug Trade. For years, the CIA has found its covert operations enmeshed with South Asia's heroin trade. Since the late 1970s, the agency has followed a policy of radical pragmatism and allied itself with local opium warlords in such countries as Afghanistan and Pakistan. These warlords serve as commanders for the CIA, which in turn protects them. Meanwhile, the U.S. Drug Enforcement Administration keeps its distance from CIA assets, even when they are major drug lords. As a flood of heroin has moved from South Asia into Europe and the United States, CIA agents have covered up for drug lord allies and even actively engaged in the transport of opium and heroin.

Perot's smart idea Michael Kramer *Time* 140:33 Jl 6'92

Ross Perot is on to something with his call for a civil war on drugs. In 1988, different journalists wrote that Perot had encouraged Dallas police to cordon off high crime neighborhoods and go block to block looking for drugs and guns. As it was reported, his scheme would probably have violated many individual rights, but the basic notion—that America's urban areas cannot be revitalized if the residents fear for their lives—is sound. Chicago Housing Authority (CHA) head Vince Lane is one of the few public officials bold enough to push crime sweeps as an essential part of securing public safety. Within weeks of taking over CHA, Lane instituted Operation Clean Sweep, under which CHA officials, backed by police, examine apartments looking for places in need of repair and for unregistered guests. If weapons or drugs are found, says Lane, the officials complain to the trailing cops, and arrests are made on the spot. Crime is down about 30 percent in the 100 CHA buildings swept so far.

How to stamp out money laundering Alfonse D'Amato *USA Today* 120:16–18 S '91

Much more must be done to prevent drug dealers from moving more than $300 billion a year through international banks. Two of the most important areas for legislators and enforcement agencies to focus on in the fight against money laundering are the international funds transfer system and illegal storefronts. The Money Laundering Enforcement Act of 1990 attempted to address these concerns. The bill required the Treasury Department to issue regulations by July 1, 1991, instructing depository institutions to identify their customers and to report their names and other information about them. The Treasury Department, meanwhile, described seven options designed to help stamp out money laundering. Any option that the department does not pursue is likely to become the subject of new legislation. The options are listed and discussed.

Drug war vs. land reform in Peru Melanie S. Tammen *USA Today* 120:50–3 Ja '92

Ending drug prohibition in the United States would make it economically feasible for Peruvian farmers to plant other crops, ending the reign of terror caused by drugs in both countries. More than 60 percent of the world's coca production takes place in Peru. Until now, all efforts on the part of the United States to support coca eradication and interdiction in Peru have failed.

The Peruvian government has begun a promising land reform program that gives farmers legal title to their land if they commit to growing alternative crops, but the prospects for a widespread and lasting switch by the farmers are dim unless the United States legalizes illicit drugs. By removing the profit, and thus the crime, from the narcotics trade, order could be restored in America, and Peru could effectively combat the violent insurgency movements that have been linked to drug trafficking.

Still a cocaine crossroads Linda S. Robinson *U.S. News & World Report* 110:47–8 Ap 15 '91

More than a year after ex-Panamanian leader Manuel Noriega was charged with aiding drug traffickers, Panama is still inundated by cocaine. Some U.S. officials say that the trafficking has increased, and some Panamanian and U.S. officials suspect that drug dealers continue to have allies in the Panamanian government. A Panamanian customs director believes that some members of his antidrug unit at Tocumen International Airport may be helping deliver drugs. In August 1990, a U.S. military informant alleged that a trafficking network was allowing cocaine to pass through the airport for fees. A U.S. Drug Enforcement Administration official says that the informant lacks credibility, however, and praises the airport antinarcotics unit.

Meanwhile, the U.S. State Department has expressed concern about official corruption in Panama. Interagency rivalries are also complicating antidrug efforts, and Panama's resources for antidrug efforts are meager.

Cracks in the drug war: why the U.S.-Andean alliance to stop the cocaine flow is in trouble Linda S. Robinson and Gordon Witkin *U.S. News & World Report* 112:49–51 Mr 2 '92

On the eve of a second drug summit with Latin leaders, to be held in San Antonio, there has been no significant reduction in the drug supply to the United States, and the initiatives of the previous summit, held just over 2 years ago, have helped destabilize Peru and Bolivia and spread the drug scourge. The Andean nations are balking at the U.S. push for a greater militarization of the drug fight, saying that it is time for more emphasis on giving farmers incentives to stop growing the coca plant, which is the source of cocaine. The article discusses the situations in Peru, where antidrug efforts are barely alive and are playing into the hands of the Shining Path guerrilla group; in Bolivia, which is a prime victim of the relocation of cocaine refining labs forced from Colombia by antidrug efforts; in Colombia, where gains in the drug war are slim; and in Miami, where making a dent in hardcore addiction is proving difficult.